AF888568

IN SEARCH OF A
MONETARY CONSTITUTION

EDITED BY

Leland B. Yeager

HARVARD UNIVERSITY PRESS
Cambridge, Massachusetts
· 1962 ·

© Copyright 1962 by the University of Virginia
All rights reserved
Distributed in Great Britain by Oxford University Press, London

Library of Congress Catalog Card Number 62–19227

Printed in the United States of America

CONTENTS

IN SEARCH OF A
MONETARY CONSTITUTION

· I ·

INTRODUCTION

LELAND B. YEAGER

THIS book is an outgrowth of eleven lectures delivered at the Thomas Jefferson Center for Studies in Political Economy of the University of Virginia in the fall of 1960.[1] Except for the first two, each of the lecturers was invited to re-examine a line of thinking on monetary reform in which he was known to be particularly interested. He was asked to tell what he thought was needed and why—whether some mere tidying up at the fringes of existing arrangements or a radical overhaul instead. He was encouraged to take the broadest possible view, without worry about political practicality or about possible accusations of extremism. He was to approach his task as if he were an advisor not merely to administrators of existing monetary arrangements, nor even to legislators considering limited changes, but rather to men engaged in shaping the basic character of a monetary system, in shaping a "monetary constitution."

All of the contributors share a roughly similar conception of the "good society" and regard the decentralized organization of economic life by means of markets, money, and prices as indispensable to human freedom. Any artificial attempt at "balanced" representation of highly divergent philosophies

[1] Professor Friedman delivered his lecture earlier, in April 1960, but the present commentary speaks of it as if it came in its intended position in the series.

would have robbed the lecture series of any coherence or focus. Far more views deserve a hearing than can fit into a single series or a single volume. Even the ones represented here show an almost perplexing diversity. They range from belief in deriving specific recommendations for a monetary system directly from first principles of social philosophy to emphasis on technical considerations only, from advocacy of a commodity money without admixture of fiduciary media to advocacy of pure fiat money, from support of 100 per cent reserve banking to judgment that such a system is unnecessary and impossible, from preference for price-level stabilization as the supreme criterion of monetary management to scorn for the very ideas of stabilization and management, from belief in allowing quasi-independent experts a broad range of discretion to belief in restraining discretion by clear-cut statutory rules, and from advocacy of devices designed to accomplish several objectives besides monetary stability all at the same time to belief in distinguishing monetary and other problems and remedies as sharply as possible.

Why is it that even men with broadly similar conceptions of the good society can disagree so profoundly on particular policies? Policy recommendations—in any field—cannot rest solely on positive analysis, however widely accepted it may be. Disagreement may hinge on specific value judgments: some economists may attach more importance than others to economic stability and be willing to pay a higher price, if necessary, in impairment of other objectives; some may worry more than others about the redistribution that results from a change in the price level, or be more fearful of the abuse of authority. Opinions on these matters may also depend partly on different understandings of the psychology of rulers, the willingness of workers occasionally to accept wage reductions, and so forth. Thus, even when the disagreement hinges on matters of fact rather than on personal values, the disputed facts may involve political science, psychology, and other fields apart from economics. Furthermore, several different ways of achieving a given policy objective may seem workable. One man may disagree with another's proposal not because he sees any flaws of fact or logic in it or any objectionable value judgments behind it but simply because he conceives of another and easier way to achieve the same end.

This is not to suggest that several different lines of policy are equally wise and that discussion of preferences is useless. If disagreement hinges on factual and logical propositions, which may well lie outside of economics, further investigation and reasoning may perhaps settle the issue. Discussion may even change lower-level value judgments by illuminating hierarchies among values and demonstrating their clashes and compatibilities.

The following commentary tries to relate the separate lectures to each other, mention significant points of agreement and disagreement, and suggest promising lines of further discussion. It draws in part on the question and answer periods that followed each lecture, but some editorial interpretation has crept in also. For this reason, the individual lecturers bear responsibility only for what they say in their own papers.

Professor Philbrook and Dr. Warburton accepted the assignment not of presenting their own views on monetary reform but rather of sketching in a background for the proposals of the other lecturers. Their theme—that the money supply is crucially important to the performance of a market economy—ought to be obvious enough, yet was widely ignored or disparaged from the 1930's until quite recent years.

Developing the concept of monetary equilibrium, Philbrook reviews how the real-balance effect refutes the original

Keynesian notion of underemployment equilibrium. He contributes a noteworthy incidental bit of doctrinal history: the real-balance effect had long been known in neoclassical economics, especially in the oral tradition at the University of Chicago; Pigou and Patinkin had little more to do than elaborate explicity on what the neoclassicals had long regarded as so obvious a corollary of ordinary price theory as to require little emphasis.

Philbrook offers an intriguing hypothesis about why the doctrine of underemployment equilibrium was able to survive as long as it did: Keynes's use of wage units rather than nominal money units bred confusion about what was supposed to be happening to the nominal quantity of money during persistent disequilibrium. The Keynesian conclusions apparently rested on a tacit assumption of disequilibrating behavior of the nominal quantity of money, and they were confusedly applied even to models in which the nominal quantity of money was supposed to be fixed.

Even in the neoclassical armor rebuilt by Patinkin, Philbrook sees one chink still left—the supposed conceptual possibility that the general equilibrium of a monetary economy may be an unstable one because the pressures of imbalance between supply and demand in one market may spill over into and disequilibrate another market. Philbrook is able to show, however, that this supposed exceptional case cannot even be conceived of in consistent detail. Technical though his analysis is, and of negligible direct importance for practical policy-making, it is a valuable contribution to theoretical tidiness and consistency.

As Philbrook explicitly recognized in the discussion following his lecture, to demonstrate pressures toward stable full-employment equilibrium in no way amounts to claiming that disturbances in the real world will meet quick and painless automatic readjustment and does not justify indifference to monetary and fiscal arrangements and policies. But policy was to be the bailiwick of later lecturers.

Dr. Warburton presents historical evidence on the crucial role of money. His own well-known statistical researches, and more recently those of Professor Milton Friedman, have shown that all but a few of the most minor downturns in American business activity have been preceded by downward deviations of the quantity of money from its long-run growth trend. But this evidence, by itself, leaves some questions unanswered. Even if changes in monetary growth did in fact merely result from rather than cause changes in business activity, the decline in the rate of growth of the money supply could, as a matter of sheer arithmetic, come before the absolute peak and downturn in business; and the apparent causation would be spurious. Besides (privately) questioning this objection on its own ground, Warburton scrutinizes the historical record to see what events caused the monetary slowdowns or contractions preceding business downturns. For almost every one of these monetary disturbances, he identifies one or more exogenous causes, such as shifts in policy or deflationary balance-of-payments developments. The initial monetary disturbances were *not* mere passive accompaniments of declining business, though declining business and a shrinkage of the money supply did react on each other once recessions were under way.

In discussion after their lectures, both Dr. Warburton and Professor Friedman emphasized the distinction between interest-rate and money-supply aspects of so-called "monetary" policy. The Federal Reserve discount rate is a deceptive indicator of tightness or ease. After some importance in influencing the volume of bank reserves in the earliest years of the Federal Reserve System, the rate lost practically all but psychological importance. The low discount rates of the early 1930's (interrupted, however, by the notably perverse increases of late 1931 and early 1933) are no evidence that a vigorous easy-money policy was tried but failed to stem the depression. On the contrary, the authorities allowed a catastrophic shrinkage of the money supply. Neither do the large accumulations of legally excess reserves after 1932 prove an easy-money policy ineffective. The banks did indeed hold reserves in excess of what the law alone required, but not beyond the requirements of the law and of bankerlike prudence combined. Grim experience after 1929, and especially in 1932–33, taught bankers not to count on the Federal Reserve for adequate help in meeting heavy deposit withdrawals. Bankers saw a further reason for unprecedented caution in the newly acquired (and, in fact, soon to be exercised) power of the Federal Reserve to raise the required percentages and so convert an adequate reserve into a deficiency on short notice. Even reserves well in excess of those currently immobilized by legal requirements were thus not truly idle; they were providing the service of availability. Finally, while the stock of bank-deposit money did not grow in the 1930's in full proportion with bank reserves, its growth was substantial and was accompanied by growth of total spending and production. Heavy but declining unemployment persisting until Pearl Harbor testifies both to the insufficient vigor of money-supply policy and to the linkage that does hold between money and total effective demand.

The first specific reform proposed in the lectures is one whose name, at least, is hallowed by tradition. Though the gold standard strikes many persons as an outmoded and extremist idea, the broad scope of the lecture series allowed the participants to go even as deeply into fundamentals as to risk anti-intellectual accusations of "trying to turn the clock back."

In Dr. Rothbard's reading of history, the state becomes an enemy whenever its activities go beyond certain narrowly defined essentials. Government is not a mere adding machine, passively recording the choices of the voters; and its functionaries, far from being mere servants of the electorate, tend to become a distinct group seeking power for themselves. Throughout the ages, the state has used inflation of the money supply as one way to wrest resources from its subjects and build its own power at their expense. It is chiefly for this reason that Rothbard yearns for a completely nongovernmental money.

Professor Kemp's argument is similar, though less emphatic. It was no coincidence, he maintains, that classical liberalism and the gold standard flourished together. Redeemability of money in gold coin restrains the self-aggrandizing propensities of the state. To maintain confidence and protect its gold reserve, the government must avoid excessive spending and excessive issues of fiduciary money. By standing ready to demand redemption, the citizens can control their government more directly and effectively than they could at the ballot box alone. Furthermore, gold coins promote human freedom by providing a durable form of wealth, high in value in relation to bulk, that can easily be hidden and protected from confiscation. Kemp waxes poetic on the acceptability of gold coins everywhere and at all times.

Even on more narrowly economic grounds, Kemp expects the gold standard to work well. He finds price-level fluctuations under the historical gold standard not too bad over the long run. The performance was far from ideal—the ideal is unattainable—but better than we can realistically expect from unfettered governmental discretion. Rothbard, in sharp contrast, rejects price-level stability as a criterion. He almost seems to count it as an advantage of a gold standard that its smooth operation would *require* breaking down institutional impediments to downward flexibility of wages and prices.

The two men disagree most sharply over the type of gold standard to be adopted. Kemp envisages one not far differene from what the world knew before 1914. Some details might be improved, perhaps by better cooperation among central banks; but paper currency and bank deposits, rather than gold itself, would still make up the bulk of the money supply. Rothbard sees grave defects in such a fractional-reserve system. It is inconsistent to link money to gold and then set about loosening the link by arrangements that "economize" on gold. Only one of the difficulties is that variations in the volume of gold reserves can require awkward multiple variations in the total money supply if redeemability is to be preserved. To maintain pure gold money, Rothbard would even stamp out banking as we know it. But Kemp, especially in the discussion after his lecture, saw little hope of enforcing 100 per cent reserves. The question of reserve requirements must be distinguished from the question of the monetary standard.[2]

Returning to points of agreement, we find Kemp leaning toward an approach that is quite evident in Rothbard's paper. For both men, the choice of a monetary system depends heavily and rather directly on their concern for preserving personal freedom against state power; strict economic analysis plays only a part—perhaps only a subsidiary part—in the choice. To judge policies by weighing their advantages and costs, conceived in narrowly economic

[2] An unkind critic might point out that one advocate of a gold standard has shown the grave defects of partial gold money while the other has recognized the impossibility of total gold money, and that the alternative is money not tied to gold (or any other commodity) at all.

terms, is what Rothbard would pejoratively label as "utilitarianism." Judgments on major policy issues require a frank application of political philosophy. Some lines of policy may be wrong and others right, he feels, almost regardless of the more obvious of the costs of pursuing them.

A very different approach underlies Professor Buchanan's paper, as well as most of the others. Buchanan would decide among rival proposals "only after a careful analysis of the relative costs and benefits expected from the operation of each system." The relevant questions fall entirely within the realm of positive economics: What are the probable effects of particular measures and institutions? Under what monetary arrangements do markets work most smoothly? Of course, this pragmatic approach does not dispense with value judgments entirely. Buchanan and other contributors presumably prefer the kind of society in which individuals can pursue their own goals and ideals with as little clash among their various pursuits as can be arranged and with the greatest possible freedom from both private and governmental coercion. This implies a preference for an economy coordinated by free markets and, in turn, for whatever monetary arrangements promise, *on purely technical grounds*, to be most workable. No further ethical premises are appropriate in appraising, say, fiat money against commodity money or fractional reserves against 100 per cent reserves. An Occam's Razor can be applied to value judgments as well as to analytical concepts: value judgments are not to be multiplied beyond necessity.

Buchanan illuminates the advantages and disadvantages of any commodity standard by exploring the characteristics of an ideal monetary commodity. While money of stable gold value tends to some extent to be stable in general purchasing power also, and while changes in gold production in depression and inflation tend to influence the volume of money in the appropriate direction, these automatic tendencies are notoriously feeble. An ideal monetary commodity, by definition, would have these characteristics in the highest conceivable degree. It would have an almost constant price ratio with other goods and services in general because its production could be contracted to expand theirs or could be expanded at their expense at almost constant opportunity cost; and its high real elasticity of supply, together with large current production in relation to accumulated monetary stocks, would ensure that automatic countercyclical variations in its production and thus in the money supply nipped deflationary and inflationary tendencies in the bud. For reasons that Buchanan explains, it is not too far-fetched to name this imaginary commodity "bricks." Rather than a reform to be actually adopted, his brick standard is a pedagogical device to emphasize certain aspects of a commodity standard stripped of historical and emotional associations.

Incidentally, Buchanan considers the idea of gradual adjustments, announced in advance, in the commodity content of the money unit. This might be a way of economizing on real resources used up to provide long-run monetary growth. In his view, predictability in the purchasing power of the money unit is more important than stability as such. Monetary changes, if fully foreseen and allowed for, leave economic calculation unimpaired and distort neither the distribution of wealth nor the pattern of production and relative prices. If stability has any special virtue, it is merely in providing predictability of the simplest, most understandable, and, if made the rule of policy, most believable kind.

The composite commodity bundle that Mr. Graham proposes may be a practical approximation to Buchanan's ideal monetary commodity. Under a composite commodity standard, growth of the money supply would automatically tend to speed up or slow down in countercyclical resistance to deflationary and inflationary tendencies. This effect would be reinforced by support of or restraint on incomes earned in primary-producing sectors of the economy when commodities were moving into or being withdrawn from monetary use.

Based on commodities of far greater importance than gold, money would have especially high "quality." Mr. Graham considers this an important advantage in comparison with mere fiat money. An incidental advantage, in his view, is that the sheer bulk of the composite commodity bundle in relation to its value would deter speculative redemption of paper money for purposes of hoarding; a feature of the gold bullion (rather than gold coin) standard would be exploited to the fullest. A composite commodity standard would be no less vulnerable to redemption than a gold standard, however, if the reserve ratio were sufficiently lower. Furthermore, deliberately to loosen the link between the reserve base and the money supply is hardly consistent with the logic of a commodity standard as expounded by Kemp and particularly by Rothbard.

Objections along this line lose most of their force when we remember that monetary reform is only tangential to Graham's main interest. His chief aims are to eliminate extreme fluctuations in the prices of primary commodities and in the incomes of their producers, to build commodity reserves against times of emergency, and to channel into foreign aid some of the surpluses that develop under individual price-stabilization or price-support schemes. Graham prizes the monetary aspects of his plan mainly because commodity reserves accumulated for other purposes could finance themselves through creation of the new money that is needed, anyway, in a growing economy. Graham's willingness to see commodities diverted from the monetary reserves in times of emergency or shortage and his willingness to have discretionary Federal Reserve policy continue in operation—everything that apparently suggests trying to hit several targets with one shot—is understandable when we realize that Graham is not really shooting at the monetary target. Monetary stability, if achieved, would be a welcome but incidental benefit of his plan.

While recognizing the attractions of a pure commodity money, Professor Friedman rejects it as both impossible to preserve from fiduciary dilution and wasteful of real resources when fiat money could serve just as well. He critically examines the familiar idea of entrusting monetary management to experts "independent" of political interference and experienced in doing the right things at the right times. Full-fledged independence would be intolerable in a democracy. "Independence" as we have known it depends too much on accidents of personality, disperses responsibility, obstructs appraisal of performance, and gives too much scope to the misdirected preoccupation of bankers with how policy affects interest rates and credit availability rather than how it affects the quantity of money. The apparent prevailing consensus in favor of discretionary countercyclical policy, as contrasted with a simple rule, is spurious: advocates of countercyclical policy cannot agree, without hindsight, on the particular actions to be taken at particular times. Not, of course, in comparison with entrusting policy to an independent authority of superhuman wisdom and powers of prophecy, but in comparison with real and meaningful alternatives, the "rule" approach scores best. Friedman sees flaws in the rule of stabilizing the price level, however, but leaves to Professor Selden a fuller discussion of the particular alternative rule with which he himself is so closely identified.

In emphasizing how a plurality of objectives, weapons, and authorities complicates the tasks of monetary management, Professor Viner implicitly endorses much of Friedman's argument against an *independent* monetary authority. He apparently is willing to move toward a greater measure of coordination among the numerous agencies currently exercising monetary powers in the United States. But he sees no hope of streamlining agencies, objectives, and weapons so completely that the tasks of monetary management would become simple enough to permit dispensing with continuous discretion on the part of some authority. Even apart from the impossibility of complete institutional streamlining, the further difficulty remains that stable functional relations just do not exist in economic affairs: the way that the economic system will respond to particular policy measures is too indefinite to justify reliance on some pre-established rule. Paradoxically, while the difficulties of forecasting are supposed to be one of the main reasons for preferring steady adherence to a given rule over discretionary attempts at short-range countercyclical action, the adoption of a rule presupposes forecasting for the long run and of an even more ambitious kind, especially since the rule itself would spell a possibly very significant change in the economic environment on the basis of which the original prophecy was made. Furthermore, trying to accomplish complex tasks in accordance with simple rules may mean that the application of a particular rule in a particular field will cause unwanted side effects, calling for the introduction of still more rules or authorities or both. A situation in which rules are continually subject to being added, repealed, modified, and circumvented might be even less stable and predictable than one in which the need for a certain amount of discretionary authority were frankly recognized.

In mentioning a "desirable range of discretion" in monetary management, the very title of Professor Viner's paper warns against excessive polarization in the discussion of "rules versus authorities." Viner commendably abstains from the all too easy caricatures which wrongly suggest that somebody actually is advocating a rigid rule to be chosen once and for all and to be adhered to through thick and thin, no matter how bad experience proves it to be. Viner also abstains from easy paradox-mongering about the impossibility of abolishing the need for discretion entirely, even from the adoption, review, and eventual modification of a rule. Every participant in the discussion recognizes that this sort of discretion is unavoidable, as well as discretion in the detailed day-to-day administration of even a precisely defined line of policy (discretion, for example, in the scale of day-to-day open-market operations and in the choice of the particular security issues to be bought or sold on each occasion). But recognizing this is a far cry from the extreme of simply telling a quasi-independent monetary authority always to do what is best. The true issue resolves into one of how specific the limitations on discretion ought to be. Professor Viner recognizes that some such limitations are desirable when he advocates "an obligation to follow an explicit code of general 'principles,'" a set of principles that is "publicly approved." What the present editor, at least, takes to be the essence of the "rules" approach is a search for a state of affairs in which prevalent expectations reinforce monetary stability because the public can count on continued observance of some established guidelines of policy and need not respond to or worry about short-run changes in intensity and direction. The key idea is perhaps "steadiness" rather than "rules." (The two issues of rules versus authorities and steadiness versus attempted countercyclicality are related but distinguishable.) In the present state of the discussion, any suggestion for a particular rule—such as a steady rate of growth in the money supply—ought to be regarded as illustrating how steadiness might conceivably be defined rather than as somebody's final pronouncement about the unquestionably best policy. To expatiate on the imperfections of some suggested rule as if these discredited the entire case for steady rather than supposedly countercyclical policy, especially without suggesting a meaningfully better alternative—and it is hardly meaningful to say that an authority ought always to do what is best in the light of business trends and other circumstances—is to attack a straw man. Professor Viner's doubts about salvation by rule are far more sophisticated than this.

One of the main advantages claimed for 100 per cent reserve banking is that it would tighten up one of the most conspicuous of the loose joints between policy actions and economic responses that make Professor Viner, among others, despair of the "rules" approach. Professor Tolley's assignment was to assess the advantages and disadvantages of this reform in the light of historical experience and theoretical understanding gained since it was first proposed. His task was not necessarily to advocate the plan, but to come up with any verdict or any proposals for modifying it that his reconsideration indicated.

The plan would give the monetary authority more complete and precise control over the quantity of money than it has now, when the actions of the commercial banks in holding or not holding excess reserves—in being fully or only partially "loaned up"—loosen the relation between the total volume of bank reserves and the volume of bank deposits.

Expansion and contraction of commercial-bank borrowing at the Federal Reserve, as well as shifts by the public in its holdings of currency and deposits and of deposits at banks with different reserve requirements, contribute to the looseness of control. Whether this looseness really amounts to very much and seriously impedes the implementation of policy is, of course, a key question. Tolley does not insist that it does (in fact, he disclaims having proved that 100 per cent reserves are desirable to the point of being urgently necessary); and he might possibly even agree with Warburton's opinion, set forth several years ago, that fractional reserves impair the authority's power to control the money supply to a trivial extent only. A more serious problem is changeable velocity—the loose relation between money and spending. Tolley does make a few remarks about what might be done to stabilize velocity. An increase in the cost of holding demand deposits (which the higher services charges necessary under some versions of the 100 per cent plan might impose) would presumably prod people to reduce their demand-deposit holdings more nearly to the bare minimum necessary for transactions purposes, would sharpen the distinction between demand deposits and other liquid assets, and so would reduce shifts in the preferences of the public as between demand deposits and assets formerly regarded as near-moneys. But as Tolley himself emphasizes, this advantage would be bought at the cost of requiring individuals and businesses to use up labor and paper and ink and communications in economizing on cash balances, even though, from the social point of view, fiat money costs essentially nothing to produce.

These matters are incidental to Tolley's main topic. After reviewing the traditional versions of the 100 per cent proposal and the arguments for and against them, he develops a variant of his own. The commercial banks would transfer their deposit liabilities to the Federal Reserve banks, obliterating the present distinction between demand deposits owned by the public and "high-powered" reserve funds. Under contract with the Federal Reserve, the commercial banks could continue the physical administration of deposits and the checking system. They could continue their traditional lending functions, except that, as intermediaries, they would be borrowing from bondholders instead of from depositors. Unlike earlier versions of the proposal, Tolley's would not strip the banks of their lending functions while leaving them indebted for the money supply. It would apparently achieve the economic advantages of 100 per cent reserves with minimum disruption of present arrangements.

Dr. King doubts any urgent need for major institutional reforms. In principle, he recognizes how much may be said for lodging all monetary powers and responsibilities with one single authority and for tidying up banking institutions and policy weapons. But if existing institutions and weapons can be made to work satisfactorily, why bother or confuse people with unnecessary changes? The main need is for general understanding and acceptance of an appropriate rule to take all but low-level discretion out of monetary management. Dr. King prefers the rule of stabilizing the purchasing power of money. Neither stability in terms of gold nor a fixed link with foreign currencies is sacred; we cannot hope to manage all the world's currencies along with our own. We want a domestically stable unit of value for much the same reason that we want well-defined units of length, weight, and volume. Instability in the price level is open to criticism on both technical and ethical grounds. A money supply managed to keep the price level stable (and this implies trying to compensate for any important uptrends or downtrends in velocity) would be growing at a rate appropriate for fully calling into play the real growth potentialities of the economy. Public confidence in a commitment to stabilize the price level would itself go a long way toward stability, toward making sharp shifts in the growth rate of the money supply unnecessary, and thus toward keeping lags in the effectiveness of monetary policy a minor problem only.

It is above all this problem of lags, as Professor Selden points out, that converted Friedman to the rule of steady monetary growth. In practice, there might be little difference between King's price-level stabilization and the rule that Warburton, Friedman, and Selden prefer. After all, the monetary growth rate is no end in itself. The objective is to promote stability of economic growth and of the price level by providing a constant and dependable monetary environment. The money supply should grow at whatever rate would avoid a persistent uptrend or downtrend in prices. Used as the immediate guide to week-by-week or month-by-month open-market operations and similar policy measures, however, the price index might call for frequent shifts back and forth between monetary ease and tightness. Because of lags between a switch in policy and its actual impact on business, attempts to counter even short-run price wobbles might well make the instability even worse. Furthermore, the monetary authorities cannot exercise as direct, tight, and immediate a control over the price level as they can over the money supply. So that there can be little excuse for deviations, the ideal rule should be one that the monetary authorities have ample power to obey.

If an initially chosen rate of monetary growth turned out to produce an unmistakable and persistent inflationary or deflationary bias, a downward or upward revision would be in order. Frequent tinkering, however, might spell a *de facto* return to discretionary policy. Selden suggests avoiding discretion even here by calculating adjustments in the monetary growth rate according to some formula involving results observed in some definite number of preceding years. Viner wonders, alternatively, whether Congress should not require the Federal Reserve to expand the money supply each year at whatever rate it judges would, if maintained during the preceding five years, have kept the price level stable over that period. As compared with an absolutely rigid rule, this flexible one might lessen the risk of marked discrepancy between objectives and results and thus enhance its own acceptability and durability. Flexibility admittedly means some discretionary judgment, and the best way of having the one while strictly limiting the other still remains to be worked out. But neither doubts about details nor an exaggerated emphasis on conflict between the "rule" and "authority" approaches should divert attention from the persuasive arguments for *steadiness* in policy, as contrasted with short-run reversibility. Slight and unspectacular corrections in one particular numerical characteristic (the monetary growth rate) of a constant policy for the long run are not at all the same thing as frequent reversals of policy in disruptive attempts to "lean against the wind" of observed or predicted short-run spurts or sags in prices and business activity.

Incidentally in his lecture and more fully in the discussion afterward, Selden rejected the 100 per cent reserve proposal. The slight extra precision of central-bank control is not worth the turmoil that would accompany its adoption. Maintaining the purity of a 100 per cent system, stamping out the creation of demand deposits in disguise or the growth of payments-clearing systems whose effects would be similar to the creation of money, would be an endless and unrewarding task.

Selden's opinion re-emphasizes the diversity of views on 100 per cent versus fractional reserves and on the private creation of money or its equivalent. The concept of "seigniorage" can be helpful in illuminating this issue, which runs through the papers and discussions of Rothbard, Kemp, Tolley, and Selden. Seigniorage is defined as the difference between the cost of bullion and the face value of coin made from it. With this definition slightly stretched for convenience, seigniorage is the value of any kind of money in excess of its cost of production. The issue of money without 100 per cent backing obviously offers a profitable opportunity to reap seigniorage—which explains why pure fiat money would quickly destroy itself through inflation in the absence of some sort of monopoly of or central control over its issue.

Under a pure commodity standard and with the supply of a competitively produced monetary commodity growing fast enough to match the total real growth of the economy and maintain price-level stability, potential seigniorage would be dissipated; the cost of real resources used up to produce the new money would entirely account for its value. In all probability, however, the supply of gold or some other monetary commodity would not be elastic enough to maintain price-level stability; growth of the total real purchasing power of the money supply would have to come about partly through a secular decline in the price level. Something akin to seigniorage would be gradually accruing to holders of cash balances. Paradoxically, this method of distributing seigniorage in a growing economy rewards the holding of cash balances and, by making velocity somewhat lower than it otherwise would be, makes necessary a somewhat larger real money supply and thus a somewhat lower price level. Problems of downward wage and price stickiness and of a negative price premium in the rate of interest would further bedevil this method of providing growth in the real money supply.

With fiat money issued only by a government monopoly,

all seigniorage goes to the government. Ideally, then, it goes to the public in the form of lower taxes or more abundant government services than otherwise. But complete government monopoly over money is hard to maintain, as commercial banking illustrates. The opportunity to borrow practically free from demand depositors and relend at interest is a powerful incentive to create demand deposits against fractional reserves. Yet banking is not an outstandingly profitable business. Competition forces banks to give demand depositors valuable services (or even interest, if it is not prohibited), or to make loans at lower rates of interest than otherwise, or both. Just how competition parcels out the seigniorage on deposit growth among the banks themselves and their depositors and borrower-customers is akin to a question in the incidence of taxes and subsidies. (Incidentally, the slight lowering of the interest rate on bank loans must affect the allocation of resources between consumption and capital formation in some way that is hardly possible to trace.) Legal reserve requirements transfer to the government or central bank part of the seigniorage that would otherwise go to bank customers and stockholders.

The higher the reserve requirements, the stronger are the incentives to find ways of issuing claims that are similar to bank deposits, yet subject to lower, if any, requirements. Since such claims are not as immediately spendable as demand deposits, people require interest as an inducement to hold them. This is simply part of the competitive distribution among the financial institutions and their customers of an amount of seigniorage that is greater for institutions subject to low or zero reserve requirements than for the more closely controlled banks. This difference is presumably the main impetus to the much-discussed rise of non-bank financial intermediaries and to the possibly declining effectiveness of central-bank controls wielded directly only over the banking system and not over its rivals. Any such difficulty lies not so much in the *existence* of quasi-money issued by non-bank intermediaries—after all, control over the volume of money in the narrow sense has a pervasive leverage effect on the entire financial structure—as in possible *instability* in the ratios of quasi-money to money held by the public, so that the leverage must work with a rubbery lever. Extending reserve requirements or similar direct controls to the most obvious non-bank financial intermediaries is no perfect solution. If the problem is not serious in the first place, the benefits are not worth the trouble; and if the problem is serious, the lure of seigniorage would lead to the relative rise of still other intermediaries. It is hard to imagine the imposition of reserve requirements not only against money but against all actual or potential quasi-moneys as well, since the dividing line between quasi-money and nonmonetary debt is inevitably a fuzzy and shifting one and since incentives would grow for the elaboration of payments-clearing systems permitting drastic economies in the use of money. (The freeing of funds from being held in cash balances provides something akin to seigniorage even when it is accomplished by new institutional arrangements rather than by the actual creation of close substitutes for money.) All these worries may seem farfetched. They admittedly have only slight relevance to an economy in which reserve requirements are relatively low, but they would come into their own if enforcement of non-interest-bearing 100 per cent reserves against money and close substitutes were ever attempted. The problem created by high reserve requirements is, in summary, one of powerful incentives for getting around the requirements, of a resulting instability in the institutional structure of the financial system, and, in turn, of rubberiness in the leverage exercised on the total financial situation by controls over the money supply narrowly defined.

One conceivable answer is low reserve requirements. The extreme solution would be free banking, under which anyone who could find customers could operate a bank, subject only to the general laws applicable to all businesses. The only reserve requirements would be those that individual banks imposed on themselves to be able to meet demands for payment and to attract customers by guarding a reputation for soundness. The reserve ratios dictated by prudence would link the size of the total money supply to the volume of either a commodity currency or a governmental fiat currency. Since banks would be no more saddled with legal requirements than any other financial institution, there would be nothing to evade as a motive for establishing quasi-banks. Institutional instability and rubbery leverage from that particular source would be avoided, though a loose linkage between basic currency and the total money supply could prove troublesome.

Another suggestion sometimes heard is that of permitting interest on demand deposits. Competition between banks and rival intermediaries could then express itself in the level of rates paid rather than in rapid changes in shares of the over-all financial structure. The spread between the net advantages of holding demand deposits and holding near-moneys would presumably be more stable if the rate of interest on demand deposits were variable instead of frozen at zero, and this would presumably reduce destabilizing shifts between bank deposits and near-moneys in the desired holdings of the public. If high reserve requirements were in effect, the central bank might even pay interest on reserve balances held with it. This interest, partly passed along to depositors under competitive pressure, would presumably lower velocity and thus, without inflation, permit some of the government securities now representing the national debt to be replaced by currency or demand deposits. If it paid interest on bank reserve balances (or if the central bank paid on its behalf), the government would, in effect, be doing some of its interest-bearing borrowing from holders of money and less from holders of government securities. Among still other advantages claimed for paying interest on money is a reduction in incentives for devoting real resources to economize on something—cash balances—that could be produced at negligible cost under a fiat system.

Several of the contributors, especially Professor Tolley,[3] touch on these issues, but none of them seeks final answers. These unanswered questions invite attention to the role of seigniorage in the circumvention of reserve requirements, in the evolution of financial institutions, and in the precision or looseness of control over the volume of money and its close substitutes. In addition to these technical matters, the partially ethical question remains of how the value of additions to the real money supply in a growing economy *ought* to be distributed. Should price-level deflation convey it to holders of existing cash balances? Should competition, as at present, convey it largely to the customers of banks? Or should—and could—a government monopoly of all money issue reserve seigniorage for keeping taxes lower or government services larger than otherwise, or for gradually reducing the national debt? In practice, no single answer can be implemented in all its purity, but a choice among alternative monetary and banking systems depends in part on a reasoned preference for one answer over the others.

[3] On the possible advantages of paying interest on money and bank reserves, see also his "Providing for Growth of the Money Supply," *Journal of Political Economy*, 65:465–485 (December 1957), and Milton Friedman, *A Program for Monetary Stability* (New York: Fordham University Press, 1959), pp. 71–75.

A great deal of contemporary monetary scholarship, notably including much of the work sponsored by the Commission on Money and Credit of the Committee for Economic Development, has concentrated on piecemeal and detailed study of our existing monetary structure and its performance. The reforms proposed have generally been correspondingly minor. Meritorious though this detailed work has been, it unfortunately tends to narrow the scope of discussion, pushing aside and even subtly disparaging a concern with broader issues. The present volume is an attempt to redress the balance. In comparison with exclusive focus on detail, broad inquiries may bear upon different aspects of monetary theory and open new avenues of possible theoretical advance. In the long run, they may even have a wholesome influence on policy. If otherwise desirable and feasible, no reform must remain "politically unrealistic" except as thinking makes it so.

· II ·

MONEY IN A NEOCLASSICAL PERSPECTIVE

CLARENCE E. PHILBROOK

THERE is a variant of the myth of Hercules and the Hydra. As the maiden Society labored to fashion a snug little house of money, she was beset with help from a monster whose heart was filled with architectural aspirations. Not the least of objections to his aid stemmed from his notoriously split personality, since each of his many heads contained more or less different notions of the correct theory of monetary stresses, while each nevertheless, with degrees of insistence which varied with heads and from time to time, gave continuing voice to his focal idea. Thus a cacophonous choral counterpoint rent the air as one head sang, "Balanced budget! Balanced budget!" and another, "Chronic unemployment!" while still others crooned or screamed various key words such as: "Sound credit conditions!" "Tight money chokes little man!" "Loans for home-builders!" "Interest cost of public debt!" "Dollar shortage!" "Dollar surplus!" Some heads, rather newly sprouted, boomed, "Growth rate, beat Russia!"—and others, "Dollar surplus!" "Buy American!" and "Raise price of gold!"

Now the Herculean task was not, in this version, to kill the monster. It was, rather, to bang heads until a helpful and harmonious ensemble was achieved. A detail on which bards differ is a belief that for this chore the muscular hero was supplanted by Athena, goddess of wisdom.

One of myriad minor heads, I myself sprouted just prior

to one of the most notable upsurges of violence in the battle, named for a commanding head called Keynes. My call was borrowed from older and wiser heads than my own, the "Chicago Heads," and most directly from two named Lloyd W. Mints and Henry C. Simons. I thought I understood the source of *their* song—a score generally termed the neoclassical theory of money. Much of what I have to say will not seem worthwhile unless one shares a belief that distortion of intellectual history is a source of danger to sound present thought. Such distortion has, I think, occurred with respect to the neoclassical tradition even, indeed, at the hands of men friendly to its conclusions. For example, the recent Patinkin book more than hints that the neoclassicals, while discussing real-balance equilibrium, almost never really understood this force—well, hardly ever! I shall start by trying to sound the essential themes as they came through to me, and then make some observations bearing upon what part these should play in an ultimate harmony which we hope the gray-eyed goddess will bring forth.

As suggested in the bitter complaint of a certain writer—now, to use his own graceful term, defunct—the neoclassical song of money was indeed in some sense a separate score or volume. What was said or left unsaid was much influenced by the fact that a prior volume, on value theory, had presumably been digested. Broadly speaking, Volume I addressed itself to the question whether the relative prices of goods, the quantities bought and sold, and the relative incomes of persons constituted a chaos or on the other hand were characterized by some approximation to systematic relations. By familiar devices it pictured an equilibrium position of each of the variables. One of these devices, which was afterwards taken for granted as background in Volume II, on money, was the concept of a society with given tastes, resources, and technical knowledge.

In deriving a picture of equilibrium in such an economy,

the student head would presumably have gone through a number of mental processes which impinged on the ensuing volume about money by tending there to obviate much otherwise essential analysis. He would have worked through thoughts related to the conception of diminishing marginal utility, and would henceforth suppose he might without sinning take for granted that diminishing marginal utility applied to anything which yielded utility, whether corn or cash balances. Given this, he would have conceived a budget-equilibrium position for each budgeting entity determined by the resources it had and the relative market values of all things involved in the budget. The budgeting process would encompass the planning of any owner of productive resources, be they labor power, capital, or land, in which the budgeter determined what portion of each of his resources he would put to use somehow through the market; that is, the student would suppose the individual to budget between "leisure" uses and income-earning uses, and to do so, of course, in the light of the market value of the use of each resource. Indeed, it was this latter budgeting process which gave meaning to the notion of an equilibrium amount—and so a full-employment amount—of use of land, of capital, or of labor. Finally, it would have become second nature to him to look for stability conditions around any equilibrium position.

Thus, before we arrived at the volume on money, a considerable universe of discourse had been developed. Just as one might neglect to mention the law of gravity as a reason not to walk the plank, so in the monetary treatment—oral or written—a point from the prior volume was often taken for granted. It may be this fact that accounts for the ancient ring of some ideas now and then offered in a lilting tone of joyful creativity.

The monetary theme came through to me somewhat as follows.

The famous Fisher equation $MV = PT$ says that the quantity of money times its velocity of circulation equals the average price of goods times the number of units exchanged. It contains elements such that through one or another of them can be introduced any factor in the economy which will influence the price level or the total of expenditures or money income. The sale of one unit of a good means that sooner or later money equal to the price is received for one unit of transactions. If we sum for the society all the products of one unit times its price, we shall of course have all receipts from sales. Or we may do this: count the number of unit transactions and call the total T, average the prices with proper weighting, and get a figure for P, the price level; naturally this average price when multiplied by T will give us the total of receipts just mentioned. Each dollar of receipts means a dollar of money handed over by someone at some time. That is not to say that this *number of dollars* has been handed over, since the average dollar may have been used more than once (or less, for that matter)—money may have a velocity of circulation different from *one*. However, the total receipts do correspond to an equal number of dollars' worth of effective demand. MV sums the effective points on those demand curves for individual goods which in Volume I we regard as entering into the determination of individual prices. And the T sums the effective points on supply curves. Thus, in using the formula we have not *forgotten* the infinite complexity of the economy—have not said the price level is determined "in a mechanical way"—but have summed elements so that, if we proceed carefully, our thinking may be aided.

No theory—quantity or other—of money income or price level is stated by the equation, beyond the assertion that the elements in it must be mutually compatible. A monetary theory is introduced only when we assert what are the determinants of the values of these summary symbols. To make the point by example, the NIRA of New Deal days might be viewed as implicitly asserting that if *P* were forcibly raised *T* and *M* or *V* would rise. This example, if followed up, points to the reason that this and related equations became identified with the quantity theory. It was taken for granted to apply to an essentially free-market economy. This fact alone has enormous methodological implications. The general implication is not that *V* or *P* or *T* cannot "independently" be the source of a change, but rather that each of these has its own appropriate determinants, which are exclusively the free decisions of individuals. On the other hand, as to the quantity of money, governments have always influenced it and perhaps cannot in any reasonably full sense avoid doing so. But to know the effect of a *change* in the quantity of money, we must know whether a particular quantity tends in any significant sense to bring about any particular money income and price level. Hence the quantity of money is to be treated as a given in the central analysis, for the usual reason that leads to the use of *ceteris paribus:* not that one believes a thing actually to *be* constant—if one believed that he probably would not mention the factor at all—but rather that we know it will vary and wish to move toward seeing the effects of its variation.

The notion that the equilibrium *T* and *V* are to be regarded as determined by things other than the quantity of money rests on reasoning such as the following.

Instead of transactions, let us in a common fashion speak of *O* for output. In a world of given tastes, resources, and technology, the output which tends to be established is that resulting from the apportionment, by each individual, of his resources between "leisure" uses and income-earning uses, as Volume I should have made clear. For imbalance will lead to bidding that makes itself felt in the market by affecting costs of doing business. These budget calculations ultimately go on in real terms. However, we can tie the matter to money by noting this: clearly, *if MV were constant*—that is, aggregate-demand constant—the market would by means of price-level changes be able just to clear whatever amount of productive services men wished to sell, which is to say, to clear the "preferred" output.

This way of putting things, however, brings up the query, "Yes, but what about velocity?" Our net conclusion is that for velocity too there is a "preferred" value which tends to come into being—to preclude equilibrium until it is matched by the actual velocity. We note that velocity is merely the ratio of aggregate money income to the existing quantity of money, that is, to total cash balances. To say that the one such ratio actually prevailing is the preferred one is to say that, with the particular total money income, men are just content with the amount of cash balances—the quantity of money—in existence. That is, they have budgeted just this holding of cash. We believe we can see farther and more dependably with this style of thought. For Volume I tells us that men with particular real incomes and other given circumstances will choose some particular *real* balances; and that allowance for the price level gives us money income and preferred cash balances in money terms. We may if we wish take the reciprocal of "preferred *V*" and, in keeping with the Cambridge tradition, call it "preferred *K*."

Thus there exists a preferred position for output (real income) and one for *K*, or *V*. And this fact constitutes that "bridge" between Volume I and Volume II which was later alleged to be wanting.

Now to the price level. With a given quantity of money, first, no resting position (equilibrium) for the price level exists as long as either of the preferences just mentioned—for output and *K*—is unsatisfied, and second, there is some price level which will cause the real value of cash balances to be such that these preferences are satisfied. From these considerations we get the notion that there is for the given quantity of money an equilibrium money income and price level.

Let us inquire into the nature of this equilibrium, for there have always been those who talked as if with the same quantity of money the price level might as well rest at one thousandth of, or a thousand times, whatever it is.

Some discussions to be heard or read would apparently question the possibility of, or even deny the very quality of meaning to, an inquiry into the effects of the departure of a price or a quantity from its equilibrium value. If a price falls, must it not be because demand has fallen or supply increased? Probably I misunderstand, for along these lines I can make no sense of our concern with things that may be symbolized by upward-sloping supply curves and downward-sloping demand curves. I take these things to be intended exactly to show that, although human error assures that the price, for example, will not stick tightly at all moments to the value which the intersection assigns it (and indeed assures that the curves themselves will wobble), there exists nevertheless a central point such that departures from it will give rise to forces tending back toward it. In short, it seems to me that we cannot do without the procedure of conceptually testing an equilibrium by assuming departures which occur through sheer error. For sellers do on occasion write prices upon their goods and must be presumed often if not typically wrong even on average, to at least some small degree, in the light of the true demand and cost conditions. And lucky indeed the man who has not to his sorrow taken his eye off his cash balance for too long a moment when deciding upon purchases.

Should sellers raise the price level by error, the real value of cash balances would be less. Actual K would be lower than preferred *K*, and men would move to rebuild their balances. But to demand larger cash balances is the same thing as to demand less of consumption goods or of investment goods; that is, with given *M*, to demand more cash is to lower expenditure and income by lowering velocity. Not only would the original output fail to clear the market at the *higher* price level, but with the lower expenditure it would not now clear even at the original price level—so that downward bidding of prices of productive services trying to clear the market would be even more marked.[1] However, as productive-service prices and thus cost curves fell, and hence prices fell toward the original level, the real value of cash balances would tend to be restored; actual *K* would move toward preferred *K* (actual *V* toward preferred *V*), and at the original price level things would come to rest.

Men make mistakes also in planning for cash balances, and must be presumed often to do so even on average. Thus actual *V* may, for example, rise above preferred *V*, so that expenditure rises and the market would clear even at somewhat higher prices. Much discussion has gone forward as if the price level then might as well remain higher. My own judgment on what is reasonable says it should be sufficient to note that men tend also to *correct* errors. However, in a full exposition one would wish to give maximum scope to that handy resort of those who love to think we live in a chaos—namely the notion of elastic expectations, meaning that men start to speculate on a further rise in the price level. Again, what I think is that a reasonable man would stop when noting that last point: the thing required merely to sustain the higher *V at a given higher level* is not simply a

[1] In so far as unemployment occurred, causing a decline of real income which tended to make men content with the low real balances, the effect would of course point to the downward pull on aggregate demand, which, in the argument above, makes impossible the continuance of the higher price level.

higher price level, but the expectation of *enough further rise* in it. This is an altogether larger order. But if we suppose that a speculative urge does somehow take hold, we must note that the assumed continued rise of velocity is also an assumed continued decline in the real value of cash balances, a fall in actual *K* still farther below the normally preferred *K;* and this process is occurring in the face of a strengthening counter force which it causes—a continuous rise in the marginal utility of dollars held in cash balances. This latter rise means that men are more and more often embarrassed by lack of cash to meet obligations—are suffering more and more pain for want of balances, are more often "broke" before payday. Yet, as soon as they even abate the rate of decrease they plan for cash balances, expenditure ceases to rise so fast and the speculator should feel at least a slightly cool draft upon his feet. To help blight the speculation, he need not sell his holdings of goods; he need only avoid going deeper *at as great a rate as before.* The end of this process is nebulous; but it is clear that there are increasingly strong forces exuding from the normally preferred *K* as real balances decline, while the speculation-creating force (the expected rate of increase of the price level) can scarcely be indefinitely increasing as it must if a continuing rise in *V* is to be maintained—especially if we remember men's propensity to suppose that what goes up often comes down. Thus, even conceding as I have to the point of absurdity, it seems patently foolish to deny an end to the rise. But once the *rise* in *V* ceases, all the temporary supports of velocity have been pulled from under it. One may be led to say no force remains but that of the normally preferred *K,* which will promptly return *V* to its original value and thus lower expenditure and so the price level to its equilibrium position. But actually the speculative force will not really be gone—it will only have reversed direction so that all forces would work toward returning the price level toward the original position.

From this kind of reasoning neoclassical economists found it sensible to conclude that for any particular set of tastes, resources, and technology a particular quantity of money carried with it a particular equilibrium price level for products and for productive services. The obverse of the central conclusion was that, if equilibrium at a pre-chosen price level were to be insisted upon (together with full employment), some particular quantity of money must be supplied—enough to satisfy the real-balance demands of the public. The possible extent of temporary deviations from equilibrium was not much discussed, although their reality was in no doubt. The main reason was empirical: it was hard to find cases of swift and marked changes in the price level except in the presence of either actual change in the relative quantity of money or conditions (for example, outbreak of war) which must be expected to lead to actual, marked change in the relative money supply. With a fairly stable money supply the price level was observed not to shoot up and shoot down but rather to vary mildly.

When the voice of the Keynes head of the Hydra was fully primed, we heard something like the following. Equilibrium requires that certain economic variables adopt values which render mutually consistent four data (all pure quantities being measured in "wage units"): the quantity of money and three functions or curves—liquidity preference, the marginal efficiency of capital, and consumption. According to the simplest interpretation things work in the following manner. Since liquidity preference is the amount demanded of real money balances, as an inverse function of the rate of interest, the existing rate of interest is the resultant of this function together with the quantity of real money balances available. Since the marginal efficiency of (rate of return on) capital is a negatively sloping function of the amount of investment per period, there exists some rate of investment which will reduce the effective marginal efficiency to equality with the existing rate of interest—and this amount of investment per period will in fact go forward. This rate of investment will assure a particular level of income, by reason of the nature of the propensity to consume—which is such that (1) a unique amount of consumption expenditure (inversely, of savings) will result from any particular amount of income and (2) any increase in income will be partially, but not wholly, spent upon consumption, thus leaving a greater residue of savings. Savings and investment must be equal; hence income (and its alter ego, employment) must assume a level such as to bring about this equality.

It is perfectly possible, the message said, that the outcome thus determined will involve "full" employment. But if so, it will be by the greatest good luck. For, should investment be in such amount that a full-employment income would cause savings to exceed it, the only possible expectation must be a lower income and the existence of unemployment. The mere need of more employment will not trigger any mechanism to equate full-employment planned savings with investment. If the rate of interest *did* fall in response to these circumstances, it would increase investment. But it will not. Indeed, one of the major intended contributions of Keynes was that the liquidity preference theory of interest gave assurance that any previously presumed influence upon the rate of interest of men's efforts to save, on the one hand, and the productivity of capital, on the other, was sheer illusion, the exorcism of which also removed any reason for supposing that the rate of interest might react in a manner to promote full employment. Finally, no influence apart from the interest rate could help. Thus, there exists no tendency toward full employment. This is of course the great theme which, sounding sonorously forth from the superhead, set up a somatic resonance in the very cells of myriad members of the Hydra, so that the song swelled deafeningly and still sounds through the plain, though often in muted echos or in variations with many ingenious minims, shakes, and trills.

In response to the Keynesian song, some crucial thoughts readily occurred even to young heads by reason of neoclassical background—thoughts hinging in general upon real-balance considerations.

The true bearing of the real-balance margin upon Keynes's theory and its common interpretation does not become plain unless we bring to the fore Keynes's ambivalence with respect to two models—let us call them A and B—which differ drastically in regard to *definition* of the quantity of money.

In model A, surely his central model, *real* money balances were given and never responded in amount, regardless of what else happened; that is, the number of dollars always cunningly changed just in proportion to the average wage rate. Thus no real-balance effect could result from a reduction of money-wage rates, and thus cleverly frustrated, such a reduction could not help employment. Evidently it was from this model A that followers derived their sense of assurance that Keynes had shown underemployment equilibrium to be independent of rigidity of wage rates; and, had this latter statement always been carefuly noted as resting on model A, little or no objection would have been forthcoming, for we gave this model itself but short shrift. No argument had been offered to show that the quantity of dollars acted with such fiendishly perverse exactitude. And indeed, we should have felt that to posit without comment a constant *real* quantity of money was to propose treating as natural and permanent in the body economic a feature which we had long viewed as a disease furthered by the "real bills" doctrine: exactly the tendency of the fractional-reserve banking system sometimes to act in a manner all too nearly related to keeping constant the real quantity of money, although by no means closely described by that rule. We should have wondered, in case this important tinge in our monetary system was to be treated as its essence, just what the ponderous new analytical apparatus was for—why we did not, Keynes and all, simply get on with the job of treating the disease of the monetary system. Keynes's monetary assumption and his apparatus could have been used exactly toward the end of concentrating attention here; but of course they were not, and policy suggestions, when they came, were such as to take attention away from, rather than directing it to, the role of the quantity of money.

Thus, we addressed our thinking to model B—that model which from Chapter Nineteen appears to approximate a fixed number of nominal dollars. Using it, Keynes visualizes a wage rate lowered during unemployment, notes the resulting rise in real balances, and reaches the neoclassical conclusion that employment will tend to be increased. For some purposes this was satisfactory. Two points should, however, be noted in passing. First, the widespread conviction that underemployment equilibrium was, "with a constant quantity of money," independent of wage rigidity must surely have stemmed from a careless transfer to model B of Keynes's conclusion from model A. There is a formal conceivability that those who long continued to reiterate this conviction did so because they really considered useful the fixed-real-balance model A. But in fact there was certainly no practice among them of distinguishing between the models; and there was no doubt that what they intended to contradict was exactly the typical neoclassical conclusion which rested on a fixed quantity of money in dollars. To insinuate that commercial-banking reactions justify a fixed-real-balance model was a late as well as disreputable arrival among the defenses of underemployment equilibrium. Second, the absence of the consumption-real-balance margin could not be accepted, and indeed was bolstered only through avoidance of discussion of the issue—by leading Keynesians on the spot as well as by the master. It had not been denied that wealth ought to influence consumption expenditure out of a given income, or that to the individual money constituted wealth. We therefore felt free to keep on tap a real-balance effect on consumption, to use when necessary, as in the theoretical extreme of infinitely elastic liquidity preference, to destroy an underemployment equilibrium.

The satisfactory part of Keynes's use of model B was his recognition that his model must say that the rise in real balances on account of lower wage rates would, in the conditions he took to be typical of the world, decrease the rate of interest and thus increase investment and employment.

Indeed, this very satisfactoriness may account for two developments in nominally Keynesian thought which involve repudiation of Keynes as well as of common sense.

One development is the assertion that the rate of interest has no effect upon investment, so that (only by implication) there was in the first place no point in an effort to demonstrate that the rate of interest was not responsive. I am as troubled as Keynes was to the last by this notion, which in effect repudiates the whole conception of equilibrium, underemployment or other, and implies that prospective revenues can influence action but costs cannot. Indeed, this idea need only be added to the often-espoused application of the same thought to wage rates in order to complete the picture of our economic world as an utter chaos. It is of course only the logical result of this kind of thinking about interest that some students of employment should restrict their efforts to discovering empirically how much investment is going to be made and thus forecasting income and employment—although it is scarcely apparent how for this purpose the consumer can be pictured as fiercely clinging to marginalism in income and consumption in a world where most other economic decisions are seemingly made with a blithesome hey-nonny-nonny.

The other development is a partial, implicit rejection of Keynes's theory of interest in favor of an even less satisfactory treatment. It shows up in a certain ambivalence to be found in the Keynesian literature, in the writings of Professor Alvin H. Hansen, for example. A speculative liquidity preference theory of interest may be offered quite straightforwardly, in a manner which to all appearances is meant to suggest that the generally relevant world for our discussion is the one which Keynes apparently thought it was—that is, the model which has been called the Keynesian "general case," and in terms of which I have been speaking. In particular, the given-real-money-supply curve is shown intersecting the liquidity preference curve in its downward-sloping range and thus in that range fixing the rate of interest. There will typically be suggested, however vaguely, the usual inference (above shown to be false) that the rate of interest is thus shown to have no tendency to respond to the needs of full employment. Yet in the discussion, suddenly and without notice, a change occurs. It comes just when we are being shown explicitly why the rate of interest will not respond in the needed way. We find ourselves in a somewhat different world, one in which Keynes seemed to say we could be but typically are not. I refer, of course, to that subworld often labeled the Keynesian "special case," that of infinitely elastic liquidity preference, where the rate of interest has reached a level so low that men will not bother to lend, but will simply hoard any additional cash they have saved. (Incidentally, it is not pointed out in such expositions that in this infinitely elastic range it cannot possibly be said that the rate of interest is a function of the quantity of money.) We must soon refer to the substance of this *latter* case; the present point is merely that the apparent uncertainty as to just what the message is intended to be may well be a product of reluctant realization that underemployment equilibrium makes no sense in the Keynesian general case.

So much for excursions into these two anti-Keynesian developments of Keynesian thought. I have alluded to the existence of two sorts of response to Keynesism with respect to the rate of interest and stated the most basic one: namely, that the *real* quantity of money cannot be treated as an independent variable.

The other response was the sense of necessity to reassert the old-fashioned theory of interest on account of the basic flaw specific to Keynes's *speculative* liquidity preference theory of interest. As Keynes actually made clear, the speculative money balances that men were presumed to demand depended not upon the rate of interest but upon the difference between the actual rate of interest and some "normal" rate—the one that men fully expected to be reified. And of course a curve which existed only on account of the rate men counted on could scarcely *account for* the rate men counted on. The author's suggestion that this rate was determined "psychologically" was of no help; for nothing that men do can be totally independent of psychology, and what we need to know is just how the psychological processes operate with respect to just what. Nor did Mabel Timlin's speaking of causation by a "psychological-institutional complex" greatly enlighten anyone, since we need to know just how men interact, in the patterns called institutions, to bring about their belief that a certain rate of interest is the "normal" one.

On the usual supposition that a hypothesis which makes

some kind of sense should not be relinquished except in favor of another which makes at least as much sense, we reactionaries clung to the idea, as a first approximation, that what men looked at when forming their notions of a "normal" rate of interest was the marginal productivity of capital. It was not, of course, assumed that this was a case of "every man his own marginal productivity watcher." Rather, as in most of economic life, men farmed this chore out to specialists—to businessmen, who, in so far as they hope to survive, had jolly well better be watchers of the marginal productivities of various productive services. Thus, in the large, men threw their savings on the market, depending on the selfish competition of enterprisers to protect the savers' interests. To be sure, where short-run considerations were under inspection, to these thoughts were added the qualifications about hoardings and dishoardings and creation and destruction of money which turned the statement into the so-called loanable-funds theory of interest, which few or none can find it in their hearts to deny.

The "special case" of Keynes—infinitely elastic liquidity preference—has received but scant mention above. To repeat, we must interpret this conjuncture as one in which the marginal productivity of capital and the interest rate have fallen until men are no longer moved to lend or invest rather than hoard. Or not quite this. Even here, on Keynesian logic, as long as any economic advance proceeded, *some* rate of investment must be going forward—enough to keep the marginal efficiency of capital down at equality with the lenders' minimum interest rate—so that some saving would, except in perfect stagnation, be consistent with equilibrium. Like Keynes, we did not take very seriously the possibility that the amount of investment at so low an interest rate—or indeed the amount at a higher rate of interest—would under usual circumstances be less than would absorb full employment savings. But more fundamentally, this dire contingency was regarded as having been covered in our discussion of real balances in relation to the consumption function: that is, it had been argued that some amount of real balances was conceivable such that the product of full employment would clear the market—if not partially in the form of investment goods, then in the form of consumption goods; and, if not provided otherwise, these real balances would tend to be created through lower prices.

In sum, then, we arrived at a conclusion which in essence was a simple reassertion of old real-balance reasoning. The conclusion was the now familiar one that, on account of the role of money, the notion of underemployment equilibrium cannot stand. We still thought certain old assertions to be defensible. There is some quantity of money in real terms which will be necessary and sufficient to make the equilibrium adjustment involve full employment. There is, for any particular price (and money-wage) level, some quantity of money in ordinary terms which will be necessary and sufficient to render the equilibrium adjustment an equilibrium involving full employment. There is, for any particular quantity of money in ordinary terms, some level of prices (and money-wage rates) which will render the real balances such as to make the equilibrium adjustment one involving full employment.

Such thoughts as these, then, were an important part of the meaning of the song which I took up. That they were caught from older Hydra heads, who themselves regarded them as old, merits emphasis. It was in the belief that they were old that from the start I offered the fundamental themes to my classes, that I greeted such writings as Lange's welcome though unsatisfying 1944 recognition of real-balance effects and Modigliani's widely heralded formulation, and that in faculty seminars of 1945 I presented these thoughts and soon thereafter included them in a dissertation. The 1947 articles of Pigou and Patinkin seemed but a restatement for the needs of the day.

It was clearly in the same spirit that Lloyd W. Mints published in 1951 his excellent but neglected *Monetary Policy for a Competitive Society* (New York: McGraw-Hill). There as a matter of course he applied the cash-balance reasoning which he had with no pretense to originality taught so many students.

At least as recently as the early 1950's one felt quite lonely in singing the song of real balances, even though some clever and important heads had published scores or partial scores for it. The loneliness has since been somewhat assuaged. There has been a less full-voiced scorn in the countersong, perhaps especially because consumption has acted in such a manner, in relation to income, as to lead men to admit additional factors—even if only bonds, as in the case of Samuelson—among the forces affecting consumption expenditure. And there has been an unmistakable increase in the number of economists who explicitly take cash-balance reasoning seriously.

One should not leave the impression that this theme was totally unaffected by the Keynesian tune. Although full-employment savings will much of the time be absorbed into capital use even at a rising rate of interest, to say nothing of a nondeclining one, it is presumable that sometimes the marginal productivity of the additions to capital will be lower than before, so that the absorption will occur at a lower rate of interest. If larger real balances are demanded on account of a lower rate of interest, then monetary conditions which, barring a decline of the interest rate, would permit full employment at the old price level would on occasion, then, require a lower price level. Now, although Keynes is read as requiring recognition of the basic point—

the dependence of real-balance demand upon the interest rate—strictly speaking he did not do so. For his transactions-and-precautionary-cash demands were not influenced by the rate of interest and his speculative demand was a function not of the rate of interest but of *differences* between the actual and the "normal" rate. However, a certain old-fashioned, meticulous regard in some quarters for discovering what was useful in a set of ideas resulted in noting that in principle it was surely true, and long recognized, that real balances demanded would tend to vary inversely with the rate of interest. This is not the place to discuss the matter of degree; we may try to hope that empirical work will yield us some convictions about it. It seems safe to say that the neoclassically oriented neglected the point exactly because they thought the degree of dependence negligible. But in our reassertions of the theory of equilibrium, we have felt obliged to be explicit about allowing for the fact that a rate of interest determined fundamentally by the marginal productivity of capital is one of the factors influencing the amount of real balances demanded.

With special respect to allowance for the rate of interest, the most arresting recent reassertion of traditional theory burst in 1956 from a head named Don Patinkin.[2] It merits being used for testing whether recent styles of thought require that we modify the crucial conclusions about the role of money.

In the post-Keynesian world, where the old universe of discourse had been lost to so many students or never opened to them, numerous teachers must have welcomed the explicitness with which Patinkin spelled out the notion of the budget equilibrium of the individual, with specific regard to the determinacy of the amount demanded of real-balance holdings, and purveyed as a net *effective* message the "right"

[2] In *Money, Interest, and Prices* (Evanston, Ill.: Row, Peterson, 1956).

answers about equilibrium. Still I shall concentrate on Patinkin's macroeconomics, to which most readers will attach the stability issue. For in spite of what I have just called his net effective message, these arguments contain elements which may yet be used effectively *against,* rather than for, that belief in the existence of stability which the author seems clearly to enjoy; and probably Patinkin can be saved from himself.

The major argument employs an aggregative model of the commodity market together with the bond market. The quantity of money (number of dollars) is held constant along with tastes, resources, and technology; and, to repeat, prices adjust to maintain full employment. In effect the following question is asked: Is there a price level which is an equilibrium one in the sense that: (1) the actual price level will at that point be compatible with the rate of interest which must then obtain; (2) should price level or rate of interest depart from these values, or both at once do so, would the departure create forces to press each back—or instead might some other value of the price level (and interest rate) prove consistent with the given quantity of money?

Old cash-balance analysis would typically disregard the interest rate and conclude that only one particular price level would create equilibrium in the commodity market. With Patinkin, however, we say that, if the rate of interest were higher, aggregate demand with the given cash balance would be *lower,* and on two accounts: namely, both investment expenditure and consumption expenditure out of given income would be lower. Thus, showing interest rates on a vertical axis, we have for a given quantity of money a downward-sloping curve displaying different equilibrium price levels—higher price levels as the interest rate is lower.

An upward-sloping bond-market equilibrium curve is

added to assert that, should the price level be lower (with the constant nominal quantity of money), conditions would result in the bond market which would cause a *lower* rate of interest to be the one which would equate the number offered and the number demanded of bonds (each a perpetual claim to one dollar a year). The key to interpretation of this phenomenon is that a lower price level (with its lower money income and total costs) will lower both the number of bonds offered and the number demanded at each conceivable interest rate, but the increase in real balances will accentuate the decline in number of bonds offered (since a firm then has real balances to spare) while moderating the decline in number demanded (because households too can then spare real balances). That is to say, the upward-sloping supply curve for bonds and the downward-sloping demand curve both move in the same direction as the price level, but the supply curve moves more than in proportion, while the demand curve moves less, and the intersection rises to a higher bond price, or lower interest rate.

Thus, with a downward-sloping commodity-market equilibrium curve and an upward-sloping bond-market equilibrium curve, the stage is set for finding simultaneous equilibrium for both the price level and the rate of interest.

The book is most often, I suspect, supposed to leave us in good position. But in fact Patinkin finally says that the stability he worked so hard to demonstrate is after all only a matter of faith (although he does perform that act of faith): certain departures of interest rate or price level from the intersection values (that is, movements into sectors II and IV of his Figure 18, page 155) may prove mutually reinforcing, so that both may rise together or fall together indefinitely and apparently without assignable (or at least without assigned) limit.

His reason runs in terms of what he calls "inter-market

pressures," and what I call a "spillover" effect, of the following sort. An interest rate below the posited equilibrium level means that there will be more bonds offered than demanded. A price level below that indicated by the commodity-equilibrium curve for an existing interest rate means unduly large real cash balances and hence an excess of commodities demanded over commodities offered. Suppose these two conditions arise simultaneously. Commodity purchasers, unable to get the amount of commodities they wish at the lowered prices, may not bid up the prices of commodities as the basic commodity-equilibrium curve says they will. They may instead buy more bonds—bidding up bond prices (instead of the prices of the things they really want) and of course pushing the rate of interest farther down. Meanwhile, what of the originally disappointed borrowers? Are they bidding up the interest rate to a rationing level? No: although panting for capital funds, the argument runs, they may sell off *extra* amounts of commodities (presumably from their working inventories) to raise funds—and at sacrificially lower prices. Thus, for example, an initial lowering of interest rate and price level may result in continuing further declines.[3]

It does seem strange that in this picture purchasers cannot get more commodities even though more are being thrown on the market, that the queues of would-be commodity-buyers do not encourage sellers at least to maintain prices, perhaps to raise them, and even to maintain or increase inventories—and strange too that would-be bond-sellers do not bid down prices of the things they really want

[3] As indicated, Patinkin gets the same result in all of his sector IV of Figure 18, page 155, which includes both the case treated above and that of a *higher* price level (within limits) along with the lower interest rate. However, the left half of sector IV—a *lower* price level with a lower rate of interest—appears to maximize the chance of sustaining the author's conclusion, and so is used here as a test case.

to sell (that is, bonds) rather than prices of the very capital goods (including inventory) which must be what they wish to buy with funds if they do obtain them. In short, it is self-contradictory to picture an excess *supply* of commodities because of frustration in bond-selling, together with an excess demand for bonds which arises exactly because of a frustrated excess *demand* for commodities. Stability cannot be rejected on such reasoning, and we may simply drop the spillover effect as it was argued in Patinkin's chapter X.

When we next meet the spillover effect in Patinkin's pages, it is in connection with a model originally intended to demonstrate the stabilizing process by means of the commodity market and, this time, what the author calls the "money market." [4] Here the illustrative disturbance takes the form of a rate of interest above the intersection, rather than below, as before, together with a price level which if changed at all may be, within limits, either above or below the original. Patinkin believes that he sees a spillover effect here, too. He does not spell this out even to the meager extent found in his first presentation of the spillover effect, but merely says that what he more or less does spell out is a manifestation of that phenomenon. What he says explicitly is this: a rise in the interest rate causes a reduction in cash balances demanded, and the act of trying to reduce cash balances must be presumed to increase not merely the demand for bonds but also the demand for commodities (page 178); hence the old, negatively sloping commodity-equilibrium curve immediately becomes suspect. Indeed, for this reason the author distinctly prefers the commodity-and-bond model.

[4] See Patinkin's Figure 26, page 176. This model supplants the bond-equilibrium curve with an upward-sloping (LL) curve which shows higher interest rates and higher price levels as counterbalancing each other to maintain equality between dollar-balances demanded and the fixed supply of dollars available.

Now, to me it seems an error to identify with the spillover effect the phenomenon which here disquiets Patinkin. The disquieting factor appears plainly to be but a recognition of the effect of the interest rate upon real cash balances demanded. If the recognition forces unwelcome inferences, we can scarcely prefer some other model by reason of its obscurity on this key point. It would be better to face the implications of the offending model with greater care and, if possible, remove the apparent contradiction. This I believe Patinkin could accomplish were he to distinguish systematically between *equilibrium* interest rates on the one hand and disequilibrium rates on the other. If I am not mistaken, the cause of his confusion is this: the models were set up to show the consequences of incipient disequilibrium; and Patinkin, inadvertently putting into them a change in the equilibrium rate of interest, is naturally unable to get a satisfactory reading.

Let us explore in order the effects, first, of changes in the *equilibrium* rate of interest, and then the effects of disequilibrium rates, that is, changed rates coming about without change in the fundamental "givens." In the first case, we shall derive the *upward*-sloping commodity-equilibrium curve which throws Patinkin into confusion; in the second case, using the disequilibrium rates which surely he intended to inspect, we may be able to derive the stability which he clearly hoped his models would show.

For the first exploration, then, let us consider in turn a series of higher equilibrium rates of interest, each according to the cause of the change.

1. Let a technological change raise the marginal productivity of capital, thus the demand for lendable funds, and so the rate of interest. If indeed men save more (spend less on consumption) at the higher rate, this factor will not fully offset the greater investment expenditure plans which

greater demand for funds reflected; for the higher interest rate is a higher genuine *opportunity cost* of holding cash, and what men want is smaller cash balances, not greater, so that they will lend (and use, in the case of entrepreneurs) not only any additional savings but something more from previous cash balances. A higher money income and price level must follow, the latter alleviated only as real output grows, although Patinkin believes the price level may be either higher or lower (page 185).

2. Suppose men become less frugal, valuing more highly present consumption, saving less out of given income and spending more on consumption goods. The rate of interest will rise exactly because there is opportunity to lend (and see invested)—at a rate of interest higher than the old one—more than the reduced amount of savings. Hence lending will be done at the expense of cash balances, while entrepreneurs also will economize balances in order to invest. Aggregate demand and the price level will be higher, although again Patinkin considers it uncertain which way the price level will move (page 185).

3. With reference to a "rise in liquidity preference," we must proceed with circumspection and, with Patinkin, separate three cases.

a. Let us explore a mere benchmark case, which involves no change in the rate of interest. Suppose that men simply become more nervous about the thought of defaulting payments. This supposition does not necessarily involve any change in the relation between the amount of real consumption budgeted and the amount of real-bond ownership budgeted; and a type-case is identified if we assume no change in this relation. Consumption expenditures in money terms will decrease; so will offers of loans in money terms, and the resulting higher rate of interest will decrease borrowings and investment expenditures in money terms. Hence the price level will be lower, as traditional reasoning would have it when cash-balance demand rises. What of the rate of interest, which we have just left in a raised position? This position is one of disequilibrium, and the rate will fall again to its old level. As long as men have not permanently decreased the real value they keep in the form of bonds—the real amount of capital they enable firms to have in use—the marginal productivity of capital and so the rate of interest must settle at the old position. In monetary terms, as the price level falls, the demand curve for bonds falls, but not as fast as the supply curve for bonds, and the interest rate declines. Thus we have merely a case of a lower price level because of stronger demand for cash balances, with no change, at equilibrium, in the rate of interest. And Patinkin agrees.

b. Suppose the initial new decision is to obtain the increase in cash balances solely at the sacrifice of consumption expenditure—so that we have an extreme case standing for any in which the means of increasing cash is more at the sacrifice of consumption plans than of lending. By this route we again get an illustration of our central proposition, although it involves a *lower* equilibrium rate of interest. The initial budget adjustment (increase of budgeted cash), by reducing the planned marginal utility of budgeted real balances in relation to that of real bonds, leads to further adjustment in the form of budgeting somewhat more real bonds in relation to the newly planned real balances, bringing more capital into use, hence a lower marginal productivity of capital, hence a lower equilibrium rate of interest. The initial move from consumption to more cash, plus the dampening of consequent movement into bonds (capital) as this movement lowers the interest rate, lowers the price level. Thus we have, at a lower equilibrium rate of interest, a lower price level—the upward-sloping commodity-equilibrium curve asserted above. Again Patinkin agrees.

c. What if the increase in demand for cash were specifically at the expense of the amount of bonds wanted? This is the type of case which estops the simple assertion that a higher equilibrium price level must always go with a higher equilibrium interest rate. The budgeting for more cash purely at the expense of bonds must *mean* a decline in the amount of real bonds budgeted—the total capital stock—and so lead to a rise in the marginal productivity of capital. This change raises the equilibrium rate of interest. The consequently reduced investment expenditure (and possibly a reduction of consumption on account of the higher interest rate) operates to *decrease* the price level, while the rise in the equilibrium rate of interest itself causes cash balances to be economized more—velocity to be greater—than would be the case if we had, along with the new, stronger taste for cash balances, the old, lower rate of interest. This analysis too is in keeping with Patinkin. But if we are to represent this case by reference to correct commodity-equilibrium curves, we must start with one which slopes upward, showing higher price levels for higher equilibrium rates of interest, move it to the left on account of the increased demand for cash balances (lower preferred velocity for each rate of interest), and move up along our interest-rate axis as the equilibrium rate rises, but not sufficiently to bring us rightward to a price level as high as the original one.[5]

In sum, an interest-rate rise incidental to adjustment to equilibrium under new conditions will tend to make the price level higher, not lower. When Patinkin says, in spite

[5] Unless, indeed, one wishes to say consumption expenditure is *increased* by the higher interest rate, and to a degree sufficient at least to offset the decline of investment. (Real balances held would then not be increased after all, and might decline.) Such a conclusion would be unwelcome, not only to Patinkin, but to all Keynesians who have regarded an ill-behaving liquidity preference as a source of danger to full employment.

of the contrary suggestion of his preferred model, that the door to fundamental instability is still open, the reason apparently is an uneasy awareness of the fact just cited, together with forgetfulness that his testing of the equilibrium should be carried on by reference to initially *disequilibrium* values of the variables. We must, then, inquire what will be the outcome when the disturbing changes involve initially disequilibrium values of the variables.

Let us again make use of the assumption of specific errors, and inspect whether such departures from equilibrium are self-correcting.

It is too often true that in economics one alleging anything but chaos will be generally presumed wrong unless he makes a perfectly overwhelming case for orderly relations. Probably no devotee of instability would be shaken in his faith, at best, unless each conceivable error and each possible combination of simultaneous errors were in turn posited and shown beyond doubt to meet correcting forces. I have in fact written down elsewhere an attempt at something about like that. The product proved impossibly long and tedious, so I have singled out three particular cases of error specifically because they seem the most favorable for deriving instability. Their earmarks are these: the rise in the interest rate accompanies a "sellers' market" for funds; the rise in the price level accompanies a "sellers' market" for commodities; and when both initially move simultaneously, they move in the same direction. It must be hoped that treatment of these cases will suffice to indicate lines of reasoning which can show that errors are not self-sustaining, mutually reinforcing, or in general destructive of equilibrium.

1. Suppose that the rate of interest rises because entrepreneurs issue more bonds—increase the demand for funds—in the *mistaken* belief that the marginal productivity of capital has risen. We get the right kind of start here (that is,

a "sellers' market"), since together with the higher interest rate there exists the intention both to borrow more funds and, through cash-balance economizing on account of higher interest, to spend a larger portion of them on investment. The higher rate of interest reflects a genuine opportunity for households to lend more. They too will budget smaller cash balances, and they will add to lendings by more saving if indeed a higher interest rate inspires less consumption. The greater lending-by-saving will of course not add to aggregate demand, but will only channel more to investment. But the cash-balance economizing *will* add, and the price level will tend to be higher. Prior to realization that the marginal productivity of capital has not after all become higher than originally, there is no reason the price level or the rate of interest should fall back. On the other hand, the rise in the price level will not cause a *further* rise in the rate of interest and through that another rise in the price level, as instability would require: the price-level rise and the consequent decline of real balances will simply have been a factor limiting the increase in the extent to which households lend, and entrepreneurs spend, out of cash balances under inspiration of high interest. There will merely be a new, temporarily higher, spurious-equilibrium velocity of money. Nor will interest rate and price level continue elevated. As the error of overoptimism becomes apparent to entrepreneurs, the amount of bonds supplied and the investment expenditure will decline, lowering the rate of interest and the price level respectively toward their original positions.

2. Now let us suppose the error consists in carelessly budgeting too much for commodities (while initially budgeting the same bonds as before) and so leaving budgeted cash balances low. This time too the rise in the price level occurs because of a "sellers' market," so that temporarily, at least, the market clears and money income is higher. Should

awareness of, and action to correct, the cash-balance error not immediately occur, the bond-supply curve will move rightward more than the bond-demand curve, and the interest rate will rise, decreasing entrepreneurs' real investment expenditure and so their money-investment expenditure in relation to the swollen money income flow, yet causing firms to aim at smaller increases in cash balances than the raised price level originally dictated.The higher interest rate stands for no genuine opportunity. Thus lower investment expenditure will reinforce a downward pull on the raised money income and price level which will make itself felt when reaction to the original, error-created cash-balance shortage occurs; and the declining price level will reverse the bond supply-and-demand movements and lower the rate of interest. Stabilizing reactions seem quite apparent.

3. Finally let us try a simultaneous combination of the two errors just discussed. Let entrepreneurs be overoptimistic about marginal productivity of capital just when men in general by error budget for too much of commodities and too little cash with respect to each possible rate of interest. Thus we have one force tending to raise the rate of interest and a partially independent one tending to raise the price level. It would seem that we need merely to add together the effects of these errors. Before the errors are recognized, the price level and the interest rate can be above the original level. The levels, however, will again reach a high point of temporary, spurious equilibrium; no interaction between them will move each continuously farther from the original equilibrium. For the rest, we merely observe again that realization of error will dawn, budgets will move toward basic equilibrium, and with them the price level and the rate of interest.

What net conclusion may be drawn? First, it should be noted that in Part One of the Patinkin book it was confidently argued, and in minute detail, that under given tastes, resources, and technology there is for a particular quantity of money one particular equilibrium price level in the sense usually implied in the quantity theory. Then, in Part Two, after painstaking effort had apparently brought us to the same conclusion in different terms, the "inter-market pressures" intruded and inspired a labeling of stability as "a matter of assumption." These pressures were quite obviously an afterthought, dealt with in an unobtrusive tone mainly suggestive of a guarding of flanks, with anything but the author's usual laboring of a point to assure us that it makes sense. Afterthoughts too can be sound; but this one seems to take its rise in a confusion which identifies a change in the *equilibrium* interest rate as the disturbance appropriate for testing the stability of the equilibrium imputed to the original set of basic "givens." As we explored deviations of interest rate and price level without changing the original "givens," we appeared to find that, after all, stability conditions are present. Perhaps then we may disregard the discordant note from this significant Hydra head, as a case of temporary tone deafness, and hear only its rather full-voiced support of the major theme of the quantity theory of money.

Thus far I have made bold myself to represent the "Chicago Heads" and those harmonious with them as they sang and as they might countersing against such major disharmonies as those of the avowedly incompatible Keynesian heads or against the mere vocal error of Patinkin. I must, however, single out for somewhat different treatment one now-leading Chicago head, the redoubtable Milton Friedman. He has greatly contributed in relatively recent years to a significant and still growing swell in the quantity-theory chorus. At the same time, his countersong is less nearly encompassed in the sounds I have offered than, I hope, are most other major, harmonious notes.

He would presumably wish to emphasize as basis for his message the empirical studies he has carried out or influenced. But in the approach to such efforts he has contributed importantly to the theoretical discussion. In his own essay in the 1956 volume, *Studies in the Quantity Theory of Money* (Chicago: University of Chicago Press), he spelled out the presumptive determinants of the demand function for money and asserted its stability. Apart from the marginal utility function for cash balances (made real balances of course by a price-level factor), the rate of interest found a role, as did the expected rate of change in the price level. A factor for "wealth" was evidently crucial—divided into "human wealth" (somehow capitalized labor income) and the "nonhuman wealth" dependent on other sources of income. It seemed that he would as lief have rested simply upon real income, at least if it were divided into "human" and "nonhuman" income. In his more recent work, summarized in the *Journal of Political Economy* for August 1959, this transition appears to have been made in a sense definitively. He had in his earlier work stipulated that the relevant income was in some sense *permanent* income; and now this factor has taken the stage almost to the point of crowding off the other actors.

It might thus seem that we were back in ordinary pre-Keynesian discussion, in which a particular real income carried with it a demand for one particular real balance. But of course there are differences. True, Friedman finds empirically little actual role for the rate of interest; and only during drastic change of the price level do expectations of such change appear to enter. In principle, however, each has a place. It might well be doubted whether this fact really constitutes a difference. But Friedman's hypothesis that permanent income may almost wholly account for the demand for cash balances both secularly and cyclically is importantly novel. His statistical findings are far from unimpressive, although I personally should like to let them season a bit, partly because Friedman's "money" includes savings deposits in commercial banks. For present purposes, the question is whether the permanent income hypothesis makes any significant difference to the assertion that monetary stability conditions are present.

On theoretical grounds it would seem that no new worries are introduced. With a given quantity of money, should men on average start by error to divest themselves of cash balances, the money income we measure will of course rise. If Friedman is right, the higher *measured* money income will not be the magnitude to which men now wish to adjust their cash balances (although the original error at least is still crying for correction). Yet this current *measured* magnitude, being the most important single factor determining *expected* (that is, "permanent") income, *has* raised the crucial magnitude; and the longer the measured money income remains high in relation to its putative equilibrium level, the more nearly "permanent" income approaches it. In more old-fashioned discussion we might have spoken as if desired cash balances immediately rose to suit the higher measured income. With Friedman we ought (if the error continued) to expect a lagging rise in the cash-balance demand, which should result in a less prompt decline in measured income as "permanent" income rose, and less jerkiness in the restoration of the original money income, perhaps with a small damped fluctuation *below* the original level.

In the case of a rise in the quantity of money there is, as Friedman points out, a reading of some interest. Since "permanent" money income, and hence cash balances demanded, will rise initially less than measured money income, measured money income will tend to rise more than it otherwise would—higher than the level at which it must settle when "permanent" income has risen enough to absorb the new money into desired balances. Thus a rise in the money supply would bring about the new equilibrium money income and price level only after a temporarily greater rise in money income. One might add that this exaggerated rise, together with upward flexibility and downward rigidity of wage rates, contains an interesting possibility for an upper turning point in the business cycle. But in the context of readily adjusting prices, which is our realm at present, no doubt is cast on the proposition that a given quantity of money tends to create a particular equilibrium money income and price level.

It would be useful, of course, to listen to the calls of other recent heads of the Hydra. I must content myself with having invited attention to a few strong voices as suggesting that the gray-eyed goddess is making progress toward unifying the monetary chorus, and that the song emerging is but a harmonious variation on the old, neoclassical theme—a variation possibly to be distinguished, at worst, as merely neo-neoclassicalism.

· III ·

MONETARY DISTURBANCES AND BUSINESS FLUCTUATIONS IN TWO CENTURIES OF AMERICAN HISTORY

CLARK WARBURTON

More than forty business cycles since the beginning of our national government are recorded by the National Bureau of Economic Research.[1] Although there is great divergence in the character of these cycles, each includes a downswing, trough, upswing, and peak. Of the downswings, several are notable because of financial panic or the length and severity of the depression. A few of the upswings, under the pressure of war, have given us serious inflation. This article is focused on the relation of disturbances in our monetary system to the great depressions and inflations, and to intervening fluctuations of lesser magnitude.

THE DEPRESSION OF THE LATE 1760'S AND EARLY 1770'S

The Revolutionary War was preceded by a decade of depression in most of the colonies.[2] Previous depressions had not been simultaneous or in close sequence throughout the Atlantic seaboard colonies. Some of the single-colony depres-

[1] Willard Thorp, *Business Annals*, publ. no. 8 (New York, 1926); Arthur F. Burns and Wesley C. Mitchell, *Measuring Business Cycles* (New York, 1946); Geoffrey H. Moore, *Measuring Recessions*, Occasional Paper 61 (New York, 1958). All published by the National Bureau of Economic Research.

[2] Thorp, p. 112.

sions and spurts of growth are known to have been associated with changes in the circulating medium. It is a reasonable assumption that the widespread character of the depression of the last half of the 1760's and first half of the 1770's was related to some common force impinging on the circulating medium of all the colonies. That such a common force was operating is known. For a quarter of a century the British Parliament had endeavored to prevent the establishment of banks in the colonies and to suppress issues of bills of credit for use as money. These efforts were intensified in 1764 by an Act of Parliament forbidding, except in emergencies, new issues as legal tender and requiring withdrawal of outstanding issues at their retirement or redemption dates. There appears to be little doubt that this act was a major factor in the widespread depression that helped to bring about the Revolutionary War.[8]

THE 1780'S AND THE BEGINNING OF BANKING UNDER THE NATIONAL GOVERNMENT

With the assumption of sovereign powers by the colonies, their legislative assemblies began to make provision for currency issues and to consider proposals for establishment of banks. Problems of war finance led them and the Continental Congress, under the Articles of Confederation, into large currency issues. These provided the nation with a rapidly expanding circulating medium, with the usual consequence of rising prices and business stimulation. But when the issues became so large that eventual redemption in specie appeared hopeless, the public lost faith in the currency. To provide a new circulating medium less likely to depreciate, Congress

[8] Bray Hammond, *Banks and Politics in America from the Revolution to the Civil War* (Princeton: Princeton University Press, 1957), pp. 25–26; Bernhard Knollenberg, *Origins of the American Revolution: 1759–1766* (New York: Macmillan, 1960), pp. 181–184; Richard A. Lester, *Monetary Experiments, Early American and Recent Scandinavian* (Princeton: Princeton University Press, 1939), pp. 24–25; John C. Miller, *Origins of the American Revolution* (Boston: Little, Brown, 1943), pp. 18–19, 264–265.

established in 1781 the Bank of North America, located at Philadelphia. The next year the bank obtained charters from Massachusetts, New York, and Pennsylvania. For the remainder of the war it was the only bank in the new nation.

The treaty of peace was signed in September of 1783. After the war a short boom occurred.[4] Specie received from British troop expenditures and French loans was in circulation. In the spring of 1784 the capital and operations of the Bank of North America were enlarged and in June and July banks were established in New York and Boston. These conditions opened the way to revival of overseas trade and expansion of domestic trade financed through a circulating medium tied to specie or sterling rather than to the depreciated "continentals." But merchandise imports, after the wartime shortages, were larger than exports and quickly led to exports of specie. The information available suggests that by the spring of 1785 the three banks had lost much of the specie obtained with their capital subscriptions the year before, with a consequent contraction of their circulating notes and deposits.[5] The postwar boom collapsed and was followed by two years of depression.

Toward the latter part of 1786 and in 1787 the banks ex-

[4] Andrew C. McLaughlin, *The Confederation and the Constitution, 1783–1789* (New York: Harper, 1905), pp. 76–77; Thorp, p. 112.

[5] Specific information regarding the specie holdings and circulation and deposits of the three banks is at hand only for the Massachusetts Bank, which in the middle of April held a third less specie than at the beginning of the year, and reduced its circulation and deposits by a similar proportion during the next two months. The specie was more than recouped later in the year, but was down again in the summer of 1786 (N. S. B. Gras, *The Massachusetts First National Bank of Boston, 1784–1934*, Cambridge, Mass.: Harvard University Press, 1937, pp. 586–588). Otto C. Lightner, *The History of Business Depressions* (New York: Northeastern Press, 1922), mentions the loss of specie; and Lawrence Lewis, in *A History of the Bank of North America* (Philadelphia: Lippincott, 1882), p. 55, refers to the drain of specie, but gives no figures for specie holdings of the bank. Hammond refers to Madison's mention in 1786 of the intense shortage of specie, and to a loss of cash by the Bank of North America after its Pennsylvania charter was repealed in September 1785, but attributes the latter to the decline of confidence in the bank (*Banks and Politics*, pp. 54, 95–96).

panded their operations.[6] In 1788 the new Constitution was ratified by enough states to make it effective. A business upswing had started, and recovery was well under way by the time the new government was organized in 1789. During the next two years the banks expanded rapidly and prosperity continued.[7]

ERA OF THE FIRST BANK OF THE UNITED STATES, 1792–1810

The first Bank of the United States was opened in December 1791 and operated until 1811. During those years the nation became dependent upon a circulating medium provided chiefly by banks. By 1800 about 30 banks, and by 1811 about 90, were in operation.[8]

The Bank of the United States, because of its size and association with the United States government, had more freedom of action than other banks in acquiring and managing specie holdings. This latitude appears to have been used, after its initial spurt of growth, to provide a steadier increase in its circulation and deposits than in its holdings of specie. The policies of the Bank also exerted pressure on other banks to maintain convertibility of their obligations into specie and hence, with the limited amount of specie available to the banks, tended to restrain the growth of the total circulating medium.[9]

[6] Again, specific information is at hand only for the Massachusetts Bank. However, the Bank of North America received a new charter from Pennsylvania in March 1787, and undoubtedly then enlarged its operations. Data for the early years of the Bank of New York are not available.

[7] In December 1791 the circulation and deposits of the Massachusetts Bank amounted to nearly eight times the amount in December 1785, the annual increases (measured from weekly figures nearest the middle of the month) ranging from 16 per cent to 93 per cent. The Bank of New York at the beginning of May 1791 had twice the circulation and deposits of the Massachusetts Bank.

[8] Hammond, *Banks and Politics*, pp. 144, 145.

[9] Hammond, pp. 198–202, and John Thom Holdsworth, *The First Bank of the United States* (in publications of the National Monetary Commission; Sen. Doc. no. 571; Washington: Government Printing Office, 1910), p. 92.

In general, the period of operation of the first Bank of the United States was a time of economic growth and prosperity. However, downswings occurred in 1796–97, 1802–03, and 1807–09. The first of these was preceded by an interruption of growth in the circulation and deposits of the Bank of the United States.[10] We do not know whether this occurred in the other two cycles.

BETWEEN THE TWO BANKS OF THE UNITED STATES, 1811–1816

In the debate on renewal of the charter of the Bank of the United States there were widespread predictions of general business collapse if the charter was not renewed.[11] A mild recession occurred in 1811–12, but the dire predictions did not materialize. The cogency of arguments regarding the impact of closing the Bank stimulated the states to charter numerous new banks; the trustees of the Bank of the United States transferred its specie and some of its business to a private bank organized by its most important stockholder; and existing banks in the larger cities endeavored to expand and attract the business of former customers of the Bank of the United States.[12] In addition, the outbreak of the

---

Available data are insufficient to provide estimates of the total circulating medium. Wholesale price indexes indicate a rise in prices of the order of magnitude of 50 per cent during the first five years, and a slightly declining price trend during the other fifteen years, of the lifetime of the first Bank of the United States.

[10] I am indebted to Professor James O. Wettereau for permission to use quarterly statements he has collected for the Bank of the United States during the years 1792–1800.

[11] Erick Bollmann, *Paragraphs on Banks* (Philadelphia: Conrad, 1810), p. 50; Mathew Carey, *Desultory Reflections upon the Ruinous Consequences of a Non-Renewal of the Charter of the Bank of the United States* (Philadelphia: Fry and Kammerer, 1810); memorials and resolutions from state banks and business groups to Congress and congressional committees, cited by Holdsworth, *First Bank of the United States*, pp. 83–87.

[12] Specific information regarding expansion of leading banks in other cities is at hand only for the Massachusetts Bank, which increased its deposits and circulation more than threefold during the year 1811 (Gras, *Massachusetts First National Bank*, pp. 606–608, 617).

War of 1812 brought serious war financing problems which were met by methods that stimulated bank expansion.

The government deficit of 1812–1815 was financed chiefly by issues of United States notes, most of which were interest-bearing and a large portion of which was acquired by the banks. Rapid expansion of the banks and loss of specie led to suspension of specie payments, except in New England, in August 1814. Some of the notes issued by the Treasury were in small denominations not bearing interest and were used as money, though not made legal tender. Their direct effect on the amount of the circulating medium was slight: the maximum outstanding was small in comparison with bank notes and bank deposits. However, their indirect effect was substantial, because they were convertible into 7 per cent government stock or 6 per cent notes. As the non-interest-bearing notes were received in the course of trade by banks or other investor groups, they were exchanged for the interest-bearing obligations and were reissued by the Treasury. This provided an indirect method of selling government obligations to the banks and a consequent increase in bank-issued circulating medium. The increase in the circulating notes of the banks, as estimated by Gallatin, was more than one half of the amount of the government deficit.

With the cessation of war financing, leading banks in New York and Philadelphia urged a reduction of loans and discounts in preparation for resumption of specie payments.[13] I have not found any information to indicate whether such a contraction was begun at that time, though this seems probable and may have been a factor in the depression of 1816.[14]

[13] Henry W. Domett, *A History of the Bank of New York, 1784–1884* (New York: Putnam, 1884), p. 71; Lewis, *Bank of North America*, pp. 88–89.

[14] The recessions of 1918 and 1945 reported in the National Bureau

ERA OF THE SECOND BANK OF THE UNITED STATES, 1817–1835

Legislation providing for establishment of the second Bank of the United States, designed to function in much the same way as the first Bank, was enacted in April 1816, and the Bank opened in January 1817. By 1829, according to Gallatin's estimate, its notes and deposits were about one fourth of the total for all banks in the country. Its large specie holdings and changes in its holdings of the obligations of other banks gave it a position of leadership in the banking structure, so that an expansionary policy by the Bank of the United States had a stimulating, and a contractive policy a retarding, impact similar in character to that of a central bank.[15]

Historians of business fluctuations recognize five business downswings, with intervening periods of recovery, during the lifetime of the second Bank of the United States. The first of these was a sequel to the means used to assure resumption of specie payments and to establish the leadership of the Bank. At the time of its chartering Congress had provided that after February 20, 1817, all payments to the United States were to be made in specie, United States Treasury notes, or notes of banks paying specie on demand. It was hoped that this would induce the state-chartered banks to resume specie payments by that date. Resumption was not accomplished until late in 1817, and the process involved a rapid expansion of the Bank of the United States. This was so large that the Bank itself was threatened with inability to maintain specie payments, and in the summer of 1818 began a process of contraction that continued for about

chronology of business cycles were postwar adjustments and not sequels to monetary contraction. This may have been the case in 1816.

[15] The central-bank character of both the first and second Banks of the United States is elucidated by Hammond, *Banks and Politics*, pp. 198–209, 286–325, 366–368, and by Fritz Redlich, *The Molding of American Banking: Men and Ideas, Part 1: 1781–1840* (New York: Hafner, 1947), pp. 96–160.

a year, during which its circulation and deposits were reduced by more than one half. The ensuing depression lasted about two years.

The Bank resumed its expansion in the latter part of 1819, and by the middle of 1821 its circulation and deposits had increased about 40 per cent. By that time business was on the upswing, but the Bank of the United States and other banks began to lose specie, inducing another period of contraction in 1822 that continued mildly into 1823, followed by a business downswing. A reversal of the Bank's specie holdings was again followed by expansion and another business upswing. But in turn, another period of loss of specie and contraction led in 1826 to the third of the five recessions during the active life of the Bank.

This sequence of changing specie holdings of the Bank of the United States, followed by expansions and contractions of bank credit, with resulting business cycles, cannot of course be satisfactorily explained without an understanding of the forces inducing the gains and losses of specie. Movements of specie between the Bank of the United States and other banks and into and out of circulation were doubtless a factor. International specie movements appear to have been more important. Some of these movements were associated with the Bank's negotiations abroad, including the handling of payments on the United States government debt held in other countries. Others were the result of shifting trade balances associated with differences in harvests and other economic factors, and of investment flows which in turn were largely the consequence of changing business prospects.[16]

After 1826 the circulating medium provided by the Bank

[16] Walter Buckingham Smith, *Economic Aspects of the Second Bank of the United States* (Cambridge, Mass.: Harvard University Press, 1953), provides much information regarding these forces.

of the United States was less dependent upon changes in its specie holdings and was more a matter of policy decisions. There was a fairly continuous expansion of the Bank's circulation and deposits until 1832, despite some large variations in specie holdings. During this period only one mild recession is recorded, following a mild reduction in the Bank's circulation and deposits.

In 1834 the fifth depression during the life of the second Bank of the United States followed contractive operations beginning in the preceding year. That contraction was not induced by loss of specie—in fact, specie holdings were increasing—but was a deliberate policy designed to fortify the position of the Bank in preparation for the pending expiration of its charter and as a guard against adverse effects of Treasury actions deemed likely to cause a specie drain.[17] Cessation of the Bank's contractive behavior shortly after mid-1834 and then expansion for nearly a year was accompanied by another business upswing. By that time the Bank's influence was no longer dominant, for it was approaching its end as a bank chartered by Congress.

ADJUSTMENT TO AN ALTERED BANKING SYSTEM AND MONETARY STANDARD, 1836–1843

Termination of business by the Bank of the United States, with liquidation of its assets, withdrawal of its circulation, and cancellation of its deposits, without offsetting developments, would have produced a serious business collapse. However, the business of its branches was taken over by various successor institutions and the bulk of its assets, at the main office in Philadelphia, by a state-chartered successor bank with continuity of management.[18] In addition, many new banks opened throughout the nation and others ex-

[17] Hammond and Smith describe this episode in considerable detail.
[18] See Smith, pp. 174–175, for these arrangements.

panded rapidly under the stimulation of a need for banking services and removal of the restraints previously exercised by the Bank of the United States.

But though expiration of the charter of the second Bank of the United States was followed by expansion of the circulating medium, other developments soon produced contraction. During the first few months of 1837 the banks of the nation lost about one fourth of their specie, and those in New York more than one half. A part of this loss, particularly by the New York banks, was a consequence of the distribution of the federal government surplus among the states. Some of the loss may have been a drain into circulation as a result of the hard money agitation of the Jacksonians, the President's order that payments for purchases of public land be made in specie, and an increased need for currency because of the business boom.[19] Taken together these forces seem sufficiently potent to have called a halt to the rapid expansion of bank circulation and deposits and consequently to have produced a depression in 1837.

In fact, however, there was a more fundamental factor at work, which in the light of events of the next several years seems to have had a greater force than is usually assigned to it. This was the Coinage Act of 1834, which changed from 15 to 16 the ratio of the amount of silver in a dollar coined from that metal to the amount of gold in a gold dollar. To understand the impact of this act, which brought the mint ratio closer to the market ratio and might be thought to have been innocuous, we need to look back to the monetary

[19] The distribution of the surplus was required by a Congressional act of June 1836, with the first installment early in 1837. The specie circular was issued in July 1836, to apply to land sales after December 15 of that year. Richard H. Timberlake, Jr., who has recently studied their impact, believes that the effect of the specie circular was negligible ("The Specie Circular and Distribution of the Surplus," *Journal of Political Economy*, 68:109–117, April 1960).

standards of the leading nations. For a third of a century prior to 1816 the United States, Great Britain, and France were all using both silver and gold as legal tender, at coinage ratios of 15.0, 15.2, and 15.5 respectively, with other countries on a silver or bimetallic standard. During this period approximately equal amounts of the two metals were coined in the United States. In 1816 the British mints were closed to silver coinage, and five years later the Bank of England resumed specie payments after operating under the Bank Restriction Act since 1797.[20] Great Britain became the only country in the world with an exclusively gold standard. As a consequence, the world's monetary gold tended to gravitate to that country, and American coinage was thereafter, until 1834, chiefly silver.

The change in the coinage ratio made it profitable to import gold into the United States for coinage, stimulated silver exports, and reduced our monetary use of silver. With most of the world on a silver standard or on a bimetallic standard with large amounts of silver in monetary use, the reduced absorption of silver by the United States was spread over a large area and did not have much impact upon the world market for silver. But our new market for gold was important.

Our imports of gold began in 1834. They were checked in 1835 by a crop failure, which reduced the favorable balance of trade, but were resumed in 1836. The gold imported came in part from the Bank of England, which was the chief holder of that metal. The Bank of England, alarmed by its loss of gold, raised its discount rate, which had been at 4 per cent for nine years, to 4½ per cent in July 1836, and to 5 per cent on September 1. In addition, toward the end of the year it

[20] *Report of the United States Monetary Commission* (1877), I, 66–67; Ralph G. Hawtrey, *Currency and Credit*, 3d ed. (London: Longmans, Green, 1928), chap. xviii.

refused to make further discounts on behalf of the firms that had been extending large credits and exporting gold to the United States, leading to a demand by those firms for payment from their American debtors. These measures resulted in a sharp reversal of the gold flow early in 1837, when the Bank of England had lost half of its gold holdings, and was an important factor in the reduction of specie holdings of the banks in this country during the early months of 1837.[21] Under this pressure and that of other forces inducing specie withdrawals, the seaboard banks could not maintain specie payments. New York and New Orleans suspended specie payments in May and were followed by banks in the rest of the country.

The impact of suspension of specie payments in 1837 was different from that in 1814. In the earlier period general banking codes had not been developed, and definite specie requirements were not included in most of the bank charters. This made it possible for banks to expand their note issues rapidly under the impact of war financing. By the 1830's most of the leading states had enacted legislation penalizing banks that failed to pay their notes in specie, or had inserted such provisions in new or renewed bank charters. Under these conditions suspension of specie payments provided relief from an immediate banking panic but led to a curtailment of bank loans and discounts and contraction of bank-supplied circulating medium.[22]

[21] John Clapham, *The Bank of England* (New York: Macmillan, 1945), II, 150–153; Richard Hildreth, *Banks, Banking, and Paper Currencies* (Boston: Whipple and Damrell, 1840), pp. 93–95; and Reginald C. McGrane, *The Panic of 1837: Some Financial Problems of the Jacksonian Era* (Chicago: University of Chicago Press, 1924), pp. 40–42.

[22] Davis R. Dewey, *State Banking before the Civil War* (Washington: Government Printing Office, 1910), pp. 73–79; Hildreth, pp. 97–100; and Lewis, *Bank of North America*, pp. 97–98. Hammond, after correctly describing the difference between suspension of specie payments in 1814 and in 1837 and bank suspensions in the twentieth century (in the former cases the banks did not close their doors, and their notes and deposits continued to be

The leading banks made strenuous efforts to increase their holdings of specie. Both gold and silver were imported. By May of 1838, a year after suspension, the banks of New York, assisted by a gold shipment directly from the Bank of England, had more than recouped their specie losses, and by the end of the year this was true for banks throughout the country.[23] Specie payments had been resumed during the summer. Expansion of circulation and deposits was under way. The Bank of England had attracted sufficient gold to meet both its own requirements and assistance to American banks and had reduced its discount rate to the customary 4 per cent.

But the next year the Bank of England experienced another drain. From March to November 1839 its specie dropped rapidly. The discount rate was raised to 5 per cent in May, 5½ per cent in June, and 6 per cent in August. This reversed the direction of the gold flow in the autumn, and American banks were in trouble again. Another and longer period of contraction followed, accompanied by one of the longest and most severe depressions in our history.

During the next few years American banks seemed unable to compete with the Bank of England in the retention of gold, and under the prevailing silver-to-gold ratio American silver imports were relatively light. Though the Bank of England reduced the discount rate to 5 per cent in January 1840, it continued that rate until April 1842. This was sufficient to attract gold from other countries or at least to prevent American banks from building up gold stocks. The

used as money), incorrectly concludes that in 1837, as in 1814, banks were free to create more deposits and more notes (*Banks and Politics*, p. 478). This was doubtless true in some parts of the country, particularly in some of the southern states, but not in the leading seaboard states.

[23] Both Clapham (*Bank of England*, pp. 164–165) and Hammond (pp. 479–485) discuss the arrangements for the gold shipment from the Bank of England, which Clapham characterizes as "without precedent."

world's monetary stock and annual production of gold in the 1830's were insufficient to serve two great nations, instead of one, without inducing banking disturbances and business depression.

The turning point came in 1842 and 1843, when increased production of gold in Russia enabled American banks to increase their gold holdings without disturbing the Bank of England. Recovery from the long depression began.[24]

STATE BANKS UNDER EXPANDING GOLD SUPPLIES, 1843–1859

In the late 1840's and in the 1850's the gold base of the American and British banking systems was greatly augmented by production from the Australian and Californian mines. For most of this period the price level was rising—creeping inflation, or faster, under the gold standard. It was a period of great economic expansion, but there were three noteworthy business downswings.[25] The chain of events leading to the first of these, in 1847–48, appears to have begun with establishment of the Independent Treasury. The law required all payments into the Treasury after December 31, 1846, and all payments from the Treasury after April 1, 1847, to be made in specie or Treasury notes. In the latter part of 1846 the Treasury rapidly reduced its balances in state banks, deposited its receipts in the newly established subtreasury offices, and shifted as rapidly as possible to use of specie in government transactions. This drew specie from the banks into circulation and the Treasury. By the beginning of 1847 the banks' holdings of specie had been reduced by one sixth in comparison with the beginning of 1846. How-

[24] The annual Russian production is reported to have increased from an amount worth $4 million in 1840 to $11 million in 1843 (*Report of the United States Monetary Commission*, 1877, I, Appendix, p. 572).

[25] Thorp's *Business Annals* also mentions a brief recession in 1845 and a mild depression in 1846. These are not mentioned in Lightner's *History of Business Depressions*.

ever, the immediate impact was small because the banks' losses were recouped from gold imports associated with large exports of grain. This produced in the summer of 1847 a drain of gold from the Bank of England, which was already subject to pressure from the Bank of France, and led to an increase in its discount rate from 4 per cent in the spring to 8 per cent in late October.[26] The gold flow was reversed. Another contraction in American bank reserves and their circulation and deposits occurred, followed by a money market panic and business recession.

Some temporary relief to the banks during the panic was given by a Treasury purchase of government obligations under a resale agreement.[27] More substantial and more permanent additions to the banks' specie holdings were made possible by the huge quantity of gold mined in California. Though a large proportion of the new gold was exported, additions to bank reserves and to gold coin in circulation in the United States were substantial. For several years American banks steadily expanded their circulation and deposits, with the longest peacetime upswing in the National Bureau chronology.[28]

In the middle 1850's, the annual rate of gold production slackened. Pressures upon bank reserves began to be felt in various parts of the world. The Bank of England had a serious gold drain in 1853 and the early months of 1854 and

[26] Clapham, pp. 200–202, 429.

[27] For a discussion of this episode, see Richard H. Timberlake, Jr., "The Independent Treasury and Monetary Policy before the Civil War," *Southern Economic Journal,* 27:92–103 (October 1960). Timberlake describes the transaction as "probably the first policy-loaded, open-market operation in government securities that a central monetary authority of this country ever conducted."

[28] The 1933–1937 upswing is measured by Burns and Mitchell, in *Measuring Business Cycles,* as 50 months; that of 1848–1853 is not measured in months, but Thorp, in *Business Annals,* indicates that it must have approached 60 months. The only upswing of longer duration is that of 1938–1945.

raised its discount rate by a series of steps from 2 per cent at the beginning of 1853 to 5½ per cent in May 1854.[29] This, together with changes in the balance of trade and accumulation of specie in the United States Treasury, brought a halt in the accumulation of specie by American banks.[30] A lull in business ensued, but the depression was mild. The Treasury released specie by rapid retirement of the Mexican War debt, including large purchases of outstanding bonds at market prices, and the banks soon resumed expansion.

In late 1856 and in 1857 more serious trouble developed. The banks, with very little increase in their specie reserves after the end of 1854, had continued to expand their operations, and some of them were highly vulnerable. Specie movements, both internal and external, became critically important. The sequence leading to downswing and crisis appears to have begun with an unusually large seasonal drain of coin from the eastern banks, particularly those in New York City, to other parts of the country, followed by insolvencies and suspension of specie payments in the East. A successful effort was then made by New York banks to accumulate specie, drawing a considerable amount from abroad. The British Bank Act of 1844 had made the Bank of England more sensitive than previously to gold drains, and with its reserve declining at an alarming rate in the

[29] The bank's annual average total specie holdings decreased each year from 1852 to 1857 (R. H. Inglis Palgrave, *Bank Rate and the Money Market in England, France, Germany, Holland, and Belgium, 1844–1900*, London: Murray, 1903, p. 15); and its "reserve" in the Banking Department from early 1853 to about mid-1854—from reserve at dates of change in the discount rate (Ralph G. Hawtrey, *A Century of Bank Rate*, London: Longmans, Green, 1938, p. 281).

[30] With a surplus of revenue over expenditures, the cash balance in the Treasury, which was held mostly in specie, increased from $15 million on July 1, 1852, to $28 million on September 30, 1853. The latter figure was nearly half the amount of specie held by the banks, which was estimated at $60 million at the beginning of 1854 (*Annual Report of the Secretary of the Treasury*, 1853, pp. 1–2, and 1854, p. 280).

autumn of 1857, its discount rate was raised in October to 8 per cent and in November to the unprecedented high of 10 per cent. This replenished the gold of the Bank of England without seriously disturbing accretions by American banks, presumably by attracting it from other uses in various parts of the world. But adjustment of the banking and credit system in the gold-standard part of the world to a diminished rate of gold production had entailed a financial crisis of extraordinary extent and severity.

WAR FINANCING AND THE BANKING SYSTEM IN THE 1860'S AND 1870'S

The initial financing of the War between the States was a loan from banks in the leading eastern cities, withdrawn by the Secretary of the Treasury in specie and resulting in immediate suspension of specie payments. The gold loan met only the government's emergency requirements, and the Treasury began issuing its own notes in denominations suitable for use as currency. These were made legal tender by Congress in March 1862. Banks operating under state laws at first hesitated to regard the legal-tender notes as equivalent to specie; but as the war went on, this became a necessity, and court decisions and legislatures legalized the practice.[31]

By the close of the war the federal government had issued

[31] There were two aspects of treatment of legal-tender notes as the equivalent of specie: (1) for meeting requirements in bank charters or state laws that bank obligations—circulating notes or deposits—be payable in specie at all times; and (2) for meeting requirements that banks keep at all times certain amounts of specie relative to their circulating notes or deposits, or both. For the former, legal-tender notes became the equivalent of specie throughout the nation. For the latter, there was at least one exception. The branches of the State Bank of Ohio were required to maintain their specie reserves at the legal ratio until they converted to national banks. "Legal tender notes may supercede coin for the purpose of *paying debts,* but not for any other purpose for which it may be required to be kept on hand" (letter from the president of the State Bank of Ohio to the president of the Summit County Branch Bank, May 13, 1864).

about half a billion dollars' worth of legal-tender notes. This was only about one sixth of the wartime borrowing, but it was about twice the amount of gold and silver in monetary use at the beginning of the war. While the legal-tender notes were used as pocket currency, they tended to accumulate in the banks, as the banks paid out their own note issues except when lawful money was demanded and held the greenbacks to meet their "specie" requirements.

Establishment of the national banking system in 1863, the prohibitive tax on state bank notes in 1865, and conversions of state banks to national banks resulted in more uniform and rigid lawful-money reserve requirements and limited the amount of circulating banknotes. Specie holdings by the banks, except for subsidiary and minor coins, were greatly reduced. Most of the specie that had been held by the banks was sold, and gold exports exceeded production.[32] For the remainder of the 1860's and throughout the 1870's the legal-tender notes and other types of Treasury obligations into which some of them were converted continued to constitute most of the lawful-money reserves of the banks and a portion of pocket currency. However, bank notes and bank deposits constituted the bulk of the circulating medium.

When the war closed an effort was made to retire the legal-tender notes rapidly by inducing their conversion into bonds. The consequent impact on business activity was so great that in 1868 further retirement was forbidden by Congress.

[32] For the four-year period ending June 30, 1866, reported net gold exports exceeded estimated domestic gold production by about $75 million, or 40 per cent. In a talk at the Southern Economic Association in 1957 (published in the *Journal of Economic History,* 18:283–297, September 1958), I said that the specie in large part accumulated in the Bank of England. This is not a correct statement. Specie holdings of the Bank of England, according to Palgrave's annual estimates (*Bank Rate and the Money Market,* p. 15) increased from a low in 1861 to a high in 1867 by an amount which was over half the estimated reduction of specie in American banks, but American exports of gold during the period, coming largely from production, were several times as large as the accumulation by the Bank of England.

Nevertheless, for many years the reserve position of the banks was under severe pressure. The National Bank Act placed a ceiling on the amount of national bank notes that could be issued. When this was removed, the amount was limited by availability of the bonds on which they were based. This meant that an increasing proportion of the legal-tender notes was needed for pocket currency. From the autumn of 1866, after most of the state banks had converted into national banks, to the autumn of 1872, the lawful-money reserves of national banks were reduced by approximately 40 per cent while their circulation and deposits had increased by about 15 per cent. State banks were also expanding their deposit obligations. Insufficiency of lawful money for use as bank reserves was the underlying factor in the crisis of 1873, though the immediate cause was the pressure to withdraw lawful money from the banks to meet currency needs in the autumn when crop movements were at their height.

In 1874 the reserve position of the banks was relieved by a moderate increase in outstanding legal-tender notes and by exemption of circulating notes from the reserve requirements for national banks, which previously had applied to both notes and deposits. The relief was temporary. During the next few years outstanding legal-tender notes and national bank notes both declined. Under these circumstances the banks did not accumulate additional legal-tender notes for use as reserves and they were not accumulating specie. As long as the legal-tender notes were inconvertible and a premium on specie existed, gold and silver from American mines were exported. The banks could not increase their reserves by acquiring specie except at a price that would lead to loss. With resumption of specie payments at the beginning of 1879 the premium on coin disappeared. Banks could then acquire gold without prospect of future loss.

THE 1880'S AND 1890'S AND THE "LIMPING STANDARD"

Resumption of specie payments took place under what has been called a "limping standard." A revision of the coinage law in 1873 made the gold dollar the unit of value and omitted the silver dollar from coinage, but silver coins remained full legal tender with no requirement for redemption in gold. In 1878 provision was made for a limited coinage of silver, but the amount of it and actions of the Treasury to maintain its convertibility into gold kept the monetary stock of silver smaller than the monetary stock of gold.

For about two years following resumption of specie payments the banks increased their reserves substantially, chiefly by using their balances abroad to pay for imports of gold. After this initial spurt, which was essentially a redistribution of the world's monetary gold stock, the increase that occurred in lawful money was insufficient to maintain continuously an adequate growth in both bank reserves and currency in circulation. Because of limitations on issue of bank notes, seasonal needs for currency tended to draw lawful money from the banks, thus providing great pressure on their reserves.

The underlying basis of the banking and business fluctuations in the 1880's and most of the 1890's was similar to that of the 1830's and early 1840's. The rate of world gold production was insufficient to provide an appropriate growth in bank reserves and hand-to-hand currency in the countries on the gold standard, even though a part of the hand-to-hand currency was supplied by silver and by circulating notes not requiring a gold backing. The lack of growth of monetary gold was reflected primarily in a tendency of the price level to decline—a creeping deflation under the gold standard. But it also provided a situation under which bank reserves were greatly affected by changes in the international balance of trade, actions of European central banks, and variation in the public demand for currency. The fluctuations in bank reserves caused occasional periods of contraction in bank deposits, with consequent business downswings superimposed on the declining price level. These circumstances gave great impetus to attempts to re-establish a bimetallic monetary base. Those efforts were unsuccessful but resulted in the law of 1890 designed to provide more basic money in the United States through additional coinage of silver and issue of circulating notes on the basis of silver. The benefits of this law were small because maintenance of convertibility of all forms of currency into gold tended to result in larger gold exports or smaller gold imports than would otherwise have occurred.

For the twenty years following resumption of specie payments the National Bureau of Economic Research records five business downswings. Information for national banks indicates that the business peaks at the beginning of these downswings were preceded by peaks, or at least an interruption to growth, in bank reserves and in deposits and circulation, with the decline in reserves usually preceding that in circulation and deposits.[33] My own studies of this period have not progressed far enough to permit description of the specific circumstances inducing each of the upswings and downswings in bank reserves.

RISING GOLD PRODUCTION AND THE GOLD STANDARD, 1896–1914

In 1900 the Gold Standard Act made all forms of money in the United States redeemable into gold at the Treasury,

[33] The national-bank data used in this comparison are for the reporting dates, five times a year, and the limitations that this places on the accuracy of the sequence should be kept in mind. The data need to be subjected to more rigorous statistical analysis to determine their cyclical characteristics than I have been able to give them. The above statement is therefore a tentative conclusion.

with provisions which led to a reduction in silver coinage without reducing the existing monetary use of silver. The world's production of gold had been increased in the late 1890's by the South African, Alaskan, and Canadian discoveries. From 1896 to 1914 the specie reserves of national banks increased at about 8 per cent a year. There was a similar increase in their deposits (excluding interbank deposits and those of the United States government). In addition, there was a faster growth of deposits in state banks than in national banks. There was thus no longer a problem of inadequate growth in the nation's circulating medium. With an average rate of increase more than the rate of growth of output, the result was a rising trend in the price level—another creeping inflation under the gold standard.

But occasional interruptions occurred. Five business peaks during the period are dated by the National Bureau. Each was preceded by a peak, or at least a halt in growth, in the lawful-money reserves of the national banks, and in their deposits.[34] I have not investigated the specific circumstances which brought about the downward deviations from an upward trend in bank reserves. However, the feature of the situation which most impressed contemporary observers was the seasonal drain of currency from the banks to meet crop movements and the consequent great pressure upon their reserves. Such seasonal movements were most serious in years when reserves were under pressure from international specie movements or other forces. The changing proportion of all lawful money in the country absorbed by currency in circulation was the chief problem of the monetary structure as viewed by the protagonists of banking reform. The panic of 1907 was a dramatic illustration of this situation and led to the Aldrich-Vreeland Act, which provided for emergency currency issues and for appointment of the National Mone-

[34] The comment in note 33 also applies to this period.

tary Commission. The studies and report of the Commission and the pressure for banking reform resulted in the Federal Reserve Act of 1913.

PURPOSE OF THE FEDERAL RESERVE SYSTEM

A survey of the literature preceding establishment of the Federal Reserve System indicates that it was designed primarily to accomplish five things: (1) to provide a method of issuing paper currency by the banking system free from the limitations on national bank notes and readily adjusted in quantity to the varying need for currency; (2) to provide for interconvertibility between such currency and bank deposits without disturbing the reserve position of the banks; (3) to pool a portion of bank reserves and to make them available for the relief of financial stringency in any area or locality; (4) to remove or at least reduce inappropriate seasonal variation in bank credit; and (5) to stabilize the total amount of bank credit and thus promote stability of the total circulating medium. It was not assumed that the system would be able to control the long-run rate of growth of the circulating medium or "stock of money," in present-day terminology; but it was intended that the impact of fluctuations in the gold holdings of the banking system would be cushioned, money panics would be eliminated, and both deflation and inflation would be restrained or prevented.[35]

Since the establishment of the Federal Reserve System,

[35] For more detailed discussions of the views of the founders of the Federal Reserve System, see Clark Warburton, "Monetary Control under the Federal Reserve Act," *Political Science Quarterly*, 41:505–534 (December 1946); "Co-ordination of Monetary, Bank Supervisory, and Loan Agencies of the Federal Government," *Journal of Finance*, 5:153–155 (June 1950); "Monetary Theory and the Price Level Trend in the Future," in Study Group on Business Income, *Five Monographs on Business Income* (New York: American Institute of Accountants, 1950), p. 182; "How Much Variation in the Quantity of Money is Needed?" *Southern Economic Journal*, 18:503–505 (April 1952); and "Monetary Difficulties and the Structure of the Monetary System," *Journal of Finance*, 7:532–535 (December 1952).

changes in the stock of money, or circulating medium, have depended primarily on changes in the policies of the Reserve authorities. In the 1930's, however, changes in the value of their gold holdings were also important. The history of the relation of banking and monetary disturbances to business fluctuations since establishment of the Reserve system may conveniently be divided into three eras, separated by radical changes in policy objectives.

THE FIRST FEDERAL RESERVE ERA: 1915–1928

During their first two years of operation the Reserve banks were concerned with an initial expansion of circulating notes and with banking adjustments to disturbances in trade patterns and international financial relationships resulting from the war in Europe. After entry of the United States into the war in April 1917, Federal Reserve powers, strengthened by concentration of the required reserves of national and other member banks in the Reserve banks, were used for war-financing purposes. War-financing operations of the Treasury continued for about a year after the armistice and entailed a rapid expansion of bank credit. By the end of 1919 effective reserves of the national banks and their deposit obligations had increased, in comparison with 1914, by about 75 per cent.[36] The stock of money, according to Friedman's estimate, had about doubled.

Toward the end of 1919, the Federal Reserve Board felt it unnecessary to continue support of Treasury operations. Discount rates at the Reserve banks were raised from the range of 4 to 4½ per cent that had been maintained throughout the period of wartime financing to a range of 6 to 7 per cent in early 1921. The Reserve authorities were also dis-

[36] Effective reserves are computed from the lawful-money reserves (specie and legal tender) of national banks on September 12, 1914, and their balances in Federal Reserve banks on December 31, 1919, adjusted for the average percentage-reserve requirements on the two dates.

turbed by the fact that some member banks were discounting large amounts of paper continuously. To exert stronger pressure on such banks a differential penalty rate was established. Many member banks were willing to incur penalty rates in order to accommodate their own customers, but most of them found it necessary to reduce their holdings of government obligations acquired during the war. In addition, the amount of member-bank reserves was reduced by a substantial reduction in Reserve bank holdings of bills bought and of government obligations.

By mid-1920 the postwar boom had collapsed and a major downswing was under way. By the spring of 1921 a serious depression had developed. This was the first experience of the Reserve authorities in credit restraint and their actions had been followed by more severe results than they had anticipated. In midsummer, their policies were reversed and the recovery process began promptly.

This sequence of events was also followed by a search, within the Reserve system, for principles to serve as a basis for their operations. The Federal Reserve Board, in its report for 1923, included a more detailed discussion of guides to policy than in any previous or subsequent report. The basic principle emerging from this report is that a central bank should keep a close scrutiny of indexes of output, inventories, employment, sales, and prices. Restrictive measures should be taken when these indexes show output pressing upon capacity, unemployment at or close to the minimum, and prices rising, with easier credit policies in order when the indexes show rising unemployment, unused capacity, and falling prices.[37] Subsequent reports in the middle 1920's show concern about re-establishment of the gold standard throughout the world, the tendency of some member banks

[37] "Guides to Credit Policy," *Annual Report of the Federal Reserve Board for 1923*, pp. 29–39.

to rediscount continuously at the Reserve banks, and increasing speculation, but none of these was at that time the major focus of policy.[38]

The reports of the Board throughout the 1920's do not express concern about a need for growth in the circulating medium, nor is there a reflection of such a concern in the operations of the Reserve banks, the assets of which remained stable, except for frequent minor fluctuations, from mid-1921 to mid-1929. But though the Reserve authorities appear to have neglected growth they did not prevent its taking place, and reversals of direction in Reserve policy were reflected in business conditions. The business peak in 1923, the downswing in 1924, the recovery of 1925, the peak in 1926, the recession of 1927, recovery from it, and the downswing beginning in 1929 were all preceded by turnabouts in Reserve policy.[39]

THE SECOND FEDERAL RESERVE ERA: 1929 TO THE 1940'S

The annual report of the Federal Reserve Board for 1929 reveals a striking change of emphasis. The focus on output, employment, and prices is absent, with speculation becoming the center of attention. The report refers to the increase in discount rates at the Reserve banks from 3½ per cent at the beginning of 1928 to 5 per cent later in the year, and to 6 per cent in New York in August 1929, and describes the "direct pressure" put on member banks in the early part of 1929 to reduce their loans in the stock market, adding that the public consequences of this pressure were not a matter with which they should be concerned.[40]

[38] See particularly the *Annual Report of the Federal Reserve Board for 1928*, pp. 3–10.

[39] See the acompanying tabulation.

[40] "It is not for the Federal Reserve Board to estimate the general expediency or the larger public consequences of its intervention by 'direct pressure' in the complex situation existing at the time" (*Annual Report of the Federal Reserve Board for 1929*, p. 4).

After the stock market crash in the autumn of 1929, discount rates were reduced, reaching a low of 1½ per cent at the Federal Reserve Bank of New York and 2 to 3 per cent at the other Reserve banks in the summer of 1931. However, the opposition to continuous borrowing by member banks persisted, rediscounting declined, and no other provision was made for growth in member-bank reserves. In the autumn of 1931 the principles for guidance of central-bank action developed and utilized in the middle 1920's were completely abandoned. In the midst of deep depression the discount rate at the various Reserve banks was raised to 3½ or 4 per cent. More than this, the Reserve authorities repudiated, during the next two years, one of the basic objectives for which the System had been established, namely, a method of responding to a public desire for more pocket currency without adversely affecting bank reserves. As currency withdrawals became large, the Board said that the system had done its duty by keeping reserve balances freely convertible into Federal Reserve notes or gold; and it showed no concern about the contraction of bank reserves that had developed.[41] As a consequence of all these measures the effective amount of bank reserves decreased from a peak in the second quarter of 1928 to an amount five years later about 30 per cent below the figure that would have been reached with a 4 per cent annual growth. Most of the contraction of the money supply from 1929 to 1933 was the result of the adjustment of the commercial banks to their inadequate reserve balances.[42]

[41] See Warburton, "Monetary Control under the Federal Reserve Act," pp. 518–521, and reference therein to the annual reports of the Federal Reserve Board for 1931, 1932, and 1933.

[42] Daily average total reserve balances of Federal Reserve member banks during the first quarter of 1929 were $2360 million, of which $47 million, or 2 per cent, were "excess reserves." By the first quarter of 1932 their total reserve balances had declined to $1928 million, or by 18 per cent, with $46 million of "excess reserves." Later in 1932 reserve balances increased, with

The periods of business upswing from 1933 to 1937 and from 1938 to the outbreak of World War II were made possible by a great increase in member-bank reserve balances at the Reserve banks. Only a small part of the increase in reserves was due to actions of the Reserve authorities; most of it resulted from the change in the price of gold and subsequent gold imports. Throughout the 1930's there is no indication in the reports of the Board that the authorities were aware of the monetary growth needed to recover from the depression or to maintain a stable price level and full employment. Moreover, in various official publications they maintained the view that their actions had comparatively little effect on changes in the level of prices or the degree of business activity. They cited statistical data to support this view, using the data in such a way as to deny the need or desirability of growth in the circulating medium.[43] This philosophy was retained into the war period and was expressed in the annual report of the Board for 1943.[44]

The one decisive policy action of the Federal Reserve authorities in the second half of the 1930's was the doubling of percentage-reserve requirements. The purpose of this action was laudable—to prevent the enormous increase in member-bank reserves due to the changed price and imports of gold from exerting a proportionate effect upon the nation's circulating medium. However, the annual report of the Board for 1936 referred to the great volume of accumulated

a substantial rise in "excess reserves," but decreased in early 1933 and at the time of the banking holiday were down to $1776 million. Data from U.S. Board of Governors of the Federal Reserve System, *Banking and Monetary Statistics* (Washington, 1943), pp. 370–371, 387. See also note d to the accompanying tabulation.

[43] Policy statements in 1937 and 1939, reprinted in a Federal Reserve pamphlet entitled *Monetary Measures and Objectives* (1939). For a more detailed discussion of the argument put forth in these statements, see Warburton, "Monetary Control under the Federal Reserve Act," pp. 531–533.

[44] *Annual Report of the Board of the Governors of the Federal Reserve System for 1943*, p. 10.

cash resources held by individuals and business concerns, describing them as in excess of current needs. This implied that the Reserve authorities were not only concerned with avoiding excessive expansion in the future, but also believed a contractive policy, or at least a policy of no additional increase in deposits, to be the proper monetary policy.

This attitude was reaffirmed in the next annual report, and the precautionary character of the increase in reserve requirements was supported by data showing that after the final increment of the increase the member banks, taken all together, still had a substantial amount of excess reserves. However, the impact on banks in the financial centers was severe in March and April 1937, when they were preparing for the final installment of the increase in required reserves.[45] The resulting interruption of expansion in the stock of money led the depression of 1937–38. Actions to improve the reserve position of member banks preceded the recovery from that depression.[46]

Little need be said here about Federal Reserve activities during World War II except to note that they were subservient, probably overly subservient, to war-financing problems. A policy was adopted of maintaining a set of support prices for the various types of marketable government obligations. The Reserve banks absorbed enough such obligations to provide a great increase in member-bank reserves, thus permitting commercial banks to acquire a large portion of the increase in the government debt.

[45] *Annual Report of the Board of Governors of the Federal Reserve System for 1936*, p. 2, and *1937*, pp. 4–7. For a more detailed discussion of the Board's attitude and of the impact of the increase in percentage-reserve requirements, see Clark Warburton, "Has Bank Supervision Been in Conflict with Monetary Policy?" *Review of Economics and Statistics*, 34:72–74 (February 1952).

[46] These included release of gold from the inactive account of the Treasury in September 1937 and a reduction of about one eighth in percentage-reserve requirements in April 1938.

Federal Reserve policies after the war-financing period deserve much more praise and credit than is usually attributed to them. Although hampered by continuing to support prices of long-term government obligations, the Federal Reserve authorities permitted a sharp rise in the rate on short-term obligations, cooperated with the Treasury to facilitate retirement of issues held largely by Reserve banks, and in 1948 raised percentage-reserve requirements. In consequence, they brought the growth of circulating medium to a halt, but did it so gently that only a minor recession occurred, and there was no great deflation as had followed other major wars.

THE THIRD FEDERAL RESERVE ERA: THE 1950'S

In the early 1950's the annual reports of the Board of Governors indicate that another radical change had taken place in the economic philosophy underlying Reserve policy. The report for 1952 contains this statement: "The objective was . . . to restrict bank credit and monetary expansion to the growth needs of the economy . . . Federal Reserve credit policy in 1952 was designed to limit bank credit expansion to amounts consistent with the requirements of a growing economy operating at a high level without inflation." [47] This aim has been repeated in numerous statements by Federal Reserve officials and has been a basic principle underlying Reserve operations in recent years.

Nevertheless, explanations of Federal Reserve policy show that actions in accordance with this principle have been tempered, or perhaps one should say interfered with, by adherence to another concept of the proper objective of central bank action. This tempering or interfering principle is described as "leaning against the wind." It is similar to the policy guide developed in the 1920's, and has produced

[47] Pp. 1–2.

similar results. Severe depression has been avoided, but we have had a succession of moderate recessions. The leadership of Reserve policy at business peaks and troughs has continued. This is shown by comparison of the turning points of business fluctuations since 1948 with the timing of shifts from restraint to ease or from ease to restraint by the Federal Open Market Committee and the timing of other actions having a direct impact upon member-bank reserves. As in previous years, reversals in Reserve policy have preceded each peak and each trough in the National Bureau chronology of business cycles (see tabulation).

In summary, two centuries of American experience, with a variety of monetary standards and various criteria for the

COMPARISON OF MONETARY POLICY AND BUSINESS CYCLE TURNING POINTS, 1919–1961

Monetary policy (change from ease to restraint)[a]	Business cycle (change from upswing to downswing)[b]	Monetary policy (change from restraint to ease)[a]	Business cycle (change from downswing to upswing)[b]
Nov. 1919–Jan. 1920	Feb. 1920	May–July 1921	Aug. 1921
Jan.–Feb. 1923	June 1923	May–July 1924	Aug. 1924
Nov. 1925–Jan. 1926	Nov. 1926	Aug.–Sept. 1927[c]	Dec. 1927
Feb.–July 1928, Feb.–July 1929	Sept. 1929	March 1933, June–Oct. 1933, Feb. 1934[d]	April 1933
Jan. 1937[e]	June 1937	Sept. 1937, April 1938	July 1938
2d quarter 1947, Dec. 1947, Sept. 1948	Dec. 1948	March, May, Aug. 1949	Nov. 1949
Jan. 1951, June 1952[f]	Aug. 1953	June–July 1953, June–July 1954	Sept. 1954
May 1955, Aug. 1956, Jan. 1957[g]	Aug. 1957	Dec. 1957, Feb.–April 1958[h]	May 1958
July 1958, May 1959	June 1960	May–Aug. 1960	March 1961

[a] Compiled from statistical data pertaining to discount rates, open-market operations, changes in percentage-reserve requirements, and monetary gold stock in *Banking and Monetary Statistics* (Board of Governors of the Federal

guidance of central-bank operations, support the conclusion that monetary disturbances have been a basic factor in bringing about our depressions and our inflations. That experience suggests that a noncyclical monetary policy is likely to give better results than the recent countercyclical policy, and that we should experiment with central-bank policies that produce a steady growth, at a reasonable rate, in the stock of money.

Reserve System, 1943) and *Federal Reserve Bulletin*, and record of policy actions and text comments in the annual reports of the Board of Governors of the Federal Reserve System, 1919–1959. Dates refer to the principal decisions of Federal Reserve authorities, or other developments, which influenced the direction of monetary policy. Where second or third dates are given, they refer to additional or stronger actions in the direction indicated. The types of action in the months indicated are as follows (see also notes c–h): 1919–1921, changes in discount rates; 1923–1929, changes in discount rates and in asset holdings acquired through open-market operations, and in 1929, "direct pressure"; 1933–34, large-scale rediscounting in March, purchase of government obligations, June–October, and revaluation of gold, February 1934; 1937–38, changes in percentage-reserve requirements and release of inactive gold; 1947–48, retirement of government obligations held by Federal Reserve banks, lowered support prices for government obligations, and increase in percentage-reserve requirements; 1949–1961, changes in percentage-reserve requirements and in directives by Federal Open Market Committee regarding transactions in the System Open Market Account. Changes in discount rates are not cited here as indicators of change in direction of monetary policy since 1933 because the volume of rediscounting has been too small for rate changes to have much influence on the amount of member-bank reserves, though on numerous occasions discount-rate changes have supported the restraint or ease policy indicated by other types of action. Except as indicated in notes below, effective bank reserves reached peaks or troughs, relative to estimated normal rate of growth, during or soon after the dates given for policy actions. Effective bank reserves are computed from total member-bank reserve balances at Federal Reserve banks by adjustment for shifts in the proportion of deposits subject to different reserve requirements and for changes in percentage requirements. For estimates of effective reserves between 1918 and 1947, see Clark Warburton, "Bank Reserves and Business Fluctuations," *Journal of the American Statistical Association*, 43:547–558 (December 1948). The author's estimates of effective reserves for 1947–1960, computed according to the same principles but differing in methodology because of differences in available data, are unpublished.

[b] Months immediately following business-cycle peaks and troughs, as given in Moore, *Measuring Recessions*, p. 260, *Fortieth Annual Report of the*

National Bureau of Economic Research (1960), p. 34, and *Forty-First Annual Report* (1961), p. 40; includes all business cycles recognized by the National Bureau of Economic Research since concentration of member-bank reserves in the Federal Reserve banks in 1917, except the brief recessions of 1918–19 and 1945, which were immediate postwar reconversion phenomena and not business cycles in the usual sense.

[c] The peak in effective reserves, because of gold movements, was in the first quarter of 1927.

[d] Reductions in discount rates had been made at various dates between November 1929 and May 1931, but were not an effective measure of ease, because "direct pressure" and other factors prevented an increase in rediscounting; and in the autumn of 1931 discount rates had been advanced. From March to July of 1932, easing action had been taken by relatively large-scale purchases of government obligations, and in the latter part of that year effective reserves had increased because of an increase in the monetary gold stock. But in early 1933 demands for currency, without offsetting action, reduced member-bank reserves by the early part of March to the lowest figure in ten years. The 1932 easing action was reflected in an intermediate business cycle which the National Bureau of Economic Research excludes from its standard business-cycle reference dates (see Burns and Mitchell, *Measuring Business Cycles,* pp. 82–83).

[e] Action increasing percentage-reserve requirements effective March 1 and May 1. The previous increase in percentage-reserve requirements (July 1936, effective in August) had not entailed monetary restraint because it did not absorb a sufficient portion of the increase in reserve balances resulting from revaluation of gold and gold imports. The additional increase entailed monetary restraint because of its impact on central reserve city banks.

[f] The Federal Open Market Committee had followed a policy described as restraint from December 1949 to October 1951, but its impact had been offset by the pressures generated by the Korean War.

[g] The Federal Open Market Committee had dropped its promotion of "ease" in January 1955, and trend-adjusted effective reserves had reached a peak in the fourth quarter of 1954.

[h] The trough in trend-adjusted effective reserves occurred in the second quarter of 1957, suggesting that the degree of restraint had lessened prior to the change to "ease" in December 1957.

· IV ·

THE CASE FOR A 100 PER CENT GOLD DOLLAR

MURRAY N. ROTHBARD

TO ADVOCATE the complete, uninhibited gold standard runs the risk, in this day and age, of being classified with the dodo bird. When the Roosevelt administration took us off the gold standard in 1933, the bulk of the nation's economists opposed the move and advocated its speedy restoration. Now gold is considered an absurd anachronism, a relic of a tribal fetish. Gold indeed still retains a certain respectability in international trade; as the pre-eminent international money, gold as a medium of foreign trade can command support. But while foreign trade is important, I would rather choose the far more difficult *domestic* battleground, and argue for a geninue gold standard at home as well as abroad. Yet I shall not join the hardy band of current advocates of the gold standard, who call for a virtual restoration of the status quo *ante* 1933. Although that was a far better monetary system than what we have today, it was not, I hope to show, nearly good enough. By 1932 the gold standard had strayed so far from purity, so far from what it could and should have been, that its weakness contributed signally to its final breakdown in 1933.

MONEY AND FREEDOM

Economics cannot by itself establish an ethical system, although it provides a great deal of data for anyone constructing such a system—and everyone, in a sense, does so in deciding upon policy. Economists therefore have a responsibility, when advocating policy, to apprise the reader or listener of their ethical position. I do not hesitate to say that my own policy goal is the establishment of the free market, of what used to be called *laissez faire,* as broadly and as purely as possible. For this, I have many reasons, both economic and noneconomic, which I obviously cannot develop here. But I think it important to emphasize that one great desideratum in framing a monetary policy is to find one that is truly compatible with the free market in its widest and fullest sense. This is not only an ethical but also an economic tenet; for, at the very least, the economist who sees the free market working splendidly in all other fields should hesitate for a long time before dismissing it in the sphere of money.

I realize that this is not a popular position to take, even in the most conservative economic circles. Thus, in almost its first sentence, the United States Chamber of Commerce's pamphlet series on "The American Competitive Enterprise Economy" announced: "Money is what the government says it is." [1] It is almost universally believed that money, at least, cannot be free; that it must be controlled, regulated, manipulated, and created by government. Aside from the more strictly economic criticisms that I will have of this view, we should keep in mind that money, in any market economy advanced beyond the stage of primitive barter, is the nerve center of the economic system. If, therefore, the state is able to gain unquestioned control over the unit of all accounts, the state will then be in a position to dominate the entire economic system, and the whole society. It will also be able

[1] Economic Research Department, Chamber of Commerce of the United States, *The Mystery of Money* (Washington: Chamber of Commerce, 1953), p. 1.

to add quietly and effectively to its own wealth and to the wealth of its favorite groups, and without incurring the wrath that taxes often invoke. The state has understood this lesson since the kings of old began repeatedly to debase the coinage.

THE DOLLAR: INDEPENDENT NAME OR UNIT OF WEIGHT?

"If you favor a free market, why in the world do you say that government should fix the price of gold?" And, "If you wish to tie the dollar to a commodity, why not a market basket of commodities instead of only gold?" These questions are often asked of the libertarian who favors a gold standard; yet the very framing of the questions betrays a fundamental misconception of the nature of money and of the gold standard. For the crucial, implicit assumption of such questions—and of nearly all current thinking on the subject of money—is that "dollars" are an independent entity. If dollars are indeed properly things-in-themselves, to be bought, sold, and evaluated on the market, then it is surely true that "fixing the price of gold" in terms of dollars becomes simply an act of government intervention.

There is, of course, no question about the fact that, in the world of today, dollars are an independent entity, as are pounds sterling, francs, marks, and escudos. If this were all, and if we simply accepted the fact of such independence and did not inquire beyond, then I would be happy to join Professors Friedman, Yeager, and others of the Chicago School, and call for cutting these independent national moneys loose from arbitrary exchange rates fixed by government and allowing a freely fluctuating market in foreign exchange. But the point is that I do not think that these national moneys should be independent entities. Why they should not stems from the very nature and essence of money and of the market economy.

The market economy and the modern world's system of division of labor operate as follows: a producer supplies a good or a service, selling it for money; he then uses the money to buy other goods or services that he needs. Let us then consider a hypothetical world of pure *laissez faire,* where the market functions freely and government has not infringed at all upon the monetary sphere. This system of selling goods for money would then be the only way by which an individual could acquire the money that he needed to obtain goods and services. The process would be: production → "purchase" of money → "sale" of money for goods.[2]

To those advocates of independent paper moneys who also champion the free market, I would address this simple question: "Why don't you advocate the unlimited freedom of each individual to manufacture dollars?" If dollars are really and properly things-in-themselves, why not let everyone manufacture them as they manufacture wheat and baby food? It is obvious that there is indeed something peculiar about such money. For if everyone had the right to print paper dollars, everyone would print them in unlimited amounts, the costs being minuscule compared to the almost infinitely large denominations that could be printed upon the notes. Clearly, the entire monetary system would break down completely. If paper dollars are to be the "standard" money, then almost everyone would admit that government must step in and acquire compulsory monopoly of money-creation so as to check its unlimited increase. There is something else wrong with everyone printing his own dollars: for then the chain from production of goods through "purchase" of money to "sale" of money for goods would be

[2] A person could also receive money from producers by inheritance or other gift, but here again the ultimate giver must have been a producer. Furthermore, we may say that the recipient "produced" some intangible service—for instance, of being a son and heir—which provided the reason for the giver's contribution.

broken, and anyone could create money without having to be a producer first. He could consume without producing, and thus seize the output of the economy from the genuine producers.

Government's compulsory monopoly of dollar-creation does not solve all these problems, however, and even makes new ones. For what is there to prevent *government* from creating money at its own desired pace, and thereby benefiting itself and its favored citizens? Once again, nonproducers can create money without producing and obtain resources at the expense of the producers. Furthermore, the historical record of governments can give no one confidence that they will not do precisely that—even to the extent of hyperinflation and chaotic breakdown of the currency.

Why is it that, historically, the relatively free market never had to worry about people wildly setting up money factories and printing unlimited quantities?[3] If "money" really means dollars and pounds and francs, then this would surely have been a problem. But the nub of the issue is this: on the pristine free market, money does not and cannot mean the names of paper tickets. Money means a certain commodity, previously useful for other purposes on the market, chosen over the years by that market as an especially useful and marketable commodity to serve as a medium for exchanges. No one prints dollars on the purely free market because *there are, in fact, no dollars;* there are only commodities, such as wheat, automobiles, and gold. In barter, commodities are exchanged for each other, and then, gradually, a particularly marketable commodity is increasingly used as a medium of exchange. Finally, it achieves general use as a medium and becomes a "money." I need not go through the familiar but still fascinating story of how gold

[3] The American "wildcat banks" did not print money itself, but rather bank notes supposedly *redeemable* in money.

and silver were selected by the market after it had discarded such commodity moneys as cows, fishhooks, and iron hoes.[4] And I need also not dwell on the unique qualities possessed by gold and silver that caused the market to select them—those qualities lovingly enunciated by all the older textbooks on money: high marketability, durability, portability, recognizability, and homogeneity. Like every other commodity, the "price" of gold in terms of the commodities it can buy varies in accordance with its supply and demand. Since the demand for gold and silver was high, and since their supply was low in relation to the demand, the value of each unit in terms of other goods was high—a most useful attribute of money. This scarcity, combined with great durability, meant that the annual fluctuations of supply were necessarily small—another useful feature of a money commodity.

Commodities on the market exchange by their unit weights, and gold and silver were no exceptions. When someone sold copper to buy gold and then to buy butter, he sold *pounds* of copper for *ounces* or *grams* of gold to buy pounds of butter. On the free market, therefore, the monetary unit—the unit of the nation's accounts—naturally emerges as the unit of weight of the money commodity, for example, the silver ounce, or the gold gram.

In this monetary system emerging on the free market, no one can create money out of thin air to acquire resources from the producers. Money can only be obtained by purchasing it with one's goods or services. The only exception to this rule is gold miners, who can produce new money. But they must invest resources in finding, mining, and transporting an especially scarce commodity. Furthermore, gold

[4] On the process of emergence of money on the market, see the classic exposition by Carl Menger in his *Principles of Economics*, translated and edited by James Dingwall and Bert F. Hoselitz (Glencoe, Ill.: Free Press, 1950), pp. 257–285.

miners are productively adding to the world's stock of gold for nonmonetary uses as well.

Let us indeed assume that gold has been selected as the general medium of exchanges by the market, and that the unit of account is the gold gram. What will be the consequences of complete monetary freedom for each individual? What of the freedom of the individual to print his own money, which we have seen to be so disastrous in our age of fiat paper? First, let us remember that the gold gram is the monetary unit, and that such debasing names as "dollar," "franc," and "mark" do not exist and have never existed. Suppose that I decided to abandon the slow, difficult process of producing services for money, or of mining money, and instead decided to print my own? What would I print? I might manufacture a paper ticket, and print upon it "10 Rothbards." I could then proclaim the ticket as "money," and enter a store to purchase groceries with my embossed Rothbards. In the purely free market which I advocate, I or anyone else would have a perfect right to do this. And what would be the inevitable consequence? Obviously, that no one would pay attention to the Rothbards, which would be properly treated as an arrogant joke. The same would be true of any "Joneses," "Browns," or paper tickets printed by anyone else. And it should be clear that the problem is not simply that few people have ever heard of me. If General Motors tried to pay its workers in paper tickets entitled "50 GM's," the tickets would gain as little response. None of these tickets would be money, and none would be considered as anything but valueless, except perhaps by a few collectors of curios. And this is why total freedom for everyone to print money would be absolutely harmless in a purely free market: no one would accept these presumptuous tickets.

Why not freely fluctuating exchange rates? Fine, let us have freely fluctuating exchange rates on our completely free market; let the Rothbards and Browns and GM's fluctuate at whatever rate they will exchange for gold or for each other. The trouble is that they would never reach this exalted state because they would never gain acceptance in exchange as moneys at all, and therefore the problem of exchange *rates* would never arise.

On a really free market, then, there would be freely fluctuating exchange rates, but only between genuine commodity moneys, since the paper-name moneys could never gain enough acceptance to enter the field. Specifically, since gold and silver have historically been the leading commodity moneys, gold and silver would probably both be moneys, and would exchange at freely fluctuating rates. Different groups and communities of people would pick one or the other money as their unit of accounting.[5]

[5] The exchange rate between gold and silver will inevitably be at or near their purchasing-power parities, in terms of the social array of goods available, and this rate would tend to be uniform throughout the world. For a brilliant exposition of the nature of the geographic purchasing power of money, and the theory of purchasing-power parity, see Ludwig von Mises, *The Theory of Money and Credit*, 2d ed. (New Haven: Yale University Press, 1953), pp. 170–186. Also see Chi-Yuen Wu, *An Outline of International Price Theories* (London: Routledge, 1939), pp. 233–234.

Since I am advocating a totally free market in money, what I am strictly proposing is not so much the gold standard as parallel gold and silver standards. By this, of course, I do not mean bimetallism, with its arbitrarily fixed exchange rate between gold and silver, but freely fluctuating exchange rates between the two moneys. For an illuminating account of how parallel standards worked historically and how they were interfered with, see Luigi Einaudi, "The Theory of Imaginary Money from Charlemagne to the French Revolution," in Frederic C. Lane and Jelle C. Riemersma, eds., *Enterprise and Secular Change* (Homewood, Ill.: Irwin, 1953), pp. 229–261.

Professor Robert Sabatino Lopez writes, of the return of Europe to gold coinage in the mid-thirteenth century, after half a millennium: "Florence, like most medieval states, made bimetallism and trimetallism a base of its monetary policy . . . it committed the government to the Sysiphean labor of readjusting the relations between different coins as the ratio between the different metals changes, or as one or another coin was debased . . . Genoa, on the contrary, *in conformity with the principle of restricting state intervention as much as possible* [italics mine], did not try to enforce a fixed relation between coins of different metals . . . Basically, the gold coinage of Genoa was not meant to integrate the silver and billon coinages but to

Names, therefore, whatever they may be, "Rothbard," "Jones," or even "dollar," could not have arisen as money on the free market. How, then, did such names as "dollar" and "peso" originate and emerge in their own right as independent moneys? The answer is that *these names invariably originated as names for units of weight of a money commodity, either gold or silver.* In short, they began not as pure names, but as names of units of weight of particular money commodities. In the British pound sterling we have a particularly striking example of a weight derivative, for the British pound was originally just that: a pound of silver money.[6] "Dollar" began as the generally applied name of an ounce weight of silver coined in the sixteenth century by a Bohemian, Count Schlick, who lived in Joachimsthal, and the name of his highly reputed coins became "Joachimsthalers," or simply "thalers" or "dollars." And even after a lengthy process of debasement, alteration, and manipulation of these weights until they more and more became separated names, they still remained names of units of weight of specie until, in the United States, we went off the gold standard in 1933. In short, it is incorrect to say that, before 1933, the

form an independent system" ("Back to Gold, 1252," *Economic History Review,* April 1956, p. 224).

On the merits of parallel standards and their superiority to bimetallism, see William Brough, *Open Mints and Free Banking* (New York: Putnam, 1898), and Brough, *The Natural Law of Money* (New York: Putnam, 1894). Brough called this system "Free Metallism." On the recent example of pure parallel standards in Saudi Arabia, down to the 1950's, see Arthur N. Young, "Saudi Arabian Currency and Finance," *Middle East Journal,* Summer 1953, pp. 361–380.

[6] The fact that there was never an actual pound-weight coin of silver is irrelevant and does not imply that the pound was some form of "imaginary" unit of account. The pound was a pound of silver bullion, or an accumulation of a pound weight of silver coins. Cf. Einaudi, "Theory of Imaginary Money," pp. 229–230. The fundamental misconception here is to place too much emphasis on coins and not enough on bullion, an overemphasis, as we shall see presently, connected intimately with government intervention and with the long slide downward of the monetary unit from weight of gold and silver to pure name.

price of gold was fixed in terms of dollars. Instead, what happened was that the dollar was *defined* as a unit of weight, approximately 1/20 of an ounce of gold. It is not that the dollar was set equal to a certain weight of gold; it *was* that weight, just as any unit of weight, as, for example, one pound of copper *is* 16 ounces of copper, and is not simply and arbitrarily "set equal" to 16 ounces by some individual or agency.[7] The monetary unit was, therefore, always a unit of weight of a money commodity, and the names that we know now as independent moneys were names of these units of weight.[8]

Economists, of course, admit that our modern national moneys emerged originally from gold and silver, but they are inclined to dismiss this process as a historical accident from which we have now been happily emancipated. But Ludwig von Mises has shown, in his regression theorem, that logically money can only originate in a nonmonetary commodity, chosen gradually by the market to be an ever more general medium of exchange. Money cannot originate as a new fiat name, either by government edict or by some form of social compact. The basic reason is that the demand for

[7] The monetary unit was not just a pure unit of weight, such as the ounce or the gram; it was a unit of weight of a certain money commodity, such as gold. The dollar was 1/20 of an ounce of *gold,* not of just any ounce. And here we find a crucial flaw in the idea of a composite-commodity money which has been overlooked: just as we cannot call the monetary unit an "ounce" or "gram" or "pound" of several different, or composite, commodities, so the dollar cannot properly be the *name* of many different weights of many different commodities. The money commodity selected by the market was a single particular commodity, gold or silver, and therefore the *unit* of that money had to be of that commodity alone, and not of some arbitrary composite.

[8] This is why, in the older books, a discussion of money and monetary standards often took place as part of a general discussion of weights and measures. Thus in Barnard's work on international unification of weights and measures, the problem of international unification of monetary units was discussed in an appendix, along with other appendixes on measures of capacity and the metric system. Frederick A. P. Barnard, *The Metric System of Weights and Measures,* rev. ed. (New York: Columbia College, 1872).

money on any "day," X, which along with the supply of money determines the purchasing power of the money unit on that "day," itself depends on the very existence of a purchasing power on the previous "day," X-1. For while every other commodity on the market is useful in its own right, money (or a monetary commodity considered in its strictly *monetary* use), is only useful to *exchange* for other goods and services. Hence, alone among goods, money depends for its use and demand on having a pre-existing purchasing power. Since this is true for any "day" when money exists, we can push the logical regression backward, to see that ultimately the money commodity must have had a use in the "days" previous to money, that is, in the world of barter.[9]

I want to make it clear what I am *not* saying. I am not saying that fiat money, once established on the ruins of gold, cannot then continue indefinitely on its own. Unfortunately, such ultrametallists as J. Laurence Laughlin were wrong; indeed, if fiat money could not continue indefinitely, I would not have to come here to plead for its abolition.

[9] Ludwig von Mises developed the very important regression theorem in his *Theory of Money and Credit*, pp. 97–123, and defended it against the criticisms of Benjamin M. Anderson and Howard S. Ellis in his *Human Action* (New Haven: Yale University Press, 1949), pp. 405–408. Also see Joseph A. Schumpeter, *History of Economic Analysis* (New York: Oxford University Press, 1954), p. 1090. For a reply to Professor J. C. Gilbert's contention that the establishment of the *Rentenmark* disproved the regression theorem, see Murray N. Rothbard, "Toward a Reconstruction of Utility and Welfare Economics," in M. Sennholz, ed., *On Freedom and Free Enterprise* (Princeton: Van Nostrand, 1956), p. 236n.

The latest criticism of the regression theorem is that of Professor Patinkin, who accuses Mises of inconsistency in basing this theorem on deriving the marginal utility of money from the marginal utility of the goods that it will purchase, rather than from the marginal utility of cash holdings, the latter approach being used by Mises in the remainder of his work. Actually, the regression theorem in Mises' system is not inconsistent, but operates on a different plane, for it shows that the very marginal utility of money *to hold*—as elsewhere analyzed by Mises—is itself based upon the *prior* fact that money has a purchasing power *in goods*. Don Patinkin, *Money, Interest, and Prices* (Evanston, Ill.: Row, Peterson, 1956), pp. 71–72, 414.

THE DECLINE FROM WEIGHT TO NAME: MONOPOLIZING THE MINT

The debacle of 1931–1933, when the world abandoned the gold standard, was not a sudden shift from gold weight to paper name; it was but the last step in a lengthy, complex process. It is important, not just for historical reasons but for framing public policy today, to analyze the logical steps in this transformation. Each stage of this process was caused by another act of government intervention.

On the market, commodities take different forms for different uses, and so, on a free market, would gold or silver. The basic form of processed gold is gold bullion, and ingots or bars of bullion would be used for very large transactions. For smaller, everyday transactions, the gold would be divided into smaller pieces, coins, hardened by the slight infusion of an alloy to prevent abrasion (accounted for in the final weight). It should be understood that all forms of gold would really be money, since gold exchanges by weight. A gold ornament is itself money as well as ornament; it could be used in exchange, but it is simply not in a convenient shape for exchanges, and would probably be melted back into bullion before being used as money. Even sacks of gold dust might be used for exchange in mining towns. Of course it costs resources to shift gold from one form to another, and therefore on the market coins would tend to be at a premium over the equivalent weight in bullion, since it generally costs more to produce a coin out of bullion than to melt coins back into bullion.

The first and most crucial act of government intervention in the market's money was its assumption of the compulsory monopoly of minting—the process of transforming bullion into coin. The pretext for socialization of minting—one which has curiously been accepted by almost every economist—is that private minters would defraud the public on the weight and fineness of the coins. This argument rings peculiarly hollow when we consider the long record of governmental debasement of the coinage and of the monetary standard. But apart from this, we certainly know that private enterprise has been able to supply an almost infinite number of goods requiring high precision standards; yet nobody advocates nationalization of the machine-tool industry or the electronics industry in order to safeguard these standards. And no one wants to abolish all contracts because some people might commit fraud in making them. Surely the proper remedy for any fraud is the general law in defense of property rights.[10]

The standard argument against private coinage is that the minting business operates by a mysterious law of its own —Gresham's Law—where "bad money drives out good," in contrast to other areas of competition, where the good product drives out the bad.[11] But Mises has brilliantly shown that

[10] Presumably, on the free market private citizens will also safeguard their coins by testing their weight and purity—as they do their monetary bullion—or will mint coins with those private minters who have established reputations for probity and efficiency.

Even in the heyday of the gold standard there were few writers willing to go beyond the bounds of social habit to concede the feasibility of private minting. A notable exception was Herbert Spencer, *Social Statics* (New York: Appleton, 1890), pp. 438–439. The French economist Paul Leroy-Beaulieu also favored free private coinage. See Charles A. Conant, *The Principles of Money and Banking* (New York: Harper, 1905), I, 127–128. Also see Leonard E. Read, *Government—An Ideal Concept* (Irvington-on-Hudson, N.Y.: Foundation for Economic Education, 1954), pp. 82ff. Recently Professor Milton Friedman, though completely out of sympathy with the gold standard, has, remarkably, taken a similar stand in *A Program for Monetary Stability* (New York: Fordham University Press, 1960), p. 5.

For historical examples of successful private coinage, see B. W. Barnard, "The Use of Private Tokens for Money in the United States," *Quarterly Journal of Economics*, 1916–17, pp. 617–626; Conant, I, 127–132; Lysander Spooner, *A Letter to Grover Cleveland* (Boston: Tucker, 1886), p. 79; and J. Laurence Laughlin, *A New Exposition of Money, Credit and Prices* (Chicago: University of Chicago Press, 1931), I, 47–51.

[11] Thus, see W. Stanley Jevons' criticism of Spencer in his *Money and the Mechanism of Exchange*, 15th ed. (London: Kegan Paul, 1905), pp. 63–66.

this formulation of Gresham's Law is a misinterpretation, and that the Law is a subdivision of the usual effects of price control by government: in this case, the government's artificial fixing of an exchange rate between two or more moneys creates a shortage of the artificially undervalued money and a surplus of the overvalued money. Gresham's Law is therefore a law of government intervention rather than one of the free market.[12]

The state's nationalization of the minting business injured the free market and the monetary system in many ways. One neglected point is that government minting is subject to the same flaws, inefficiencies, and tyranny over the consumer as every other government operation. Since coins are a convenient monetary shape for daily transactions, the state's decree that only X, Y, and Z denominations shall be coined imposes a loss of utility on consumers and substitutes uniformity for the diversity of the market. It also begins the long disastrous slide from an emphasis on weight to an emphasis on name, or tale. In short, under private coinage there would be a number of denominations, in strict accordance with the variety of consumer wants. The private stamp would probably guarantee fineness rather than weight, and the coins would circulate by weight. But if the government decrees just a few denominations, then weight begins to be disregarded, and the name of the coin to be considered more and more. For example, the problem persisted in Europe for centuries of what to do with old, worn coins. If a 30-gram coin was worn down to 25 grams, the simplest thing would be for the old coin to circulate *not* at the old and now mis-

[12] See Mises, *Human Action,* pp. 432n, 447, 754. Mises was partly anticipated at the turn of the century by William Brough: "The more efficient money will always drive from the circulation the less efficient if the individuals who handle money are left free to act in their own interest. It is only when bad money is endorsed by the State with the property of legal tender that it can drive good money from circulation" (*Open Mints and Free Banking,* pp. 35–36).

leading 30 grams but at the new, correct 25 grams. The fact that the state itself had stamped 30 grams on the new coin, however, was somehow considered an insuperable barrier to such a simple solution. And, furthermore, much monetary debasement took place through the state's decree that new and old coins be treated alike, with Gresham's Law causing new coins to be hoarded and only old ones to circulate.[13]

The royal stamp on coins also gradually shifted emphasis from weight to tale by wrapping coinage in the trappings of the mystique of state "sovereignty." For many centuries it was considered no disgrace for foreign gold and silver coins to circulate in any area; monetary nationalism was yet in its infancy. The United States used foreign coins almost exclusively through the first quarter of the nineteenth century. But gradually foreign coins were outlawed, and the name of the national state's unit became enormously more significant.

Debasement through the centuries greatly spurred a loss of confidence in money as a unit of weight. There is only one point to any standard of weight and measure: that it be eternally fixed. The international meter must always be the international meter. But using their minting monopoly, the state rulers juggled standards of monetary weight to their own economic advantage. It was as if the state were a huge warehouse that had accepted many pounds of copper or other commodity from its clients, and then, when the clients came to redeem, the warehouseman suddenly announced that henceforth a pound would equal 12 ounces instead of

[13] The minting monopoly also permitted the state to charge a monopoly price ("seigniorage") for its minting service, which imposed a special burden on conversion from bullion to coin. In later years the state granted the subsidy of costless coinage, overstimulating the transformation of bullion to coin. Modern adherents of the gold standard unfortunately endorse the subsidy of gratuitous coinage. Where coinage is private and marketable, the firms will of course charge a fee covering approximately the true costs of minting (such a fee is known as "brassage").

16, and paid out only three fourths of the copper, pocketing the other fourth for his own use. It is perhaps superfluous to point out that any private agency doing such a thing would be promptly branded as criminal.[14]

THE DECLINE FROM WEIGHT TO NAME: ENCOURAGING BANK INFLATION

The natural tendency of the state is inflation. This statement will shock those accustomed to viewing the state as a committee of the whole nation ardently dispensing the general welfare, but I think it nonetheless true. The reason seems to me obvious. As I have mentioned above, money is acquired on the market by producing goods and services, and then buying money in exchange for these goods. But there is another way to obtain money: creating money oneself, without producing—by counterfeiting. Money-creation is a much less costly method than producing; therefore the state, with its ever-tightening monopoly of money-creation, has a simple route that it can take to benefit its own members and its favored supporters.[15] And it is a more enticing and less disturbing route than taxes—which might provoke open opposition. Creating money, on the contrary, confers

[14] Besides the minting monopoly, the other critical device for government control of money has been legal-tender laws, superfluous at best, mischievous and a means of arbitrary exchange-rate fixing at worst. As William Brough stated: "There is no more case for a special law to compel the receiving of money than there is for one to compel the receiving of wheat or of cotton. The common law is as adequate for the enforcement of contracts in the one case as in the other" (*The Natural Law of Money*, p. 135). The same position was taken by T. H. Farrer, *Studies in Currency, 1898* (London: Macmillan, 1898), pp. 42ff.

[15] This is a corollary of Franz Oppenheimer's brilliant distinction between the two basic alternate routes to wealth, production and exchange, which he called "the economic means"; and seizure or confiscation, which he called "the political means." Inflation, which I am defining here as the creation of money (i.e., an increase of money substitutes not backed 100 per cent by standard specie), is thus revealed as one of the major political means. Oppenheimer defined the state, incidentally, as the "organization of the political means" (*The State*, New York: Vanguard Press, 1926, pp. 24ff).

open and evident benefits on those who create and first receive it; the losses it imposes on the rest of society remain hidden to the lay observer. This tendency of the state should alone preclude all the schemes of economists and other writers for government to issue and stabilize the supply of paper money.

While countries were still on a specie standard, bank notes and government paper were issued as redeemable in specie. They were money substitutes, essentially warehouse receipts for gold, that could be redeemed in face value on demand. Soon, however, the issue of receipts went beyond 100 per cent reserve to outright money-creation. Governments have persistently tried their best to promote, encourage, and expand the circulation of bank and government paper, and to discourage the people's use of gold itself. Any individual bank has two great checks on its creation of money: a call for redemption by non-clients (that is, by clients of other banks, or by those who wish to use standard money), and a crisis of confidence in the bank by its clients, causing a "run." Governments have continually operated to widen these limits, which would be narrow in a system of "free banking"—a system where banks are free to do anything they please, so long as they promptly redeem their obligations to pay specie. They have created a central bank to widen the limits to the whole country by permitting all banks to inflate together—under the tutelage of the government. And they have tried to assure the banks that the government will not permit them to fail, either by coining the convenient doctrine that the central bank must be a "lender of last resort" of reserves to the banks, or, as in America, by simply "suspending specie payments," that is, by permitting banks to continue operations while refusing to redeem their contractual obligations to pay specie.[16]

[16] It is a commonly accepted myth that the excesses of wildcat banks in

Another device used over the years by governments was to persuade the public not to use gold in their daily transactions; to do so was scorned as an anachronism unsuited to the modern world. The yokel who didn't trust banks became a common object of ridicule. In this way, gold was more and more confined to the banks and to use for very large transactions; this made it very much easier to go off the gold standard during the Great Depression, for then the public could be persuaded that the only ones to suffer were a few selfish, antisocial, and subtly unpatriotic gold hoarders. In fact, as early as the Panic of 1819 the idea had spread that someone trying to redeem his bank note in specie, that is, to redeem his own property, was a subversive citizen trying to

---

America stemmed from free banking; actually, a much stronger cause was the tradition, beginning in 1814 and continuing in every economic crisis thereafter, of permitting banks to continue in operation without paying in specie.

It is also a widespread myth that central banks are inaugurated in order to *check* inflation by commercial banks. The second Bank of the United States, on the contrary, was inaugurated in 1817 as an inflationist sop to the state-chartered banks, which had been permitted to run riot without paying in specie since 1814. It was a weak substitute for compelling a genuine return to specie payments. This was correctly pointed out at the time by such hard-money stalwarts as Daniel Webster and John Randolph of Roanoke. Senator William H. Wells, Federalist from Delaware, said that the Bank Bill was "ostensibly for the purpose of correcting the diseased state of our paper currency by restraining and curtailing the overissue of bank paper, and yet it came prepared to inflict upon us the same evil; being itself nothing more than simply a paper-making machine" *Annals of Congress,* 14 Cong., 1 sess., April 1, 1816, pp. 267–270. Also see *ibid.,* pp. 1066, 1091, 1110ff.

As for the Federal Reserve System, the major arguments for its adoption were to make the money supply more "elastic" and to centralize reserves and thus make them more "efficient," i.e., to facilitate and promote inflation. As an additional fillip, reserve requirements themselves were directly lowered at the inauguration of the Federal Reserve System. Cf. the important but totally neglected work of C. A. Phillips, T. F. McManus, and R. W. Nelson, *Banking and the Business Cycle* (New York: Macmillan, 1937), pp. 21ff., and *passim.* Also see O. K. Burrell, "The Coming Crisis in External Convertibility in U.S. Gold," *Commercial and Financial Chronicle,* April 23, 1959, p. 5.

For a discussion of the historical arguments on free or central banking, see Vera C. Smith, *The Rationale of Central Banking* (London: King, 1936).

wreck the banks and the entire economy; and by the 1930's it was thus easy to denounce gold hoarders as virtual traitors.[17]

And so by imposing central banking, by suspending specie payments, and by encouraging a shift among the public from gold to paper or bank deposits in their everyday transactions, the governments organized inflation, and thus an ever larger proportion of money substitutes to gold (an increasing proportion of liabilities redeemable on demand in gold, to gold itself). By the 1930's, in short, the gold standard—a shaky gold base supporting an ever greater pyramid of monetary claims—was ready to collapse at the first severe depression or wave of bank runs.[18]

[17] During the Panic the economist Condy Raguet, state senator from Philadelphia, wrote to a puzzled David Ricardo as follows: "You state in your letter that you find it difficult to comprehend, why persons who had a right to demand coin from the Banks in payment of their notes, so long forbore to exercise it. This no doubt appears paradoxical to one who resides in a country where an act of parliament was necessary to protect a bank, but the difficulty is easily solved. The whole of our population are either stockholders of banks or in debt to them . . . An independent man, who was neither a stockholder or debtor, who would have ventured to compel the banks to do justice, would have been persecuted as an enemy of society . . ." Raguet to Ricardo, April 18, 1821, in David Ricardo, *Minor Papers on the Currency Question, 1809–23*, ed. Jacob Hollander (Baltimore: The Johns Hopkins Press, 1932), pp. 199–201.

In 1931, for example, President Hoover launched a crusade against "traitorous hoarding." The crusade consisted of the Citizens' Reconstruction Organization, headed by Colonel Frank Knox of Chicago. And Jesse Jones reports that, during the banking crisis of early 1933, Hoover was seriously contemplating invoking a forgotten wartime law making hoarding a criminal offense. Jesse H. Jones and Edward Angly, *Fifty Billion Dollars* (New York: Macmillan, 1951), p. 18. It should also be noted here that the Hoover administration's alleged devotion to retaining the gold standard is largely myth. As Hoover's Undersecretary of the Treasury has declared rather proudly: "The going off [gold] cannot be laid to Franklin Roosevelt. It had been determined to be necessary by Ogden Mills, Secretary of the Treasury, and myself as his Undersecretary, long before Franklin Roosevelt took office." Arthur A. Ballantine, in the *New York Herald-Tribune*, May 5, 1958, p. 18.

[18] Currently, the worst example of government aid to banks is the highly popular deposit insurance—for this means that banks have virtual carte blanche from government to protect them from any redemption crisis. As a

100 PER CENT GOLD BANKING

We have thus come to the cardinal difference between myself and the bulk of those economists who still advocate a return to the gold standard. These economists, represented by Dr. Walter E. Spahr and his associates in the Economists' National Committee on Monetary Policy, essentially believe that the old pre-1933 gold standard was a fine and viable institution in all its parts, and that going off gold in 1933 was a single wicked act of will that only needs to be repealed in order to re-establish our monetary system on a sound foundation. I, on the contrary, view 1933 as but the last link in a whole chain of unfortunate actions; it seems clear to me that the gold standard of the 1920's was so vitiated as to be ready to collapse. A return to such a gold standard, while superior to the present system, would only pave the way for another collapse—and this time, I am afraid, gold would get no further chance. Although the transition period would be more difficult, it would be kinder to the gold standard, as well as better for the long-run economic health of the country, to go back to a stronger, more viable gold standard than the one we have lost.

I daresay that my audience has been too much exposed to the teachings of the Chicago School to be shocked at the idea of 100 per cent reserve banking. This topic, of course, is worthy of far more space than I can give it here. I can only say that my position on 100 per cent banking differs considerably in emphasis from the Chicago School. The Chicago group basically views 100 per cent money as a technique—as a useful, efficient tool for government manipulation of the money supply, unburdened by lags or friction in the banking system. My reasons for advocating 100 per cent banking

result, virtually all natural market checks on bank inflation have been destroyed. Query: If banks are thus protected from losses by government, to what extent are they still private institutions?

cut much closer to the heart of our whole system of the free market and property rights.[19] In my view, issuing promises to pay on demand in excess of the amount of goods on hand is simply fraud, and should be so considered by the legal system. For this means that a bank issues "fake" warehouse receipts—warehouse receipts, for example, for ounces of gold that do not actually exist in the vaults. This is legalized counterfeiting; this is the creation of money without the necessity for production, to compete for resources against those who have produced. In short, I believe that fractional-reserve banking is disastrous both for the morality and for the fundamental bases and institutions of the market economy.

I am familiar with the many arguments for fractional-reserve banking. There is the view that this is simply economical: the banks began with 100 per cent reserves, but then they shrewdly and keenly saw that only a certain proportion of these demand liabilities were likely to be redeemed, so that it seemed safe either to lend out the gold for profit or to issue pseudo warehouse receipts (either as bank notes or as bank deposits) for the gold, and to lend out those. The banks here take on the character of shrewd entrepreneurs. But so is an embezzler shrewd when he takes money out of the company till to invest in some ventures of his own. Like the banker, he sees an opportunity to earn a profit on *someone else's* assets. The embezzler knows, let us say, that the auditor will come on June 1 to inspect the accounts; and he fully intends to repay the "loan" before then. Let us assume that he does; is it really true that no one has been the loser and everyone has gained? I dispute this;

[19] The other very important difference, of course, is that I advocate 100 per cent reserves in gold or silver, in contrast to the 100 per cent fiat paper standard of the Chicago School. 100 per cent gold, rather than making the monetary system more readily manageable by government, would completely expunge government intervention from the monetary system.

a theft has occurred, and that theft should be prosecuted and not condoned. Let us note that the banking advocate assumes that something has gone wrong only if everyone should decide to redeem his property, only to find that it isn't there. But I maintain that the wrong—the theft—occurs at the time the embezzler takes the money, not at the later time when his "borrowing" happens to be discovered.[20]

Another argument holds that the fact that notes and deposits are redeemable on demand is only a kind of accident; that these are merely credit transactions. The depositors or noteholders are simply lending money to the banks, which in turn act as their agents to channel the money to business firms. And why repress productive credit? Mises has shown, however, the crucial difference between a *credit transaction* and a *claim transaction;* credit always involves the purchase of a *future good* by the creditor in exchange for a present good (money). The creditor gives up a present good in exchange for an I O U for a good coming to him in the future. But a claim—and bank notes or deposits are claims to money —does not involve the creditor's relinquishing any of the present good. On the contrary, the noteholder or deposit-holder still retains his money (the present good) because he has a claim to it, a warehouse receipt, which he can redeem at any time he desires.[21] This is the nub of the prob-

[20] I want to make it quite clear that I do not accuse present-day bankers of conscious fraud or embezzlement; the institution of banking has become so hallowed and venerated that we can only say that it allows for legalized fraud, probably unknown to almost all bankers. As for the original goldsmiths that began the practice, I think our opinion should be rather more harsh.

[21] "It is usual to reckon the acceptance of a deposit which can be drawn upon at any time by means of note or cheques as a type of credit transaction and juristically, this view is, of course, justified; but economically, the case is not one of a credit transaction. If *credit* in the economic sense means the exchange of a present good or a present service against a future good or a future service, then it is hardly possible to include the transactions in question under the conception of credit. A depositor of a sum of money who acquires in exchange for it a claim convertible into money at any time

lem, and this is why fractional-reserve banking creates new money while other credit agencies do not—for warehouse receipts or claims to money function on the market as equivalent to standard money itself.

To those who persist in believing that the bulk of bank deposits are really saved funds voluntarily left with the banks to invest for savers, and are not just kept as monetary cash balances, I would like to lay down this challenge: If what you say is true, why not agree to alter the banking structure to change these deposits to debentures of varying maturities? A shift from uncovered deposits to debentures will of course mean an enormous drop in the supply of money; but if these deposits are simply another form of credit, then the depositors should not object and we 100-percent theorists will be satisfied. The purchase of a debenture will, furthermore, be a genuine saving and investment of existing money, rather than an unsound increase in the money supply.[22]

In sum, I am advocating that the law be changed to treat bank notes and deposits as what they are in economic and social fact: claims, warehouse receipts to standard money—in short, that the note- and deposit-holders be recognized as

which will perform exactly the same service for him as the sum it refers to has exchanged no present good for a future good. The claim that he has acquired by his deposit is also a present good for him. The depositing of money in no way means that he has renounced immediate disposal over the utility that it commands." Mises, *Theory of Money and Credit*, p. 268. What I am advocating, in brief, is a change in the juristic framework to conform to the economic realities.

[22] Professor Beckhart has recently called our attention to the long-standing and successful practice of Swiss banks of issuing debentures of varying maturities, and the recent adoption of this practice in Belgium and Holland. While Beckhart contemplates debentures for long-term loans only, I see no reason why banks cannot issue short-term debentures as well. If business needs short-term loans, it can finance them by competing with everyone else in the market for voluntarily saved funds. Why grant the short-term market the special privilege and subsidy of creating money? Benjamin H. Beckhart, "To Finance Term Loans," *New York Times*, May 31, 1960.

owners-in-law of the gold (or, under a fiat standard, of the paper) in the bank's vaults. Now treated in law as a debt, a deposit or note should be considered as evidence of a bailment.[23] In relation to general legal principles this would not be a radical change, since warehouse receipts are treated as bailments now. Banks would simply be treated as money warehouses in relation to their notes and deposits.[24]

[23] "A *bailment* may be defined as the transfer of personal property to another person with the understanding that the property is to be returned when a certain purpose has been completed . . . In a sale, we relinquish both title and possession. In a bailment, we merely give up temporarily the possession of the goods." Robert O. Sklar and Benjamin W. Palmer, *Business Law* (New York: McGraw-Hill, 1942), p. 361.

Nussbaum surely begs the question when he says, "Only in a broad and non-technical sense may the relationship of the depositary bank to the depositor be considered a fiduciary one. No trust proper or bailment is involved. *The contrary view would lay an unbearable burden upon banking business*" (italics mine). But if such banking business is improper, this is precisely the sort of burden that should be imposed. This is but one example of what happens to jurisprudence when pragmatic considerations of "public policy" supplant the search for principles of justice. Arthur Nussbaum, *Money in the Law, National and International* (Brooklyn: Foundation Press, 1950), p. 105.

[24] On warehouse receipts as bailments, cf. William H. Spencer, *Casebook of Law and Business* (New York: McGraw-Hill, 1939), pp. 661ff.

Perhaps a proper legal system would also consider all "general deposit warrants" (which allow the warehouse to return any homogeneous good to the depositor) as really "specific deposit warrants," which, like bills of lading, establish ownership to specific, earmarked objects.

As Jevons, noting the superiority of specific deposit warrants and realizing their relationship to money, stated: "The most satisfactory kind of promissory document . . . is represented by bills of lading, pawn-tickets, dock-warrants, or certificates which establish ownership to a definite object . . . The important point concerning such promissory notes is, *that they cannot possibly be issued in excess of the goods actually deposited, unless by distinct fraud* [italics mine]. The issuer ought to act purely as a warehouse-keeper, and as possession may be claimed at any time, he can never legally allow any object deposited to go out of his safe keeping until it is delivered back in exchange for the promissory note . . . More recently a better system [than general deposit warrant] has been introduced, and each specific lot of iron has been marked and set aside to meet some particular warrant. The difference seems to be slight, but it is really very important, as opening the way to a lax fulfillment of the contract . . . Moreover, it now [with general warrants] becomes possible to create a fictitious supply of a commodity, that is, to make people believe that a supply exists which does not exist . . .

Professor Spahr often uses the analogy of a bridge to justify fractional-reserve money. The builder of a bridge estimates approximately how many people will be using it daily. He builds the bridge on that basis and does not attempt to accommodate all the people in the city, should they all decide to cross the bridge simultaneously. But the most critical fallacy of this analogy is that the inhabitants do not then have a legal claim to cross the bridge at any time. (This would be even more evident if the bridge were owned by a private firm.) On the other hand, the holders of money substitutes most emphatically do have a legal claim to their own property at any time they choose to redeem it. The claims must then be fraudulent, since the bank could not possibly meet them all.[25]

To those who want the dollar convertible into gold but are content with the pre-1933 standard, we might cite the analysis of Amasa Walker, one of the great American economists a century ago: "So far as specie is held for the payment of these [fractional-reserve-backed] notes, this kind of currency is actually convertible, and equivalent to money; but, in so far as the credit element exceeds the specie, it is only a promise to pay money, and is inconvertible. A mixed [fractional-reserve] currency, therefore can only be regarded as partially convertible; the degree of its convertibility de-

It used to be held as a general rule of law, that any present grant or assignment of goods not in existence is without operation" (*Money and the Mechanism of Exchange*, pp. 206–212; see also p. 221).

[25] A bank that fails is therefore not simply an entrepreneur whose forecasts have gone awry. It is a business whose betrayal of trust has finally been publicly revealed. Furthermore, a rule of every business is to adjust the time-structure of its assets to the time-structure of its liabilities, so that its assets on hand will match its liabilities due. The only exception to this rule is a bank, which lends at certain terms of maturities, while its liabilities are all instantly payable on demand. If a bank were to match the time-structure of its assets and liabilities, all its assets would also have to be instantaneous, i.e., would have to be cash.

pending upon the proportion the specie bears to the notes issued and the deposits."[26]

For a believer in free enterprise, a system of "free banking" undoubtedly has many attractions. Not only does it seem most consistent with the general institution of free enterprise, but Mises and others have shown that free banking would lead not to the infinite supply of money envisioned by such Utopian partisans of free banking as Proudhon, Spooner, Greene, and Meulen, but rather to a much "harder" and sounder money than exists when banks are controlled by a central bank. In practice, therefore, free banking would come much closer to the 100 per cent ideal than the system we now have.[27] And yet if "free trade in banking is free trade in swindling," then surely the soundest course would be to take the swindling out of banking altogether. Mises' sole argument against 100 per cent gold banking is that this would admit the unfortunate precedent of government control of the banking system. But if fractional-reserve banking is fraudulent, then it could be outlawed not as a form of administrative government intervention in the monetary system, but rather as part of the general legal prohibition of force and fraud.[28] Within this general prohibition of fraud,

[26] *The Science of Wealth*, 3d ed. (Boston: Little, Brown, 1867), p. 139. In the same work, Walker presents a keen analysis of the defects and problems of a fractional-reserve currency (pp. 126–232).

[27] See Mises, *Human Action*, pp. 439ff. Mises' position is that of the French economist Henri Cernuschi, who called for free banking as the best way of suppressing fiduciary bank credit: "I want to give everybody the right to issue banknotes so that nobody should take banknotes any longer" (*ibid.*, p. 443). The German economist Otto Hübner held a similar position. See Smith, *Rationale of Central Banking, passim.*

[28] In short, our projected legal reform would fully comply with Mises' goal: "to place the banking business under the general rules of commercial and civil laws compelling every individual and firm to fulfill all obligations in full compliance with the terms of the contract" (*Human Action*, p. 440). Another point about free banking: to be tenable, it would have to be legal for 100 per cent reserve partisans to establish "Anti-Bank Vigilante Leagues," publicly calling on all note- and deposit-holders to redeem their obligations because their banks were really and essentially bankrupt.

my proposed banking reform would leave the private banks entirely free.[29]

OBJECTIONS TO 100 PER CENT GOLD

Certain standard objections have been raised against 100 per cent banking, and against 100 per cent gold currency in particular. One generally accepted argument against any form of 100 per cent banking I find particularly and strikingly curious: that under 100 per cent reserves, banks would not be able to continue profitably in business. I see no reason why banks should not be able to charge their customers for their services, as do all other useful businesses. This argument points to the supposedly enormous benefits of banking; if these benefits were really so powerful, then surely the consumers would be willing to pay a service charge for them, just as they pay for travelers' checks now. If they were not willing to pay the costs of the banking business as they pay the costs of all other industries useful to them, then that would demonstrate the advantages of banking to have been highly overrated. At any rate, there is no reason why banking should not take its chance in the free market with every other industry.

The major objection against 100 per cent gold is that this would allegedly leave the economy with an inadequate money supply. Some economists advocate a secular increase of the supply of money in accordance with some criterion: population growth, growth of volume of trade, and the like; others wish the money supply to be adjusted to provide a stable and fixed price level. In both cases, of course, the

[29] Cf. Walker, pp. 230–231. In *A Program for Monetary Stability*, p. 108, Milton Friedman has expressed sympathy for the idea of free banking, but oddly enough, only for deposits; notes he would leave as a government monopoly. It should be clear that there is no essential economic difference between notes and deposits. They differ in technological form only; economically, they are both promises to pay on demand in a fixed amount of standard money.

adjusting and manipulating could only be done by government. These economists have not fully absorbed the great monetary lesson of classical economics: that the supply of money essentially does not matter. Money performs its function by using a medium of exchange; any change in its supply, therefore, will simply adjust itself in the purchasing power of the money unit, that is, in the amount of other goods that money will be able to buy. An increase in the supply of money means merely that more units of money are doing the social work of exchange and therefore that the purchasing power of each unit will decline. Because of this adjustment, money, in contrast to all other useful commodities employed in production or consumption, does not confer a social benefit when its supply increases. The only reason that increased gold mining is useful, in fact, is that the large supply of gold will satisfy more of the nonmonetary uses of the gold commodity.

There is therefore never any need for a larger supply of money (aside from the nonmonetary uses of gold or silver). An increased supply of money can only benefit one set of people at the expense of another set, and, as we have seen, that is precisely what happens when government or the banks inflate the money supply. And that is precisely what my proposed reform is designed to eliminate. There can, incidentally, never be an actual monetary "shortage," since the very fact that the market has established and continues to use gold or silver as a monetary commodity shows that enough of it exists to be useful as a medium of exchange.

The number of people, the volume of trade, and all other alleged criteria are therefore merely arbitrary and irrelevant with respect to the supply of money. And as for the ideal of the stable price level, apart from the grave flaws of deciding on a proper index, there are two points that are generally overlooked. In the first place, the very ideal of a stable price level is open to challenge. Hoarding, as we have indicated, is always attacked; and yet it is the freely expressed and desired action on the market. People often wish to increase the real value of their cash balances, or to raise the purchasing power of each dollar. There are many reasons why they might wish to do so. Why should they not have this right, as they have other rights on the free market? And yet only by their "hoarding" taking effect through lower prices can they bring about this result. Only by demanding more cash balances and thus lowering prices can the dollars assume a higher real value. I see no reason why government manipulators should be able to deprive the consuming public of this right. Second, if people really had an overwhelming desire for a stable price level, they would negotiate all their contracts in some agreed-upon price index. The fact that such a voluntary "tabular standard" has rarely been adopted is an apt enough commentary on those stable-price-level enthusiasts who would impose their ambitions by government coercion.

Money, it is often said, should function as a yardstick, and therefore its value should be stabilized and fixed. Not its value, however, but its *weight* should be eternally fixed, as are all other weights. Its value, like all other values, should be left to the judgment, estimation, and ultimate decision of every individual consumer.[30]

[30] The totally neglected political theorist Isabel Paterson wrote as follows on the "compensated" or "commodity" dollar scheme of Irving Fisher, which would have juggled the weight of the dollar in order to stabilize its value: "As all units of measure are determined arbitrarily in the first place, though not fixed by law, obviously they can be altered by law. The same length of cotton could be designated an inch one day, a foot the next, and a yard the next; the same quantity of precious metal could be denominated ten cents today and a dollar tomorrow. But the net result would be that figures used on different days would not mean the same thing; and somebody must take a heavy loss. The alleged argument for a 'commodity dollar' was that a real dollar, of fixed quantity, will not always buy the same quantity of goods. Of course it will not. If there is no medium of value, no money, neither

PROFESSOR YEAGER AND 100 PER CENT GOLD

One of the most important discussions of the 100 per cent gold standard in recent years is by Professor Leland Yeager.[31] Professor Yeager, while actually at the opposite pole as an advocate of freely-fluctuating fiat moneys, recognizes the great superiority of 100 per cent gold over the usual pre-1933 type of gold standard. The main objections to the gold standard are its vulnerability to great and sudden deflations and the difficulties that national authorities face when a specie drain abroad threatens domestic bank reserves and forces contraction. With 100 per cent gold, Yeager recognizes, none of these problems would exist:

> Under a 100 per cent hard-money international gold standard, the currency of each country would consist exclusively of gold (or of gold plus fully-backed warehouse receipts for gold in the form of paper money and token coins). The government and its agencies would not have to worry about any drain on their reserves. The gold warehouses would never be embarrassed by requests to redeem paper money in gold, since each dollar of paper money in circulation would represent a dollar of gold actually in a warehouse. There would be no such thing as independent national monetary policies; the volume of money in each country would be determined by market forces. The world's gold supply would be distributed among the various countries according to the demands for cash balances of the individuals in the various countries. There would be no danger of gold deserting some countries and piling up excessively in others, for each

---

would a yard of cotton or a pound of cheese always exchange for an unvarying fixed quantity of any other goods. It was argued that a dollar ought always to buy the same quantity of and description of goods. It will not and cannot. That could occur only if the same number of dollars and the same quantities of goods of all kinds and in every kind were always in existence and in exchange and always in exactly proportionate demand; while if production and consumption were admitted, both must proceed constantly at an equal rate to offset one another" (*The God of the Machine,* New York: Putnam, 1943, p. 203n).

[31] Leland B. Yeager, "An Evaluation of Freely-Fluctuating Exchange Rates," unpublished Ph.D. dissertation, Columbia University, 1952.

individual would take care not to let his cash balance shrink or expand to a size which he considered inappropriate in view of his own income and wealth.

Under a 100 per cent gold standard . . . the various countries would have a common monetary system, just as the various states of the United States now have a common monetary system. There would be no more reason to worry about disequilibrium in the balance of payments of any particular country than there is now reason to worry about disequilibrium in the balance of payments of New York City. If each individual (and institution) took care to avoid persistent disequilibrium in his personal balance of payments, that would be enough . . . The actions of individuals in maintaining their cash balances at appropriate levels would "automatically" take care of the adequacy of each country's money supply.

The problems of national reserves, deflation, and so forth, Yeager points out, are due to the fractional-reserve nature of the gold standard, not to gold itself. "National fractional reserve systems are the real source of most of the difficulties blamed on the gold standard." With fractional reserves, individual actions no longer suffice to assure automatically the proper distribution of the supply of gold. "The difficulties arise because the mixed national currencies—currencies which are largely paper and only partly gold—are insufficiently international. The main defect of the historical gold standard is the necessity of 'protecting' national gold reserves." Central banking and its management only make things worse: "In short, whether a Central Bank amplifies the effects of gold flows, remains passive in the face of gold flows, or 'offsets' gold flows, its behavior is incompatible with the principles of the full-fledged gold standard . . . Indeed, any kind of monetary management runs counter to the principles of the pure gold standard." [32]

In view of this eloquent depiction of the 100 per cent

[32] *Ibid.*, pp. 9–17.

gold standard, why does Yeager flatly reject it and call instead for freely fluctuating fiat money? Largely because only with fiat money can each governmental unit stabilize the price level in its own area in times of depression. Now I cannot pause to discuss further the policy of stabilization, which I believe to be both fallacious and disastrous. I can only point out that contrary to Professor Yeager, price declines and exchange rate depreciation are not simple alternatives. To believe this is to succumb to a fatal methodological holism and to abandon the sound path of methodological individualism. If, for example, a steel union in a certain area is causing unemployment in steel by insisting on keeping its wage rates up though prices have fallen, I consider it at once unjust, a cause of misallocations and distortions of production, and positively futile to try to remedy the problem by forcing all the consumers in the area to suffer by paying higher prices for their imports (through a fall in the area's exchange rate).

One problem that every monetary statist and nationalist has failed to face is the geographical boundary of each money. If there should be national fluctuating fiat money, what should be the boundaries of the "nation"? Surely political frontiers have little or no economic meaning. Professor Yeager is courageous enough to recognize this and to push fiat money almost to a *reductio* by advocating, or at least considering, entirely separate moneys for each region or even locality in a nation.

Yeager has not pushed the *reductio* far enough, however. Logically, the ultimate in freely fluctuating fiat moneys is a different money issued by each and every individual. We have seen that this could not come about on the free market. But suppose that this came about by momentum from the present system or through some other method. What then? Then we would have a world chaos indeed, with "Rothbards," "Yeagers," "Joneses," and billions of other individual currencies freely fluctuating on the market. I think it would be instructive if some economist devoted himself to an intensive analysis of what such a world would look like. I think it safe to say that the world would be back to an enormously complex and chaotic form of barter and that trade would be reduced to a virtual standstill. For there would no longer be any sort of monetary medium for exchanges. Each separate exchange would require a different "money." In fact, since money *means* a general medium of exchanges, it is doubtful if the very concept of *money* would any longer apply. Certainly the indispensable economic calculation provided by the money and price system would have to cease, since there would no longer be a common unit of account.[33] This is a serious and not farfetched criticism of fiat-money proposals, because all of them introduce some of this chaotic element into the world economy. In short, fluctuating fiat moneys are disintegrative of the very function of money itself. If every individual had his own money, the disintegration of the very existence of money would be complete; but national—and still more regional and local—fiat moneys already partially disintegrate the money medium. They contradict the essence of the monetary function.

Finally, Professor Yeager wonders why such "orthodox liberals" as Mises, Hayek, and Robbins should have insisted on the "monetary internationalism" of the gold standard. Without presuming to speak for them, I think the answer can be put in two parts: (1) because they favor monetary

[33] Professor Yeager indeed concedes that an independent money for each person or firm would be going too far. "Beyond some admittedly indefinable point, the proliferation of separate currencies for ever smaller and more narrowly defined territories would begin to negate the very concept of money." But our contention is that the "indefinable point" is precisely definable as the very first point that fiat paper enters to break up the world's money. See Yeager, "Exchange Rates within a Common Market," *Social Research,* Winter 1958, pp. 436–437.

freedom rather than government management and manipulation of money, and (2) because they favored the existence of money as compared to barter—because they believed that money is one of the greatest and most significant features of the modern market economy, and indeed of civilization itself. The more general the money, the greater the scope for division of labor and for the interregional exchange of goods and services that stem from the market economy. A monetary medium is therefore critical to the free market, and the wider the use of this money, the more extensive the market and the better it can function. In short, true freedom of trade does require an international commodity money—as the history of the market economy of recent centuries has shown—gold or silver. Any breakup of such an international medium by statist fiat paper inevitably cripples and disintegrates the free market, and robs the world of the fruits of that market. Ultimately, the issue is a stark one: we can either return to gold or we can pursue the fiat path and return to barter. It is perhaps not hyperbole to say that civilization itself is at stake in our decision.[34]

THE 100 PER CENT GOLD TRADITION

I therefore advocate as the soundest monetary system and the only one fully compatible with the free market and with

[34] Other criticisms by Yeager are really, as he recognizes at one point, criticisms of any plan for 100 per cent banking, fiat or gold. There is, for example, the problem of how to suppress new forms of demand liabilities that might well arise to evade the legal restrictions. I do not think this an important argument. Fraud is always difficult to combat, and indeed continues in numerous forms to this day (as does all manner of crime). Does this mean that we should give up outlawing and punishing fraud and other crimes against person and property? Secondly, I am sure that the practical problems of law enforcement would be greatly reduced if the public were to receive a thorough education in the fundamentals of banking. If, in short, 100-per-cent-money advocates were allowed to form Anti-Bank Vigilante Leagues to point out the shakiness and immorality of fractional-reserve banking, the public would be much less inclined to evade such restrictions than it is now.

the absence of force or fraud from any source a 100 per cent gold standard. This is the only system compatible with the fullest preservation of the rights of property. It is the only system that assures the end of inflation, and with it, of the business cycle.[35] And it is the only form of gold standard that fully meets the following argument of the Douglas subcommittee against a return to gold: "An overriding reason against making gold coin freely available is that no government [or banks?] should make promises . . . which it would not be able to keep if the demand should arise. Monetary systems for over a century . . . have expanded more rapidly than would be permitted by accretions of gold." [36]

While this is undoubtedly a "radical" program for this day and age, it is important to note briefly that this program is squarely in a great tradition: not only in the economic tradition of the classical economists and the Currency School, but also in the American political tradition of the Jeffersonians and the Jacksonians. In essence, this was their program. In passing it should be noted that almost all historians, with the notable exceptions of William Graham Sumner and Joseph Dorfman, have misinterpreted the Jeffersonians and Jacksonians as economically ignorant and anticapitalist agrarians lashing out at a credit system they failed to understand. Whether one agrees with their position or not, they wrote in full and sophisticated knowledge of classical economics and were fully devoted to capitalism and the free market, which they believed were hampered and not aided by the institution of fractional-reserve banking.[37] In fact, it

[35] *Pace* the Mises-Hayek theory of the trade cycle, which was shunted aside but not refuted by the Keynesian Revolution.

[36] *Report of the Subcommittee on Monetary, Credit, and Financial Policies of the Joint Committee on the Economic Report,* 81 Cong., 2 Sess. (Washington, 1950), pp. 41ff.

[37] The conservative economic historians of the late nineteenth century saw Jackson as an ignorant agrarian trying to destroy capitalism and calling for inflation against the central bank. The progressives of the Beard school took

might almost be said that these Americans were unterrified members of the Currency School, lacking the almost blind devotion to the Bank of England of their more pragmatic British cousins. Indeed, the Currency Principle was enunciated in America several years before it made its appearance in England.[38] And such founders of the Currency Principle in America as Condy Raguet realized what the more eminent British tragically failed to see: that bank deposits are just as fully money substitutes as bank notes, and are therefore part of the broad money supply.[39]

After the Civil War, hard-money economists were preoccupied with battling the new greenback and free-silver problems, and the idea of 100 per cent gold virtually faded from view. General Amasa Walker, however, wrote into the 1860's and even he was surpassed in acumen by the brilliant and neglected writings of the Boston merchant Charles H. Carroll, who advocated 100 per cent gold reserves against bank deposits as well as notes, and also urged the replace-

much the same approach, except that they applauded the Jacksonians for their alleged anticapitalist stand. The most recent Bray Hammond-Thomas Govan school have again shifted their praise to the Whigs and the Bank of the United States, which they view as essential to a modern credit system as against the absurdly hard-money views of the Jacksonians.

[38] During the Panic of 1819, for example—several years before Thomas Joplin's enunciation of the Currency Principle in England—Thomas Jefferson, John Adams, John Quincy Adams, Governor Thomas Randolph of Virginia, Daniel Raymond (author of the first treatise on economics in the United States), Condy Raguet, and Amos Kendall all wrote in favor of either a pure 100 per cent gold money, or of 100 per cent gold backing for paper. See Murray N. Rothbard, "The Panic of 1819: Contemporary Opinion and Policy," Ph.D. dissertation, Columbia University, 1956. John Adams considered the issue of paper beyond specie as "theft," and Raymond called the practice a "stupendous fraud." Similar views were held by the important French ideologue and economist, and friend of Jefferson, Count Destutt de Tracy. Cf. Michael J. L. O'Connor, *Origins of Academic Economics in the United States* (New York: Columbia University Press, 1944), pp. 28, 38.

[39] Failure of the British Currency School to realize this led to the discrediting of Peel's Act of 1844, which required 100 per cent reserve for all further issue of bank notes, but left bank deposits completely free.

ment of the name "dollar" by gold ounce or gold gram.[40] And an official of the United States Assay Office, Isaiah W. Sylvester, who has been completely neglected by historians, advocated a 100 per cent dollar and parallel standards.[41] In the present century the only economist to advocate a 100 per cent gold standard, to my knowledge, has been Dr. Elgin Groseclose.[42]

[40] On Carroll, see Lloyd W. Mints, *A History of Banking Theory* (Chicago: University of Chicago Press, 1945), pp. 129, 135ff., 155–156; and especially a forthcoming collection of Carroll's writings, edited by Professor Edward C. Simmons.

[41] Isaiah W. Sylvester, *Bullion Certificates as Currency* (New York, 1882). On parallel standards, also see Brough, *Open Mints and Free Banking, passim*. For Brough's attack on the disruption caused by independent currency names, see *ibid.*, p. 93.

[42] Thus Groseclose: "The practice of the goldsmiths, of using deposited funds to their own interest and profit, was essentially unsound, if not actually dishonest and fraudulent. A warehouseman, taking goods deposited with him and devoting them to his own profit, either by use or by loan to another, is guilty of a tort, a conversion of goods for which he is liable in . . . law. By a casuistry which is now elevated into an economic principle, but which has no defenders outside the realm of banking, a warehouseman who deals in money is subject to a diviner law: the banker is free to use for his private interest and profit the money left in trust . . .

"Sooner or later we must abandon the pretense that we can eat our cake and have it, that we may have money on deposit ready to be withdrawn at any moment, and at the same time loaned out in a thousand diverse enterprises, and recognize that the only assurance of liquidity of bank deposits is to have the actual money waiting on the depositor at whatever moment he may appear. This would not mean the extinction of credit, nor the disappearance of lending institutions. But it would mean the divorcement of credit from the money mechanism, the cessation . . . of the use of credit instruments as media of exchange . . . It would mean the disappearance of the most insidious form of fictitious credit. We could still have investment banking, providing credit at long term, and bill brokers and finance companies, providing credit at short term; but such credit would not be the transfer of a fictitious purchasing power drawn from the reservoirs of a banking system whose own sources derive from the use of the bank check; the credit available would be true credit, that is, the transfer of actual, existing wealth in exchange for wealth to be created and returned at a future time. Such credit would not be inflationary, as is bank credit, for every dollar made available as purchasing power to the borrower would be the result of the abstinence from the exercise of purchasing power on the part of the lender; it would be merely the transfer of purchasing power, not the creation of purchasing power by fiction" (*Money, The Human Conflict*, Norman: University of Oklahoma Press, 1934, pp. 178, 273).

THE ROAD AHEAD

Having decided to return to a 100 per cent gold dollar, we are confronted with the problem of how to go about it. There is no question about the difficulty of the transition period required to reach our goal. But once the transition period is concluded, we will have the satisfaction of possessing the best monetary system known to man and of eliminating inflation, business cycles, and the uneconomic and immoral practice of people acquiring money at the expense of producers. Since we have many times the number of dollars as we have gold dollars at the present fixed weight of the dollar, we have essentially two alternative, polar routes toward 100 per cent gold: either to force a deflation of the supply of dollars down to the currently valued gold stock, or to "raise the price of gold" (to lower the definition of the dollar's weight) to make the total stock of gold dollars 100 per cent equal to the total supply of dollars in the society. Or we can choose some combination of the two routes.

Professor Spahr and his associates wish to return to the

Professor F. A. Hayek, in his *Monetary Nationalism and International Stability* (New York: Longmans, Green, 1937), was highly sympathetic to 100 per cent gold, and demonstrated, in some excellent analysis, the superiority of 100 per cent gold to the mixed, fractional-reserve gold standard, and to independent fiat moneys. In the end, he apparently set aside the proposal because of the difficulties of bank evasion; moreover, he concluded, rather inconsistently, by considering the ideal monetary system as directed by an international central bank, with the gold standard as only second best. Robbins, while not discussing 100 per cent money, was more sympathetic to free banking under a gold standard. Lionel Robbins, *Economic Planning and International Order* (London: Macmillan, 1937), pp. 269–305. In recent years, Hayek has abandoned the gold standard completely on behalf of a composite-commodity standard: "A Commodity Reserve Currency," in his *Individualism and Economic Order* (Chicago: University of Chicago Press, 1948), pp. 209–219. Since Hayek's major reason for the shift is that the total supply of gold is not flexible enough to change when demanded (and since, even in his earlier work, Hayek wrote of a "rationally" determined total supply of world money, regulated by an international monetary authority), it is clear that Hayek does not see that no specific total supply of money is better than any other, and that therefore no governmental manipulation of the supply is desirable.

gold standard (though not to 100 per cent gold) at the current "price" of $35 an ounce, stressing the importance of fixity of the weight of the dollar. If this were before 1933 and we were still on a gold standard, even if a defective one, I would unhesitatingly agree. The principle of a fixed weight for the dollar, and above all the principle of the sanctity of contract, are essential to our entire system of private property, and therefore would have been well worth the difficulties of a severe deflation. Aside from that, we have built deflation into an absurd ogre, and have overlooked the healthy consequences of a deflationary purgation of the malinvestments of the boom, as well as the overdue aid that fixed income groups, hit by decades of inflationary erosion, would at last obtain from a considerable fall in prices. A sharp deflation would also help to break up the powerful aggregations of monopoly unionism, which are potentially so destructive of the market economy. At any rate, while the deflation would be nominally sharp, to the extent that people would wish to save much of their present cash holdings, they would increase voluntary savings by purchasing bank debentures in lieu of their deposits, thereby fostering "economic growth" and mitigating the rigors of the deflation.

On the other hand, there is no particular reason to be devoted to the $35 figure at the present time, since the existing "gold standard" and definition of the dollar are only applicable to foreign governments and central banks; as far as the people are concerned, we are now on a virtual fiat standard. Therefore, we may change the definition of the dollar as a preliminary step to returning to a full gold standard, and we would not really be disturbing the principle of fixity. As in the case of any definition of weight, the *initial* definition is purely arbitrary, and we are so close now to a fiat standard that we may consider any dollar in a new gold standard as an initial definition.

Depending on how we define the money supply—and I

would define it very broadly as all claims to dollars at fixed par value—a rise in the gold price sufficient to bring the gold stock to 100 per cent of total dollars would require a ten- to twentyfold increase. This of course would bring an enormous windfall gain to the gold miners, but this does not concern us. I do not believe that we should refuse an offer of a mass entry into Heaven simply because the manufacturers of harps and angels' wings would enjoy a windfall gain. But certainly a matter for genuine concern would be the enormous impetus such a change would give for several years to the mining of gold, as well as the disruption it would cause in the pattern of international trade.

Which course we take, or which particular blend of the two, is a matter for detailed study by economists. Obviously little or none of this needed study has been undertaken. I therefore do not propose here a detailed blueprint. I would like to see all of those who have become convinced of the need for a 100 per cent gold standard join in such a study of the best path to take toward such a goal under present conditions. Broadly, the desired program may be summarized as follows:

1. Arrival at a 100 per cent gold dollar, either by deflation of dollars to a gold stock valued at $35 per ounce, or by revaluation of the dollar at a "gold price" high enough to make the gold stock 100 per cent of the present supply of dollars, or a blend of the two routes.

2. Getting the gold stock out of the hands of the government and into the hands of the banks and the people, with the concomitant liquidation of the Federal Reserve System, and a legal 100 per cent requirement for all demand claims.

3. The transfer of all note-issue functions from the Treasury and the Federal Reserve to the private banks. All banks, in short, would be allowed to issue deposits *or* notes at the discretion of their clients.

4. Freeing silver bullion and its representative in silver

certificates (which would now be issued by the banks) from any fixed value in gold. In short, silver ounces and their warehouse receipts would fluctuate, as do all other commodities, on the market in terms of gold or dollars, thus giving us "parallel" gold and silver moneys, with gold dollars presumably remaining the chief money as the unit of account.

5. The eventual elimination of the term "dollar," using only terms of weight such as "gold gram" or "gold ounce." [43] The ultimate goal would be the return to gold by every nation, at 100 per cent of its particular currency, and the subsequent blending of all these national currencies into one unified world gold-gram unit. This was one of the considered goals at the abortive international monetary conferences of the late nineteenth century.[44] In such a world, there would be no exchange rates except between gold and silver, for the national currency names would be abandoned for simple weights of gold, and all the world's money would at long last be freed from government intervention.

6. Free (but presumably not gratuitous) private coinage of gold and silver.

I must here differ with Professor Mises' and Henry Hazlitt's suggestion for returning to the gold standard by first establishing a "free market" in gold by cutting the dollar

[43] For an eloquent plea for using pure units of weight for money instead of national names, see Jean-Baptiste Say, *A Treatise on Political Economy*, New American ed. (Philadelphia: Grigg and Elliot, 1841), pp. 256ff. Say also favored a freely fluctuating market between gold and silver.

More recently, Everett R. Taylor has advocated private coinage of gold and silver, and a 100 per cent gold dollar, while another writer, Oscar B. Johannsen, has favored private coinage and free banking under a gold standard. Taylor, *Progress Report on a New Bill of Rights* (Diablo, Cal.: privately published, 1954; Johannsen, "Advocates Unrestricted Private Control Over Money and Banking," *Commercial and Financial Chronicle*, June 12, 1958, pp. 2622ff.

[44] See Barnard, *Metric System of Weights and Measures*, and Henry B. Russell, *International Monetary Conferences* (New York: Harper, 1898), p. 61.

completely loose from gold, and then seeing, after several years, what gold price the market would establish.[45] In the first place, this would cut the last tenuous link that the dollar still has to gold and yield us a totally fiat money. Second, the market would hardly be a "free" one, since almost all the nation's gold would be sequestered in government hands. I think it important to move in the reverse direction. The Federal government, after all, seized the people's gold in 1933 under the guise of a temporary emergency. It is important, for moral and economic reasons, to permit the people to reclaim their gold as rapidly as possible. And since the gold is still held as hostage for our dollars, I believe that the official link and official convertibility between dollars and gold should be re-established as soon as Congress can be so persuaded. And finally, since the dollar is merely a weight of gold, properly speaking, it is not at all appropriate to establish a "market" between dollars and gold, any more than there should be a "market" between one-dollar bills and five-dollar bills.

There is no gainsaying the fact that this suggested program will strike most people as impossibly "radical" and "unrealistic"; any suggestion for changing the status quo, no matter how slight, can always be considered by someone as too radical, so that the only thoroughgoing escape from the charge of impracticality is never to advocate any change whatever in existing conditions. But to take this approach is to abandon human reason, and to drift in animal- or plant-like manner with the tide of events. As Professor Philbrook pointed out in a brilliant article some years ago, we must frame our policy convictions on what we believe the best course to be and then try to convince others of this goal, and

[45] Mises, *Theory of Money and Credit*, pt. 4; and Henry Hazlitt, *Return to Gold* (New York: Newsweek, 1954).

not include within our policy conclusions estimates of what other people may find acceptable.[46] For *someone* must propagate the truth in society, as opposed to what is politically expedient. If scholars and intellectuals fail to do so, if they fail to expound their convictions of what they believe the correct course to be, they are abandoning truth, and therefore abandoning their very *raison d'être*. All hope of social progress would then be gone, for no new ideas would ever be advanced nor effort expended to convince others of their validity.

[46] Clarence Philbrook, " 'Realism' in Policy Espousal," *American Economic Review*, December 1953, pp. 846–859.

· V ·

THE GOLD STANDARD: A REAPPRAISAL

ARTHUR KEMP

WE HAVE been subjected in the recent past to a variety of opposed statements concerning, among other things, money, prices, inflation, gold exports and gold prices, budgets, economic growth, employment, and the independence of our monetary system. The more academic discussions of these questions have taken place for years and have shown as little unanimity of opinion as the popular and political ones. Some of our colleagues in the economic profession have forcefully argued for gradual increases in the general price level. Unless there is an increase in the general price level of some 2 to 3 per cent per year, they say, there will be chronic unemployment. A brief glance at any table of the mathematics of finance ought to convince us that, although 2 or 3 per cent per year sounds low, it would mean a doubling of the price level about once in each generation. Other colleagues, not long ago, appeared before a Washington hearing concerning monetary and fiscal affairs and advocated adopting the stability of prices as the most important element to govern our monetary policies. Still other economists, appearing before the same group, issued rejoinders in somewhat heated debate to the effect that monetary policies should be based upon the objective of "full employment" or of "economic growth" alone, and blamed inflation on the combination of "administered prices" and tight money policies.

How is it possible to get such widely differing views? Does the preservation of freedom depend on avoiding inflation? Is inflation a price that must be paid in order to achieve full employment or economic growth?

It is probably wise to remind ourselves occasionally that controversy in these matters does not always rest upon a dearth of factual material, or even upon false interpretation of existing data. Sometimes controversies stem from differences concerning the basic principles and values involved, and such controversies cannot be resolved by additional quantities of factual investigation. This is particularly evident in monetary matters. The nature of the monetary system is dependent, at least in part, upon the nature of the underlying social philosophy. Recommendations by one economist will be criticized severely by another not so much because of the monetary principles but because of the ideological and political convictions of the individual. Moreover, these ideological views and political convictions are frequently beyond logical argument. The nature of the monetary system is dependent, at least in part, upon the nature of the entire politico-economic structure. There are economists (and others) who believe it desirable to have a planned or centrally directed economy. They should favor, if they are logical, the use of planned money for social ends. Their monetary proposals are, and ought to be, quite different from those made by economists who believe in a free economy, an autonomous price mechanism, political decentralization, and limitations on the concentration of all power, economic or political.

To argue the relative efficacy of the basic values would be both improper and a waste of time. So, too, would be attempts to refute monetary arguments and proposals based upon a lack of faith in freedom itself—for this lack of faith I do not share. But familiarity with the writings, the lectures, and, in some instances, the personal philosophies of my colleagues in the present series of lectures, suggests that we all have an underlying preference for a free society over a totalitarian regime by whatever label is applied to it. I assume that we all place chief emphasis upon the individual or family as the basic unit in society, and upon freedom as the essential goal of relations among individuals. We prefer to settle questions, so far as possible, outside the political arena with a minimum of governmental intervention and coercion of one man by his fellow men. In brief, I assume we are all seeking to maintain a free society without further specifying the details of our respective philosophies.

Unfortunately, those who actively profess an adherence to the principles of a free society speak with many voices concerning monetary standards, monetary policies, and the problems of maintaining a stable monetary system. There are few other areas, if any, involving so large an amount of disagreement among those devoted to the principles of a free society as do questions of monetary affairs. This has had the unfortunate effect, at times, of stirring bitter controversy among those whose common enemy would concentrate discretionary monetary power in the hands of those who already wield concentrated political power. It appears self-evident that we can scarcely preserve the blessings of liberty to ourselves, let alone to our posterity, if monetary power of a discretionary nature is concentrated in the same hands, in the same groups, as have political power in a modern mass democracy. Perhaps these disagreements among the proponents of a free society are due to the very seriousness of the problem; perhaps they are due to our varying concerns with the many facets of monetary functions; perhaps we are unable to conceive of a fully satisfactory solution; perhaps we are faced with the dilemma of choosing among evils.

History tells us quite clearly that money originated not in the actions of governments but from the voluntary actions of merchants to facilitate their commercial exchanges, to promote preservation of purchasing power, and to aid in the formation of capital.[1] In the first instance, government stepped in to supply legal sanction to monetary practices the community had already adopted. The legal certification of weight and fineness, the specification of means of payment for settlement of disputes involving contracts impossible of positive performance, and the specification of means of settling actions of trover, trespass, slander, libel, or other acts involving damages to one individual by another greatly improved the function of government in acting as an arbiter of private disputes; they did not involve any necessary coercion.[2] Very soon governments made it known that they would not be satisfied with a purely passive role in monetary affairs. Few things are more irksome to governments, either today or in past centuries, than the hindrances placed in their way by the necessity of obtaining money. There appears to be no limit to the number and variety of socially desirable projects governments can devise. Each one can be clothed in the most delightful and attractive raiment, so that arguments against these individual projects are often made to resemble attacking one's sister and burning down the old homestead. In fact, much of our monetary experience relates to the efforts of governments, whether popular or autocratic, to free themselves from the shackles which money imposes and to use

[1] The published historical investigations of ancient and medieval periods are remarkable for their quantity and variation. Some of the more useful and generally available treatises are: W. W. Carlile, *The Evolution of Modern Money* (London: Macmillan, 1901); J. R. McCulloch, *Odd and Scarce Tracts on Money* (London: King, 1933); William Ridgeway, *The Origin of Metallic Currency and Weight Standards* (Cambridge, Mass.: Wilson, 1892); Arthur R. Burns, *Money and Monetary Policy in Early Times* (New York: Knopf, 1927); E. H. Kemmerer, *Gold and the Gold Standard* (New York: McGraw-Hill, 1944), chap. i.

[2] Cf., however, Milton Friedman's argument that this function is essentially private: *A Program for Monetary Stability* (New York: Fordham University Press, 1959), p. 5.

money, as the proponents put it, as an instrument of economic control. Much of our political experience relates to the efforts of individuals to keep the very active hands of government from emptying both their pocketbooks and their bank accounts.

Whether properly or not, a government has always been able to utilize, directly or indirectly, the money of citizens for its own purposes. Debasing the coinage, a practice widely described in monetary history, is comparatively insignificant when contrasted with modern issues of paper money, centralized control of credit, and deficit financing. While debasing the coinage was sporadic and obvious, giving rise on some occasions to a request for a tax as a substitute, the ever-increasing debts of modern governments have induced them to engage in almost continuous devaluation or even outright repudiation. In Western civilization the period of exception to this generalization coincides with the liberal revolution of the eighteenth and nineteenth centuries, forcing governments either to share some of their power over money and credit or to exercise it more carefully and with restraint. The mechanism used to bring about this decline in political influence in monetary affairs was the international gold standard of Western civilization. Turning to the twentieth century, it should be obvious that the restraints imposed by the liberal revolution were accepted grudgingly. The quantity of speeches, articles, and books relating to monetary maneuvering for political purposes suggests a variety of devices today that in other times might have stirred both admiration and envy in the breast of Tiberius Caesar or Henry VIII—or indeed, even of John Law.

Some believers in a free society have regretted that government ever was permitted to assume any role in monetary matters; they would prefer the spontaneous forces of market action to supply the means of performing all monetary functions. Perhaps they are right. But it seems already too late to turn back; the spontaneous forces that might have developed in the monetary process cannot now consciously be called into being. Virtually every country gives to government a high degree of responsibility in providing a monetary framework—presumably a stable monetary framework, although it is not always clear what stability means in this context.[3] Few areas of economic activity have had so long a record of agreement as to the appropriateness of governmental intervention. Of course, there is not agreement as to what *kind* of government intervention. Some prepare theories having academic respectability that extol the omniscience and omnipotence of the state with a monetary system based on irredeemable paper money, with its uses and values determined solely in the interests of political expediency. Such a state can promote either the formation or the destruction of capital; it can impose incentives or deterrents upon its most productive citizens; it can liquidate upper or middle classes; it can encourage or discourage thrift; it can, in effect, seize property without direct legal authority and without limit. Carried to the extreme, it can deprive the individual of the control of his own person by denying him his means of independence.

The United States, whether it is called a free society or not, is no exception to the general trend. From a limited government formed by virtue of a revolt against autocratic rule, we have "progressed" to the point where our national government's powers over money are close to being complete.

[3] On this point cf. Ludwig von Mises, *Human Action* (New Haven: Yale University Press, 1949), pp. 429–445, and the counterarguments, more detailed than I have expressed, in F. A. Hayek, *The Constitution of Liberty* (Chicago: University of Chicago Press, 1960), pp. 324–326, and Friedman, pp. 4–9. Interestingly enough, each of us—Mises, Hayek, Friedman, and myself—is unalterably opposed to governments having undisputed and unlimited power over money; yet each of us offers a different solution as to how best to avoid it.

Are there any limits to the national government's power to spend, to borrow, to tax, to determine the quantity and quality of all kinds of coin, paper currency, and even bank credit? If there be such, they are difficult to define. From successive decisions of the Supreme Court of the United States and by other federal courts, it appears that Congress can determine the unit of account and its physical form, if any; it can exclude the individual states from any authority whatever in monetary matters; it can charter banks; it can create a central banking system under the direct supervision of the national government; it can declare anything it pleases legal tender for its own and private debts; it can violate its own pledged word; it can borrow money without limit and tax without limit; it can call anything it pleases money and can deny possession of it to its private citizens.[4]

It follows, then, given this almost unlimited power of government, that it can be exercised in one of two ways: by certain general rules applicable to all and not subject to the whims of administrators or to the vagaries of the political arena; or it can be exercised so that some individual or group or agency has a high degree of administrative discretion over the determination and execution of monetary policy. This discretion may or may not involve specific restraints. It is based on the assumption that the motives of such an authority are always commendable and that actions based on these motives are invariably and infinitely wise.

The monetary history of the United States shows attempts to follow both paths, somewhat unsatisfactorily. More and more we have moved toward greater and greater discretionary authority, not only in the sphere of monetary policy but in other governmental activities as well. We have moved, and seem still to be moving, toward accepting a vast

[4] I have tried to present the evidence for this in *The Legal Qualities of Money* (New York: Pageant Press, 1956), chaps. 2–5.

variety of governmental activities, each of which is superficially plausible or even meritorious, but which collectively are aimed at multiple and often mutually incompatible objectives. The clear-cut danger is that in this multitude of socially desirable projects we may end up having none of them in an effort to have all of them.

There is something common to all of the suggestions made by those of us who favor the preservation, protection, and promotion of a free society. It is the desire to eliminate, or at least to minimize, the amount of administrative discretion available to monetary authorities and to substitute some more or less automatic system of general rules. Of the several varieties proposed, I prefer the traditional form of a gold coin standard with a monetary unit defined as a fixed weight of gold of specified fineness and both domestic and foreign redemption in gold coin and bullion. It is, and was, a much better system than its critics will admit. With some exercise of ingenuity, most of the criticisms leveled at it could be overcome. Many of its friends, unfortunately, have done it a disservice from time to time by implying that it is a cure-all and even suggesting that its acceptance is more or less a mystic faith.

Even under a gold coin standard, of course, there is considerable opportunity for the exercise of administrative discretion. Yet its real virtue lies in constantly imposing upon monetary authorities the necessity for facing reality rather than myth. Yet there still remains the problem of how to minimize the amount of administrative discretion within the structure of the limitations imposed upon monetary authorities under a gold coin standard. I am reminded of the story of the chap who visited his psychiatrist. "Doctor," he said, "I've been worried about many problems lately: about the elections, Cuba, bomb testing, the missile gap with Soviet Russia, the growing export of gold, our balance of payments, increasing unemployment, economic growth, inflation and taxes. But that's not why I'm here. What really bothers me is that last week I began to think I had come up with some perfectly marvelous solutions for all of them!" So, I confess, I do not think the gold coin standard is a perfectly marvelous solution for all our problems, but it appears to me to be a step in the right direction and more likely to succeed in establishing a modus vivendi for a free society than some of the perfectly marvelous solutions suggested by others.

The advocate of a gold coin standard, if he is at all sophisticated, regards it less as an end in itself than as an institution within which the monetary and credit system functions. A gold coin standard performs the function of a standard of value, a standard of deferred payments, and provides a historically efficient means of storing value over time. It also provides a mechanism for furnishing the necessary quantity of medium of exchange, the means of payment, and in modern complex credit economies the means of providing reserves against bank notes and bank deposits. It is convenient to divide these functions into two groups: those relating to establishment of the *standard* of value, and those relating to the means or media for measuring such value. The development of a gold coin standard requires determining the weight and fineness of the monetary unit, its multiples, and its fractional parts. This is exactly analogous to determining the selection and definition of units of measurement. We have many such standards to measure force, weight, distance, mass, and other magnitudes. The means of measuring value bears a relation to the standard monetary unit similar to that which a ruler or tape measure bears to a yard or meter; this is not to say that the means *is* the standard. The standard meter, for example, was for years a certain platinum-iridium bar supported in a specified manner, at the temperature of melting ice, and at standard atmospheric pressure. Obviously, most measurements in the metric system have been made by other means than this bar—by pieces of wood, steel, cloth, or plastic, each of which more or less imperfectly represents the standard. Similarly, under a gold coin standard the relation of certain forms of money to the standard (including the coins themselves by virtue of limits of tolerance) is akin to the relation of the steel, cloth, or plastic to the platinum-iridium bar. Although there is no need to enforce the use of the particular bar in measurements, there is a definite need for assuring that the measuring medium is an accurate representation of the standard. This is the basic reason for the redemption feature of the gold coin standard, as well as for other legal qualities, such as legal tender. It is also the basic reason for the emphasis placed upon fixity by those of us who advocate a gold coin standard.[5] A platinum bar of oft-changing length would scarcely function efficiently as the standard for the metric system.

One expert put the general rule as follows: "The gold standard breaks down only when governments interfere with its operation by declaring other money legal tender, and issuing or permitting other money to be issued in excess, or by interfering with exports or imports of gold." [6]

There can be little doubt that some form of gold usage as money (or at least as a store of value) has existed over a very large part of the world since the earliest times. Thus, in its cruder forms, the gold standard may be said to have existed

[5] For example, by Walter E. Spahr, James Washington Bell, Donald L. Kemmerer, Frederick A. Bradford, and the late E. W. Kemmerer, Leonard Ayres, B. M. Anderson and Joseph Schumpeter—to mention only a few. A so-called "free" gold market, in which the price of gold moves up and down in response to demand and supply without definition in fixed terms, is not a gold standard at all. To the extent that gold is used for international reserves under such circumstances, it constitutes a very limited sort of international gold-reserve standard.

[6] John Parke Young, *European Currency and Finance* (Commission of Gold and Silver Inquiry, United States Senate; Government Printing Office, 1925), vol. I, p. 10.

before man invented a medium of exchange called a coin. Gold served (and still serves) as an attraction to primitive peoples unversed in the thrilling possibilities of inconvertible managed paper standards. Its durability, cognizability, acceptability, malleability, divisibility, scarcity, and portability or high specific value have long been recognized as unique combinations of metallic qualities. No other commodity, and no other metal among the great variety that has been experimented with over thousands of years, has had the acceptance given to gold; no other commodity or even arrangement has stood the test of time, of trial and error, of variations and substitutions, as has gold. Even today, with gold coins issued by some long-dead monarch whose legions have long since perished, whose kingdom is mythical, whose palace is dust, we could travel almost anywhere in the civilized (and even uncivilized, at least in part) world and exchange those coins for current moneys sufficient to pay our way and to acquire clothing, shelter and other commodities. Nor would the cost and trouble of converting, or even the chance of being defrauded, be appreciably higher than it is for some modern paper moneys. Without arguing that gold should be utilized now as a standard merely because it has been used before, it is nevertheless of some significance to consider thousands of years of usage in monetary matters when considering the possible alternatives for future monetary standards. The qualities of gold suggest that people have used it for money for good reason; but even if this were not so, even if its long use were the result of ignorance, myth, and illusion, the historical significance of the metal could not be disregarded. Perhaps if gold did not exist we should have been forced to invent it; but as long as it does exist, I am in favor of using it.

Quite aside from the historical aspects of gold standards, there are three problems related to monetary mechanisms to which gold and gold standards have contributed viable, if not perfect, solutions. The first is the problem of inflation; the second is the problem of effective stable relations between currencies of different nations; the third is the protection given to private property and private enterprise against government encroachment, intervention, and confiscation.

Without discussing reasons, it seems apparent that the long-run trend of prices has been upward. Taking into account only the movement of prices in the twentieth century, or more properly since World War I, a substantial but varying degree of inflation has taken place in all countries of the world.[7] There is a period of time, however, corresponding roughly to the period of the effective functioning of the organized gold coin standard, when the historical trend of inflation did not take place. During the period from 1821 to 1914 the range of British wholesale prices on a 1913 base was from 72 (1896) to 126 (1821); for 80 of the 94 years the wholesale price index stood between 80 and 120, and for 33 of these years it stood between 90 and 110; it fell below 80 or above 120 in only 14 years.[8] During the 36 years before World War I the United States experienced a similar stability in wholesale prices, and general prices did not rise above 100 or fall below 71 (1913 = 100).[9]

John Maynard Keynes, certainly not noted for his defense of the gold standard, wrote: "The remarkable feature of this long period was the relative *stability* of the price level. Approximately the *same* level of price ruled in or about the years 1826, 1841, 1855, 1862, 1867, 1871, and 1915. Prices were also level in the years 1844, 1881, and 1914. If we call the index number of these latter years 100, we find that for

[7] For measurements of the extent of the inflationary trends and a discussion of "chronic inflation" see Hayek, *Constitution of Liberty*, pp. 428–433, 521.

[8] Kemmerer, *Gold and the Gold Standard*, pp. 189–190; Young, p. 450.

[9] Kemmerer, p. 191.

close on a century from 1826 to the outbreak of war, the maximum fluctuation in either direction was 30 points, the index number never rising above 130 and never falling below 70. No wonder that we came to believe in the stability of money contracts over a long period." [10]

Similarly, looking at a longer period and one not associated with a strict gold coin standard in the United States or Great Britain but a period during which both countries were loosely or tightly tied to gold, Hayek points out: "During the two hundred years preceding 1914, when Great Britain adhered to the gold standard, the price level, so far as it can be meaningfully measured over such a period, fluctuated around a constant level, ending up pretty well where it started and rarely changing by more than a third above or below that average level (except during the period of the Napoleonic wars, when the gold standard was abandoned). Similarly, in the United States, during the period 1749–1939 there also does not seem to have occurred a significant upward trend of prices. Compared with this, the rate at which prices have risen during the last quarter of a century in these and other countries represents a major change." [11]

Both logic and experience seem to me to indicate that a gold coin standard contributes to a greater stability in price levels than exists under other monetary standards and arrangements, and that this greater degree of stability is probably the result of a tendency on the part of the gold coin standard to bring up sharply severe movements in either direction. This is not to say that the gold coin standard will bring about a perfectly stable price level. Indeed, such a state of affairs, particularly if it is brought about by conscious effort, is undesirable. Unchanging price levels would be de-

[10] *A Tract on Monetary Reform* (London: Macmillan, 1923), pp. 11–12.
[11] Hayek, pp. 329–330.

sirable only if prices were, in fact, free to change and if the lack of change represented harmony of price relations—an ideal fondly to be wished but seldom realized in practice.

The evidence strongly suggests that the international gold standard (with most of the important financial countries being on a gold *coin* standard) provided a remarkable international standard prior to 1914. Foreign trade increased among nations; there were fewer obstacles to the free and unfettered movements of goods from one country to another than existed before that time or since; there was no such thing as a problem of "convertibility" in the present sense of the word; and the legal convertibility of monetary balances into gold provided a degree of confidence internationally that has not been seen since, and probably not before; for long periods of time there existed essentially stable systems of foreign exchange rates, although, as in the case of stability of price levels, not absolutely fixed ones. There can be little dispute with the fact that the Western world, or the free world, as we call it today, was more closely intertwined in terms of prices, exchange rates, capital movements, interest rates, and the like, than it has ever been under our formal attempts to accomplish this with such devices as the International Monetary Fund, International Bank for Reconstruction and Development, and other planned institutions of our times.

Keynes, after World War I, did not advocate a return to the gold standard because he believed it impractical and because he did not think central banks would follow the "rules of the game." But he recognized its virtues: "If gold standards could be reintroduced throughout Europe, we all agree that this would promote, as nothing else can, the revival not only of trade and production but of international credit and the movement of capital to where it is needed most. One of the greatest elements of uncertainty would be lifted. One of the most vital parts of prewar organization would be restored." [12]

If the promotion of economic internationalism as opposed to economic nationalism is a desirable objective, national gold coin standards and an international gold standard seem an eminently practical way to achieve it. Although space does not permit discussion of it here, there are certainly possibilities for weaknesses in such an arrangement. The errors of the international gold-exchange standards following World War I are well known. But in spite of a willingness to admit that the international gold standard is not perfect, it seems to me that on balance the experience with the use of gold for these purposes is more encouraging than the experience associated with other mechanisms, particularly when these mechanisms involve a high degree of administrative discretion on the part of international central bankers whose discretion, it would seem, had something to do with the severity of the Great Depression. It is most regrettable that the Bank for International Settlements had almost no time to operate before the onset of the depression and to demonstrate to the world the direction which improvements upon the international gold standard might have taken.

I have been most impressed, in advocating a gold coin standard, with the relation of gold to individual freedom—particularly to private property and enterprise. Whether accidentally or not, the establishment of free societies and the development of the classical liberal tradition went hand in hand with the development of formalized gold standards. Monetary history is replete with examples of the most fundamental violations of individual rights when governments were strong enough to throw off the shackles imposed upon their actions by the necessities of redemption in fixed, standard coin. The American states, under the loose association of

[12] *Manchester Guardian Commercial*, Reconstruction supplement, April 20, 1922.

the Articles of Confederation, and freed from the restraining hand of the English Parliament, assessed various penalties for refusing to accept the paper Continental currency. Some of them strike the student as exceedingly barbaric—ranging from forfeiting the debt and confiscation of property to pillorying, or even the loss of one's ears. John Stuart Mill contributed the following to a description of certain monetary practices:

> Profligate governments . . . until a very modern period, seldom scrupled, for the sake of robbing their creditors, to confer upon all debtors a license to rob theirs, by the shallow and impudent device of lowering the standard; that least covert of all modes of knavery, which consists in calling a shilling a pound, that a debt of one hundred pounds may be canceled by the payment of a hundred shillings. It would have been as simple a plan, and would have answered the purpose as well, to have enacted that "a hundred" should always be interpreted to mean five, which would have effected the same reduction of all pecuniary contracts, and would not have been at all more shameless. Such strokes of policy have not wholly ceased to be recommended, but they have ceased to be practised; except occasionally through the medium of paper money, in which case the character of the transaction, from the greater obscurity of the subject, is a little less barefaced.[13]

Mill's statement was written well over a hundred years ago, firmly in the period of the British gold coin standard. He may be forgiven for his optimism regarding the moral rejuvenation of governments.

It is revealing to read the piecemeal reports of gold "markets" in countries on the verge of being absorbed into the Soviet orbit after World War II; for example, Poland, Czechoslovakia, and Rumania. Gold became the most attractive commodity, in any form, as a protector against confiscation and as a form of wealth capable of preserving value and

[13] *Principles of Political Economy*, ed. Sir W. J. Ashley (New York: Longmans, Green, 1909), pp. 486–487.

transporting it. The father of Henry Bessemer, inventor of the Bessemer steel process, caught in the disorder of the French Revolution, was able to re-establish himself as a die-maker in England by virtue of a supply of gold coins. The vastly larger proportion of his wealth in French assignats turned out to be worthless. Gold, in no small manner, was responsible for the Bessemer process. Examples could be multiplied and, although in themselves they do not signify that gold will prevent evil doings, they do suggest the reason for the old adage "We have gold because we cannot trust governments."

Perhaps the best brief statement of the relation of the gold coin standard to property rights, private enterprise, and individual freedom has been made recently by Walter E. Spahr:

> If a person, living under the degree of freedom inherent in a gold standard, is disturbed by, or disapproves of the policies or practices of his government or banks, he may preserve his property by presenting non-gold currency for redemption. If many people demand redemption, the banks and government are forced to respect the fears or disapproval of those who are demanding redemption. The government is thus placed in a position in which it must be careful not to disturb unduly, or incur the disapproval of many people with property to protect.
>
> Thus do a people with a gold standard and right of redemption or conversion at their disposal have the power to keep a check-rein on the fiscal powers and practices of their central government. Thus do they obtain and maintain responsible government. The people may utilize that power wisely or unwisely; but it is a power they must have if they are to be able to protect themselves from improper government encroachment or tyranny.[14]

Perhaps the vaunted advantages of gold are a figment of people's imaginations. If so, it is a lively figment for its age.

For the purposes of this paper I have avoided most of the areas of conflict with my colleagues' papers and presenta-

[14] "The Gold Standard and Its Significance," *Modern Age*, 4:297–298 (Summer 1960).

tions. Some of these, I suspect, are irreconcilable; others could be resolved. The question of 100 per cent reserves, for example, is to me a different question from that of the determination of the monetary standard. To some extent the questions of favoring an inconvertible, irredeemable paper standard with a locked-in money supply, or one having a constant percentage increase per year in money supply, are similar. But in part, too, understanding and reconciliation depend upon what functions of money one emphasizes and considers most important, and upon the intent to which one believes particular policies to be practical, or politically possible. Perhaps at some future time, the various and sundry "solutions" to the monetary problems of our times can be debated directly in such a manner as to focus upon the real differences that exist among those who are devoted to the principles of a free society. It is not necessary for those who are not so devoted; indeed, nothing could be more obvious than the nature of the differences that exist between those who believe in freedom and those who do not.

· VI ·

PREDICTABILITY: THE CRITERION OF MONETARY CONSTITUTIONS

(Illustrated with reference to the proposal for a common-brick monetary standard)

JAMES M. BUCHANAN

As I interpret the organization of these articles, the several authors are examining monetary policy in the broadest possible sense of this term. We are considering the alternatives for monetary policy independently of the many political-institutional-historical constraints that may serve, and have served, to inhibit discussion at many levels. We are, in other words, engaged in a discussion of constitutional law; we are analyzing the alternative monetary constitutions that may be appropriate to the functioning of a competitive or enterprise economy.

If we conceive our efforts, our separate contributions, in this manner, the question of criteria emerges at the outset of our discussion. What results do we desire to see accomplished? How may the comparative performances of the separate monetary frameworks be evaluated? If we can initially agree upon, and accept, a single criterion for judging the performance of a set of monetary institutions, we should already have made a major step toward securing the required consensus on the more specific elements of monetary reform.

I submit that we can reach agreement on such a criterion,

agreement not only among ourselves but among scholars generally. In other words, I am stating that the issues in monetary policy can be resolved wholly into issues of means, not ends. Contrary to other areas of economic policy, there is, or should be, no basic value conflict on matters of monetary policy. Having said this, I am now obliged to define the criterion about which I speak. I suggest that the most meaningful criterion for monetary policy, regardless of the level of discussion, is *predictability* in the value of the monetary unit, or, reciprocally, in the absolute level of prices.

PREDICTABILITY AND STABILITY AS NORMS

It will be useful to compare and contrast *monetary predictability* with *monetary stability* as the criterion of policy. As we know, the latter has been more often advanced. Note that, with monetary stability, we encounter immediately the issue of definition. What is meant by stability, even in some "ideal" sense? Is stability to be defined in terms of a product or a factor price level? These questions could, no doubt, be answered satisfactorily, and significant agreement reached among large numbers of monetary theorists. But the necessity for such questions to arise at this level of discussion can be eliminated by the substitution of predictability for stability as the appropriate monetary norm. More importantly for our purposes, however, this substitution widens considerably the consensus on criteria that is required for genuine progress. Even those who have argued in favor of creeping inflation should agree on the predictability criterion. In fact, a major virtue of predictability as a criterion lies in the obvious difficulty which confronts the serious monetary scholar who proposes to refuse acceptance. As we shall discuss in the following section, predictability in the value of the monetary unit is required for maximum economic efficiency, as normally defined, and, of course, for economic growth, which has become the modern equivalent of the efficiency norm when considered in a dynamic context.

Perhaps the greatest advantage of the proposed substitution of *predictability* for *stability* lies in the fact that it allows us to isolate problems and issues relating to the monetary constitution from those which introduce problems and issues concerned with the efficacy of monetary policy in producing specific effects on the so-called macroeconomic variables. Monetary policy, either at the constitutional framework level or at the institutionally constrained level, may or may not produce the effects called for by some stabilization criteria. The quantity of money may or may not be the key control variable in an over-all macroeconomic policy model. The variation in this quantity may or may not satisfactorily explain historical experience as to fluctuations in economic magnitudes. The point is that issues such as these, regardless of individual views, *need not be raised* in the basic consideration of alternative monetary constitutions. And I think that the air would be cleared substantially if we should agree to leave aside these essentially subsidiary issues until the more basic ones are settled.

PREDICTABILITY AND EFFICIENCY

It is difficult for me to understand how anyone could seriously reject predictability as an appropriate norm for monetary policy. And yet I think that the consensus on this norm represents much more than empty agreement on such other economic policy goals as "efficiency," "rapid growth," and the like. With the latter, the fundamental agreement on goals merely puts aside argument and dispute until problems of specifying and defining the agreed-on goals are faced. Monetary predictability is not a norm of this sort. The predictability of the value of money is quite precise as a conceptual notion. Problems of definition do, of course, arise, but these are problems that are subject to discussion and, presumably, to solution. In other words, reasonable men can readily agree on the meaning of monetary predictability.

The analogy which comes to mind is weather. Predictability in weather is a widely accepted criterion for meteorologists, and we all know what is meant by improved weather prediction. I have seen no claim or argument to the effect that improvement in weather forecasting, in predictability, will not also "improve" over-all efficiency in resource usage. The correspondence between improvements in predictability here and improvements in economic performance generally is, in fact, taken for granted and rarely mentioned explicitly at all. Improved weather forecasting is acknowledged to be one of the "desirable" results to be expected from greater investment in scientific research.

This accords strictly with common-sense notions. If man can further his skills in predicting the weather, economic resources will be more effectively employed; major mistakes will be avoided. Note particularly that this conclusion holds quite independently of the trend in the weather over time. The winters in the northern hemisphere may gradually be getting "worse" or "better" by certain commonly accepted standards of "worseness" or "betterness." But the direction of change in the weather, described in this way, is irrelevant to the conclusion that improved predictability can lead to greater economic efficiency.

Our analogy becomes even closer if we move forward in time and imagine ourselves in a situation where the weather can be deliberately controlled. It is relatively easy to see that, under such circumstances, serious disputes might arise concerning criteria for betterness. But the improvements in predictability should still be recognized as universally desirable, regardless of the particular criterion of betterness that is adopted.

The analogy, as modified, seems almost perfect, but, as with all analogies, it is treacherous unless it is carefully handled. The meteorologist can direct his efforts toward improving predictability in the current situation, quite independently of his efforts toward securing greater control over the elements. The monetary theorist can, of course, do likewise. He can accept the institutional complex as it exists and devote his energies to improving forecasting techniques. But this is clearly relatively unproductive if he can, at a lower cost, devise means of modifying the institutional structure itself in such a way as to ensure greater predictability as a result. The monetary theorist would probably have much more difficulty than the meteorologist of the future, however, in separating the predictability aspects of a proposed "constitutional" change from the "improvements in results" that he might be able to secure through the change. The situation here should, of course, be reversed when we consider the relative importance of predictability and improvements in results in the two cases. With the weather, significant "improvement" can be contemplated by most people, quite apart from improved forecasting. With a monetary framework or constitution, if predictability were to be ensured, there would seem to be relatively little difference among alternative patterns of performance. There should be relatively little difference in the social costs of organizing a monetary system that would, for example, produce stability in the product price level, one that would produce a gradual decline in the product price level, and a system that would produce a gradual increase, *provided that the predictability was equivalent in the several cases.*

This is not to suggest that the choice among alternative monetary systems, independent of predictability elements, is not an important one. I should emphasize only that this choice, when constrained to a system among those that are expected to produce substantially the same predictability, is considerably less important than the initial choice between systems expected to generate monetary predictability and those which are not.

PREDICTABILITY AND PERFECT FORESIGHT

I doubt that I have said anything up to this point with which issue could be taken. I should insist, however, that the emphasis on predictability is more important than it may at first appear. But objections may be raised on the grounds that predictability is a norm that can be useful for analytical purposes but which is unattainable and, therefore, not practicable in any policy sense. Is monetary predictability as a norm not similar to the requirement for perfect foresight when we discuss the efficiency with which the competitive economic system organizes resource use? We agree that the ideally operating competitive system requires perfect foresight on the part of all or at least a substantial number of participants, but rarely do we introduce such foresight as an organizational norm. We recognize that little can be done toward substantially increasing the "predictability" of the whole economic organization, considered over all. Such efficiency as the competitive order produces is ensured through its flexibility and adaptability to changes in tastes, in resource supply, and in technology: changes that are, almost by their nature, unpredictable. The structure of relative prices responds to such of these changes as happen to occur, and any attempt to "freeze" the future course of relative price relations in some misguided efforts to increase predictability, that is, to reduce uncertainty, would make little logical sense. The act of fixing the course of relative price movements in advance would do nothing toward reducing the uncertainties that are inherent in the movements of the wholly unpredictable exogenous variables of the free economy. Surplus disposal and rationing problems would surely arise from such an attempt to increase predictability, and, rather than accomplishing this result, the reductions in responsiveness of the system to unexpected changes would be measured in avoidable inefficiency.

The pre-fixing of the course of the absolute price level would, however, be completely different. If predictability in the level of absolute prices, that is, in the value of the monetary unit, could be introduced, net gains in efficiency would surely follow. Such predictability implies, of course, *continuous monetary equilibrium.* And if this were accomplished, the actual course of change in the absolute price level would become largely irrelevant.

In comparing positions of full equilibrium, the classical dichotomy between relative prices and the absolute price level is valid. And by imposing the assumption of predictability at the outset, I am ensuring that an equilibrium state is continuously maintained. Changes in the absolute price level may, of course, require accompanying changes in the supply or quantity of money. Implicit in my argument to this point is the idea that this variable might be employed to accomplish the goal desired. The main point is that, as the neoclassical writers emphasized, the absolute price level is independent of the structure of relative prices. It follows from this that the movements in the absolute price level over time can be varied without affecting the relative price structure. And, contrary to the situation applicable to the latter, the actual course of movement is largely unimportant in relation to the predictability of this movement.

But I am not yet in the clear, since I have not really got over the possible objection that the assumption of predictability in the absolute price level is analogous to the assumption of perfect foresight in the competitive model and, as such, useful analytically but not helpful normatively. Predictability as an appropriate policy norm must still be shown to be practicably achievable or, at the least, approachable.

The unique difference between potential predictability in the absolute price level and the potential satisfaction of the perfect foresight condition lies in the Walrasian recognition that one commodity or service in an interrelated economy must be selected as a *numéraire* in order to prevent underdetermination in the solution of the system of equations describing the economy. Until and unless one such commodity or service is selected, relative price relations can be expressed only in ratios or relatives; no common denominator of value exists. The selection of such a *numéraire* does not reduce the flexibility or the adaptability of the system to changes in the exogenous variables. Quite the contrary; agreement on a *numéraire* becomes a necessary condition for organizational efficiency. It follows directly from this that the imposition of predictability in the value of this *numéraire*, when computed in terms of other commodities and services, does not substantially reduce the flexibility allowed the other variables in the system.

"IDEAL" ASPECTS OF PRICE-LEVEL PREDICTABILITY

If the predictability norm is accepted as appropriate for monetary policy, and if it is accepted that this represents a meaningful and conceptually attainable norm, the next question to be faced involves the choice of means to implement it. In one sense, everything I have said to this point is introductory to this latter question, which is the main part of my discussion. For it is on the means of attaining monetary predictability that the various students of constitutional monetary policy may, and do, differ sharply. Before discussing some of these differences, I should like to emphasize again that the attainment of predictability, under any monetary framework, is more important than the means through which the goal is accomplished. Despite the amount of discussion devoted to arguments for or against various means of introducing monetary predictability, the underlying and central importance of ensuring predictability, *by any means*, should never be overlooked.

The result we seek is not difficult to define. What we want a monetary framework to produce is predictability in the value of money. We desire a monetary system that will allow the individual decision-maker, whether he be consumer, entrepreneur, seller of productive services, or speculator, to remove from his calculus uncertainty about the future course of the absolute price level. He will face quite sufficient and necessary uncertainty in his efforts to predict the future course of relative prices, uncertainty which, quite properly, should enter directly into his calculus.

We define the result desired in terms of the value of money, or reciprocally, the absolute price level. These are conceptual abstractions, however, not physical units of measure. These magnitudes assume arithmetical meaning only after some averaging process is undertaken, a process that utilizes movements in the prices of real physical commodities and services. The predictability about which we speak is predictability in the movement of an average over time. This average can be expressed in terms of an index number, but this number can never be expected to serve for more than an arbitrary scale factor. As such, movement in the index number can provide a criterion to suggest the suitability of action being taken on *other* variables, real or physical variables. The index itself cannot be acted upon in any direct manner.

We may provide an illustration by an analogy with temperature. The thermometer measures temperature, but temperature as such can do nothing other than to provide us with a criterion for taking action directly on other variables. We cannot directly increase temperature; we must instead take action on other variables, such as the quantity of coal in the furnace, which will, in turn, influence the heat index, or temperature, that we are observing.

Fundamentally, there exist two ways in which predictability in the movement of a price index can be incorporated into a monetary constitution. First, we may utilize the price index as the *instrumental* criterion for policy changes, changes that must involve action taken on other variables of the system. Second, and alternatively, we may try to organize the institutions of private decision-making in such a way that the desired monetary predictability will emerge spontaneously from the ordinary operations of the system.[1]

It is easy to see that the first approach possesses somewhat greater appeal when the problem is conceived in its "ideal" sense. If, in fact, the "ideal" or "norm" can be defined with some precision, as we have said is the case with monetary predictability, it can always be achieved by "ideal" men operating under "ideal" conditions. Hence the tendency in this area, as in others, is for students to jump somewhat too quickly into support of the first approach suggested above. When, however, we recognize that in all matters of economic policy specific actions can only be taken by individual human beings, and that these human beings are fallible and subject to mistakes and error, we begin to sense the merit of the second, alternative, approach, that which aims at securing the desired results spontaneously rather than instrumentally.

MANAGED VERSUS AUTOMATIC SYSTEMS

This represents the difference between what we call a "managed" monetary system and what we call an "automatic"

[1] An analogy with economic efficiency, defined in the orthodox way, will be useful. In so far as such efficiency is a norm for competitive economic organization, it is achieved as a result that emerges from the operation of the economy and not as a result of instrumentally oriented attempts to achieve this goal in any direct manner.

monetary system. I am aware that these terms introduce still further questions; all monetary systems are, in a sense, managed; none can be wholly automatic. For our purposes, however, we may think of a managed system as one that embodies the instrumental use of price-level predictability as a norm of policy, either loosely by discretionary authorities possessing wide latitude for independent decision-making powers, or closely in the form of specific rules constraining discretionary authority within narrow limits. On the other hand, we may think of an automatic system as one which does not, at any stage, involve the explicit use of the absolute price level, the price index, or any other macroeconomic variable,[2] in guiding monetary policy. In the automatic system, monetary policy as such consists solely of the designation of a single commodity or service as the basis for the monetary unit, as the standard, and the firm fixing of the future course of the price, in money units, of this commodity. Note that I do not, in this description of an automatic system, require that the money price of the commodity chosen as the standard be stabilized over time. All that is required is that this price be fixed at each particular moment in time and that its level be known in advance. The price of the standard commodity may, of course, be stabilized, which is the case usually analyzed, but my point is that the normative argument for such stability arises at a level of discussion different from that considered here. Predictability is the important normative element that must first be incorporated into either a managed or an automatic system.

The ultimate policy decision as between a managed monetary system and an automatic system should be made only after a careful analysis of the relative costs and benefits ex-

[2] A system characterized by the *exclusive* attention of stabilization authorities being given to other macroeconomic variables, such as an employment index, could hardly be called a monetary system at all. Nevertheless, in so far as it should become necessary to classify such a system, it would clearly fall within the managed set.

pected from the operation of each system. Comparisons must be made on the basis of the expected properties of the alternative systems in the real world, not on the basis of properties of ideally constructed models. But we do not get very far until and unless we specify quite carefully and precisely the nature of the alternative systems that we propose to compare. There are many institutions described by the term "managed system," and there are many different commodities and services that are possible standards. Too often generic evaluations will be made as a result of comparisons between a particular managed system and some poorly working automatic system or between a particular automatic system and some poorly working managed system.

THE "IDEAL" MANAGED SYSTEM

We may avoid this difficulty, to some extent, by commencing with a comparison between the best or "ideal" managed system and the best or "ideal" automatic or commodity-money system.

I do not propose here to argue the case for any particular managed system. I shall state my conviction that some such scheme as that proposed by Henry Simons and Lloyd Mints would come closest to introducing predictability in the absolute price level. That is to say, I should opt squarely in favor of some predetermined, quasi-constitutional "rule" that would define quite precisely the task of the monetary authority, the "managers." This authority would then be charged with the responsibility of following the rule or set of rules. This system would, ideally, produce divergencies between observed and predicted values for money only as a result of errors and miscalculations stemming from the attempts of the authorities to follow the predetermined rules. By contrast, under a discretionary managed system, divergencies between observed and predicted values would arise not only from this source but also from the additional one involving departures of the actually followed rules from predicted ones. But, as suggested, it is not my function to argue this point.

THE "IDEAL" AUTOMATIC SYSTEM

Those monetary theorists who generally tend to favor managed systems of one sort or another have not, as a rule, specified the alternative automatic standard or system with which their mental comparisons are made. Too often, I suspect, they have dismissed automatic systems, generically, because they associate all such systems with one specific member of a very large set, a member that is known to have produced undesirable results when it was partially operative. I speak here, of course, of the gold standard. As we know, the historical gold standard was not even a good model of a monetary system based on the commodity gold. But this need not concern us here. My point is that we should always specify carefully the characteristics of the alternative monetary system under consideration, and until and unless we have examined the "best" practicable automatic system, we should not opt for managed systems out of hand.

I propose, therefore, that we think first in terms of the characteristics of an "ideal" commodity system of money. If it could be found, what commodity or service would "ideally" accomplish the goal of monetary predictability? Viewed in this light, it seems that we should seek some commodity that is perfectly representative of the production of goods and services over the whole economy. That is, we need to locate some commodity whose production embodies some appropriately weighted set of coefficients that are representative of production processes for all goods and services in the economy. The elasticity of supply of this ideal monetary commodity would be equivalent to that possessed by production as a whole. The production of this ideal monetary commodity would be in a real sense an image of the whole economy in operation. Or, to use a mathematical metaphor, the whole economy would be "mapped" into the single production process.

The weights that would be implicit in this ideal commodity must in some manner reflect the relative importance of the various goods and services produced. But this relative importance can only be judged in terms of values. We must introduce market prices as the only meaningful reflection of consumer evaluation. We are led in this way to the conclusion that the ideal commodity for a monetary constitution utilizing some automatic or indirect means of achieving monetary predictability must be some commodity whose price, in the absence of its designation as the standard commodity, would move *pari passu* with movements in the absolute level of prices, that is, with the price index.

If there should exist such a commodity, that is, one whose price varies in perfect correspondence with the absolute price level in the absence of its designation as the monetary standard or basis, the achievement of monetary predictability to the degree desired would require a relatively simple institutional change. The government could state simply that the monetary authority, in this case, the Mint, would stand ready and willing to buy and to sell for money units unlimited quantities of this ideal commodity at a schedule of prices fixed in advance (and not necessarily to be stabilized over time). The economy would, as a result, be operating on a basis of monetary predictability, since the decentralized and impersonal forces of the competitive mechanism could be depended upon to produce and to destroy "money" as the economy required. If the absolute price level fell below predicted values, production and sale of the ideal commodity would take place. The quantity of money units in circulation would increase, and this increase would continue until observed and predicted values for the absolute price level roughly coincided. Conversely, if the absolute price level rose above predicted values, purchase of the ideal monetary commodity from the Mint would be stimulated. This purchase would continue until observed and predicted values for some price index were roughly in equivalence. Note that predictability under this system would be achieved without the instrumental usage of any price index as a criterion of policy action. The primary virtue of any "automatic" or commodity standard of money lies in the fact that only in such a system would the forces of the competitive market be directly utilized to achieve monetary predictability. In one sense, there would be no explicit monetary policy involved in the operation of such a system.

THE PRICE-LEVEL RULE AS A SIMULATED IDEAL COMMODITY STANDARD

For purposes of comparative analysis, we may conceive the operation of the Simons-Mints rule for price-level predictability in terms of such an "ideal" commodity standard. In one sense, the system of managed money in accordance with this type of rule is designed to simulate the more automatic system. Under such a rule-oriented system, the government is essentially "selling" units of an ideal composite commodity at a schedule of predetermined prices and "buying" units of this commodity at the same schedule of prices. If the administrators of such a managed system make few errors, the results will be substantially equivalent to those produced under the operation of an actual ideal commodity standard. But there are no market checkreins on the behavior of the monetary authorities. This important control feature of an actual commodity standard is missing. Decisions must be centralized.

Some of the monetary theorists who support such a rule for

monetary management will argue convincingly that, given some predictability in the future course of the absolute price level, the forces of the competitive market mechanism will become operative. The profit-seeking actions of speculators will tend to ensure that the predictability implicit in the rule-as-directive to the monetary authorities will, in fact, characterize the rule-as-result. The phenomena here have been referred to as self-reinforcing expectations. If people are sufficiently sure that a particular result is to be achieved, their own private actions will tend to guarantee that their prediction becomes true. I do not want to go further into the interesting philosophical issues raised by the question of rules as predictions.

There is, however, one important factor that prevents self-reinforcing speculation from being fully effective under the operation of a rule for monetary predictability. Even if we can discount the major problems involved in crossing the "belief threshold," that is, the problems of convincing speculators that the predetermined rule will in fact continue to be employed as the overriding criterion for policy, the force of competitive counterspeculation will be reduced because individuals are unable to buy or sell "an average," "a price level," or "a price index." The general expectation that the over-all price level will, for example, rise to some predicted value (as indicated in the rule-as-criterion) from some currently observed value will cause speculators to shift their asset holdings from money into real goods, but in such a shift, the absence of any ideal composite commodity necessitates taking on relative price uncertainties. Some choices must be made among the many possible real assets that may be purchased. On the other hand, if there exists a general expectation that the price level will decline to some predicted value from some currently observed value, speculators will shift from real goods into money, thereby shedding some relative price uncertainties. The actions of speculators will, on balance, seem to exert a slight downward bias on the price-level that the monetary authorities would have to discount, assuming of course that individuals, on the average, prefer certainty to uncertainty. I do not want to explore here this interesting area of speculation in a system characterized by a set of rules for ensuring monetary predictability. I think that I have discussed self-reinforcing speculation sufficiently for it to be compared briefly with that which would take place under a regime of an ideal commodity standard.

STABILIZING SPECULATION UNDER AN "IDEAL" COMMODITY STANDARD

Let us now examine again the monetary system that bases the value of the monetary unit on the "ideal" commodity discussed above. Leave aside for a bit longer the attempt to locate such an "ideal" commodity. Assume that one such commodity does exist. In effect, this system utilizes the forces of the free market to ensure predictability. The market price for the designated standard commodity cannot diverge significantly from the Mint price, which is predetermined. The absolute price level can, of course, move above or below a certain predictable trend value. But the phenomena of self-reinforcing expectations will be equivalent to those arising under a system of predetermined rules for monetary management. But these market forces, which should not be underestimated in either case, become *secondary* to the main competitive force in the automatic standard, this main force being represented by the direct shifts into and out of the designated standard commodity as its price in relation to other prices (costs) moves upward or downward. The speculative forces, secondary to this main force, increase predictability to the extent that speculators in the nonstandard commodities share a general faith in the strength of economic motives in the calculus of those individuals who are potential direct traders in the money commodity. In other words, the relevant comparison here is the one between the average or representative speculator's faith in the forces of the market as stabilizing devices and his faith in the monetary authority's success in following a predetermined rule.

COMMON BRICK AS THE STANDARD COMMODITY

Having gone through ten sections of this paper, I come now to the place where I had intended to begin. I hope that by this time some of the groundwork has been laid for a more careful consideration of what must seem, at first glance, to be a proposal of a monetary extremist.

There exists no "ideal" commodity for purposes of achieving monetary predictability under an automatic system. There is no single real commodity or service that serves at all adequately to represent composite production over the whole economy, or that could appropriately be used as an image of the economy. Having recognized this, however, we should not dismiss all automatic or commodity money systems as unworkable and impracticable. There are still better and worse commodity standards, "better" and "worse" being measured in terms of the degree to which specific real commodities possess the characteristics required of the "ideal" commodity discussed above.

It is in this sense that the use of common brick as the standard commodity should be considered. Among existent real commodities, a good argument can be made out for common building brick as the best practicable commodity that could be employed as the basis for an automatic monetary system. The ingenious proposal that the value of money be based on common building brick was first advanced by Dr. C. O. Hardy, one of the seminal minds in monetary theory during the interwar and early postwar years. So far as I can discover, Dr. Hardy never published the proposal in a formal paper.[3] It has, however, come to be recognized as one of his many important contributions to monetary theory, and its substance has been passed along in an oral tradition by several scholars, among them Professor Lloyd Mints and a few of his former students, who have been impressed by the logical completeness and, confessedly, by the shock value of the common-brick proposal.

It will be useful to consider the advantages and disadvantages of common brick as the basis for an automatic monetary system. First let us specify briefly but carefully the structure of the system as it is expected to operate. The government sets a schedule of money prices for common building brick of specified quality. For simplicity in exposition, let us assume that this schedule of prices can be represented by a single price that is to be held constant over time. Again I should emphasize, however, that neither a single price nor constancy over time is significant to the proposal. At the same time that this price is announced, a public authority, which we shall call the Mint, announces its willingness to buy and sell units of common brick at the specified price in unlimited amounts. Money is issued from the Mint only in exchange for common brick, and money proceeds from the sale of common brick by the Mint are impounded in the Mint. Every individual has the assurance that he can, at any time, take a common brick, or any quantity of common brick (or a certificate of ownership of brick) to the Mint and receive in exchange a monetary unit, say, a paper dollar. He also knows that he can, at any time and in any desired amount, go to the Mint and purchase, for paper dollars, common brick of the specified quality. No additional monetary or fiscal policy need take

[3] In my search for some published version of the original proposal, I am indebted to Mrs. Myra M. Hardy of Washington, D.C., and to Dr. William H. Moore of the staff of the Joint Economic Committee.

place. Having no powers to create or to destroy money other than those implicit in the rules governing the operations of the Mint, the government has to finance expenditures through taxation or through real borrowing. Commercial banks may be assumed to operate on the basis of 100 per cent reserves behind deposits, although this assumption is not essential to the analysis of the brick standard itself.[4]

This sort of monetary system could be predicted to work in a manner analogous to any other monetary system based upon a commodity standard. When the general level of prices rises above some presumed initial or "equilibrium" level, it becomes profitable for traders in common brick to *purchase* physical units of the standard commodity from the Mint. They can do so readily by exchanging paper money for brick or certificates of ownership of brick. As these traders turn in units of paper money to the Mint, the money supply outside the Mint is reduced, since the Mint is obligated to destroy or neutralize paper so received. As the supply of money in the system is reduced, the upward pressure on general prices is changed into downward pressure, and the price level begins to fall toward a predicted value. At the same time, of course, the brick-production industry becomes depressed in relation to other industries. The rate of brick production is reduced and resources tend to shift to other industries. This induced increase in the supply of nonstandard commodities and services does, of course, exert an effect that is substantially less significant than the demand effect resulting from the monetary contraction generated by the expansion of brick purchases from the Mint. Both the demand and the supply processes continue until they, along with supporting specula-

[4] I should point out that the brick-standard proposal as outlined here, and the analysis of its operation that follows, represent my own version of the original proposal. I should like to give Dr. Hardy the full credit due him for originating the proposal without attributing to him any of the possible errors that might be present in this version.

tion in nonstandard commodities, are successful in bringing the absolute price level back into some accepted relation with a generally expected or predicted value. This result is accomplished, however, without any agency, authority, business firm, or single individual paying explicit attention to the absolute price level as such. Traders and potential traders in the standard commodity, brick, are guided by profit-maximization criteria, not by any private or public concern for monetary stability.

The system is fully symmetrical in the case of a fall in the absolute price level below some predicted value. This fall generates offsetting equilibrating behavior. Firms find it profitable to sell brick to the Mint. As this takes place, additional money finds it way into the payments stream of the economy. This primary effect tends to increase aggregate demand for all nonstandard goods and services. It is supplemented by a supply-side effect generated by the shift of resources away from the production of nonstandard commodities, reducing the excess supplies forthcoming, and into the production of brick, the standard commodity. Again, the process continues until the absolute price level returns to some expected or predicted value or, to state the same thing in terms of the criteria directing private actions, until the relative profitability of production and sale of brick to the monetary authority disappears.

To this point, the same analysis might be applied to any physical commodity designated as the standard for an automatically operating monetary system. Indeed one of the points in discussing this analysis in terms of an everyday commodity like common building brick is the demonstration that a commodity standard need not be conceived in terms of precious metals. But we may go much further than this. There are many positive advantages of the brick-standard system in comparison with other possible commodity systems.

In reviewing some of these advantages, it is useful to compare and contrast common brick with gold as the basis for an automatic monetary system.

First of all, common brick can be produced advantageously in almost every local area in the United States. The required adjustments in the industry producing the standard commodity would not, therefore, be localized in particular regions or areas. When general inflationary or deflationary pressures in the economy imposed depression or boom on this brick-producing industry, the dispersion of production over space would tend to prevent differential regional impact. Contrast this situation with one involving a standard commodity, such as gold or anthracite coal, which is produced only in highly localized areas. In periods of incipient depression or recession, the employment effects of the brick-standard system would be noteworthy. Opportunities for employment in local brickyards would tend to mitigate the necessity for the accelerated labor mobility that would be required in the shifting of resources into a regionally localized industry. This advantage is symmetrical with respect to the unemployment effects during periods of inflation.

A second major advantage lies in the fact that production processes for common brick do not seem to be overly complex, although I plead technical ignorance here. Efficient producing plants probably need not be of extremely large size, and entry into and egress from the industry should not be difficult. For these and other reasons, reactions to relative price and cost changes should take place rapidly and without serious dislocation of resources. A closely related third advantage is that production seems to require relatively few highly specialized resources. These three features combine to ensure that the elasticity of supply would be reasonably high.

A final advantage that should not be overlooked is that

common building brick would probably not be suitable for adjusting international balances of payments. The system would, in this way, facilitate rather than hinder the separation of the domestic monetary system from the international payments mechanism, a separation whose impossibility would seriously restrict the use of gold as the standard commodity. The brick-standard system would be a suitable companion to a system of floating exchange rates.

On each of the four counts noted, a monetary standard of common building brick would seem superior to one of gold or any other precious metal.

There would, of course, be some offsetting disadvantages to the brick-standard system. Any commodity standard must involve some storage costs not present under managed systems: some proportion of the resources of the economy must of necessity be devoted to maintaining a stock of the commodity designated as the monetary standard, a stock over and above that which would be normal for nonmonetary uses. With brick, there would be little deterioration or depreciation involved in storage over time, but the sheer bulk of the commodity could make storage costs substantial. Economic resources would be tied up in maintaining unused a sizable stock of common brick. This stock need not go entirely unused, however. A substantial proportion could be devoted to the construction of government buildings. If in fact it could be predicted that the system would operate effectively on some fractional-reserve withdrawal, that is, if it could be predicted that the required responses to general upward or downward pressures would involve no more than, say, one fourth of the existing stock of "money brick," then three fourths of this stock, against which the Mint would at some time have issued dollars, could be employed in the construction of government buildings. In this way, the general taxpayer would secure some indirect benefit. As a recognized ultimate reserve or backing for the outstanding money issues, the brick used in such construction projects would have to be carefully distinguished from those government bricks acquired through ordinary market channels, and a potential withdrawal of this "money brick" would have to be acknowledged. Should a general wave of dishoarding on the part of the public generate serious inflationary pressure, thus making it highly profitable for private buildings to be constructed with brick purchased from the Mint, then offsetting destruction of some government buildings might have to take place. It is difficult to imagine that such major swings around a predicted norm would take place, however, once a monetary system of this nature came to be in full operation. For this reason there would seem to be little grounds for concern about the periodic possible destruction of private or public buildings.

One of the major disadvantages of any commodity standard, especially when viewed in the light of the predictability norm, lies in its vulnerability to unpredictable changes in the relative costs of producing standard and nonstandard commodities. A major technological improvement in production processes in the brick industry could, for example, be the source of serious inflation in the economy. We know that one of the disadvantages of the historical gold standard was its subjection of general economic conditions to the sometimes fortuitous discoveries of new gold fields. While brick would on this count clearly be superior to gold, the possible inflation that could result from a differential technological breakthrough should not be neglected in any thorough comparative evaluation. There would seem to be little chance of such a depletion of suitable raw materials as to make deflation from this source a serious possibility.

A second disadvantage of any commodity standard lies in its potential vulnerability to unpredictable shifts in the nonmonetary demand for the standard commodity. For example, an upsurge in the fashionableness of brick houses would, under the operation of a brick standard, impose deflationary pressure on the economy generally. To some extent, however, these unpredictable shifts in the private demand for the monetary commodity could be offset by variations in the government demand. In so far as such demand shifts occur and are not effectively offset, the commodity standard will not be able to produce monetary predictability. But broadly considered, such shifts are different in degree only from shifts in the desire to hold money, that is, hoarding and dishoarding, which seem to reduce the predictability of any monetary system.

A LABOR STANDARD OF VALUE?

It seems clear that common brick would be a more desirable monetary commodity than gold. But are there other commodities or services that might serve the desired purposes as well as, or perhaps better than, common brick? Before and after the time of Adam Smith, economists have been intrigued with and attracted by the idea that, of all existent commodities and services, common labor provides the best single measure of value in an economy. I should like to explore briefly the idea of utilizing common labor as the basis for an automatic monetary system.

In thinking about pedagogical devices for clarifying the logic of such a standard, I have toyed with an idea jokingly suggested by Professor Armen Alchian. He proposed that the general unemployment problem could be solved quite simply by installing money machines on each street corner. Each machine would be equipped with a crank or foot pedal, and upon turning the crank or pumping the pedal anyone could secure money at a fixed rate in exchange for effort measured solely by energy inputs. The energy generated by turning the crank or pumping the pedal could, perhaps, be turned into electricity by tying each machine into a power grid of some sort. This proposal represents one side of an automatic monetary system that bases the value of money on common-labor units. As a substitute for the Alchian machine, we could think of the Mint purchasing common labor at a fixed price in unlimited quantities. The labor so purchased could then be "sold" at auction to private entrepreneurs, or used to construct public works.

The other half of a common-labor-standard system is somewhat more difficult to conceive. Labor is not a storable commodity but a service. A fully automatic system would require that the Mint stand ready to sell as well as to buy units of the service. How could the Mint "sell" labor in unlimited quantities during times of threatened inflation? The idea is not wholly implausible. We could think of a scheme in which the government obligates itself to "sell" common labor to business firms without a stock of labor being maintained. For example, if the market price of common labor should rise above the "standard" price, the business firm could "purchase" labor services from the government. To meet this demand the government would have to purchase, at the market wage rate, sufficient labor services to meet business demands on it. This public outlay would have to be financed wholly from general tax revenues. The government would be obligated to neutralize the fixed money sum turned in by the business firm in "purchasing" each unit of labor service. I do not have the space to discuss further the interesting features of a scheme such as this, but I should emphasize the importance of considering all possible alternatives.[5]

PREDICTABILITY AND CONSTITUTIONAL ATTITUDE

I am convinced that an automatic monetary system utilizing some basic commodity or service, such as common brick

[5] Dr. Francesco Forte has suggested to me that the proposal for a labor standard has been discussed at length by P. Jannaccone. I have not, however, been able to consult Jannaccone's work.

or common labor as the standard of value, would work. And by this I mean that such a system would embody a high degree of predictability about the course of movements in the absolute level of prices, in the value of money. I am also convinced that a managed system characterized by some specific rules for action would work; and I make no strong argument for one alternative over the other. Both alternatives will work, or both will fail, for the same reason.

I recall a statement once made by Professor F. A. Hayek to the effect that "nothing is inevitable but thinking makes it so." I should paraphrase this to apply here as "nothing is predictable, but thinking makes it so." The implementation of a monetary constitution that will produce predictability requires more than consensus among experts. Even if we could substantially agree on the most practicable monetary reform, and even if we were given the power to institute such reform, we would have no assurance that the continuing monetary problem would be solved. We should never lose sight of the fact that the average man knows little of economics and, worse than this, he does not know how little he does know. Man has, throughout modern history, tended to blame the monetary system for many of his economic ills, and he has been quite right on many occasions. But by now he has learned through observation that his own actions, or the actions of men acting "for him," the government, can change, modify, and reform the monetary system. Thus, with respect to monetary matters, we find the average man able to raise objections, to criticize, without being able himself to provide rationally motivated alternatives to existing institutions. No longer is the average man willing to adopt a quasi-fatalistic attitude, to attribute the workings of the monetary system to the gods, to accept some mythology of money. To some small extent, such a mythology, such an attitude, was engendered by the operation of the historical gold standard. This system was to many people sacrosanct, and even today there is within all of us some of this mythology of gold as the appropriate monetary metal. It is this mythology that makes us look upon any such proposal as the one for a brick standard as amusing, and which causes us to dismiss such a proposal before we have seriously considered its working properties.

Careful observation should convince us, however, that even the mythology of the gold standard is substantially gone, and once gone, a mythology can never be reconstructed. If it could be, it would, by definition, not constitute a mythology. Nor can the wisest of monetary reforms create a monetary mythology surrounding a brick standard, a price-level rule, a Federal Reserve Board, or whatever.

Yet without something that serves the same purposes, *no* monetary reform can be expected to work, to ensure the predictability in the value of money that we all should accept as the appropriate norm. I suggest that what is required, what is essential here, is a "constitutional attitude"; that is to say, people must agree on the basic rules that define the operation of a monetary system and then agree to abide by these rules as adopted. The attitude of which I speak is one that prevents continual tampering with the rules as adopted. This constitutional attitude seems to me to be one of the most difficult of human behavioral characteristics to adopt, or even to explain and to understand. Since the Enlightenment men have refused to acknowledge the validity of any absolutes, either in terms of ethical principles or in terms of social institutions. Ideas, laws, social structures: all have been subjected to discussion and to question, and through these, to deliberately organized modification and change. Chaos is likely to result if change is made too quickly and not for rational reasons. Until and unless we know what changes are in fact "best," it is far better to accept certain "relatively absolute absolutes," both in ethics and in the rules defining the social order. And we cannot really know what fundamental or constitutional changes are needed until we are able to observe the working of a given set of institutions over time, through a long succession of events. The willingness to do this, to play a series of games by the same rules in order to evaluate properly the rules themselves, is the essential attitude that is required. The need for this attitude is not, of course, confined to the monetary problem. The monetary problem does serve, however, to point up sharply the general relevance of the attitude that is more generally required for the maintenance of orderly civilized life.

Specifically, with the emergence of a genuinely constitutional attitude, there are many possible monetary systems that would work well, that would ensure an adequate degree of monetary predictability. Without the emergence of this attitude, there is no monetary system that will work well, and continued monetary chaos, of sorts, can be expected to prevail.

· VII ·

THE COMMODITY-RESERVE CURRENCY PROPOSAL RECONSIDERED

BENJAMIN GRAHAM

THE PROPOSAL: SUPPORT AND CRITICISM

SIXTEEN years have passed since my last major formulation of the commodity-reserve proposal, in *World Commodities and World Currency*.[1] I now wish to present a reconsideration of the commodity-reserve scheme in the light of developments since World War II.

It seems desirable to begin with a brief description of the plan and a summary of the attitude of economists towards it. I shall then discuss some significant postwar developments as they affect the proposal. My more detailed consideration of its various aspects will then be divided into two sections, the first dealing with its monetary and price-level implications and the second with its commodity implications.

The plan—familiar to most economists, I assume—calls for stabilizing the market value of a composite group of important, storable raw materials. There would probably be between 15 and 25 components, selected in accordance with objective criteria of aggregate dollar value of production or exports, or both, as well as of storability. The relative quantities of each commodity in the unit or "market basket" would be similarly determined. Provision would be made for grad-

[1] New York and London: McGraw-Hill, 1944.

ual changes in the composition of the unit to keep it reasonably up to date. A base or "normal" value for the unit would be established in the same way that a normal or central price level would be agreed on in any stabilization plan. A designated agency would purchase or accept complete commodity units whenever obtainable at some discount—say 5 per cent—from the base price, and would dispose of complete units when their price reached a similar premium above the base. Purchase of the units would be self-financing by issuance of currency backed by the commodity holdings; upon sale of units corresponding amounts of currency would be retired. The scheme could be put into effect on a single-nation, a multi-nation, or an international basis. Operating costs of the plan, chiefly storage, would be paid for as far as possible out of the profit realized on sales of units at above cost; the balance, if any, would have to be provided by nations sponsoring the plan.

In sum, the scheme proposes to give to a composite group of basic commodities exactly the same monetary status that is now enjoyed by gold, adding thereto the two-way convertibility of the old gold standard.

Advantages are claimed for the plan in five main areas: price stabilization, balanced economic expansion, protective stockpiles, sounder currency, and aid to underdeveloped countries. I shall not go into further detail at this point regarding these asserted benefits, except to emphasize the central advantage that the mechanism would operate to stabilize the price level of the commodity basket as a whole, while permitting whatever variations in the prices of the individual components were necessary to reflect constantly changing technology and other supply-demand factors.

This concept first occurred to me in the depression of 1921–22 but was not published until early 1933 in article form and in 1937 in my book *Storage and Stability.* In the meantime virtually the same idea had occurred to Professor Jan Goudriaan of Holland, who proposed it in a pamphlet *How to Stop Deflation,* published in London in 1932.[2] Thus Dr. Goudriaan must be awarded credit for prior publication.

Among economists our proposals have received a considerable amount of attention, both favorable and the reverse. My non-relative but dear friend, Frank Graham of Princeton, early became its enthusiastic adherent and integrated it with other ideas of his own, including the 100 per cent money proposal. (Understandably, not a little confusion developed about our respective roles in this movement, and even about our identities.) Other adherents of note have been Friedrich Hayek, A. G. Hart of Columbia, and Colin Clark of Australia and Cambridge. The chief criticisms are found in articles by Messrs. Beale, Kennedy and Winn of the Wharton School, and by Milton Friedman of the University of Chicago. Lord Keynes added a rather puzzling comment to Hayek's approving article, in which he appeared to reject the proposal because of its implications as to wage policy.[3] (Keynes's attitude was subsequently clarified somewhat in a letter he wrote me, which is now published as Appendix I to this paper.)

A full-scale study of the plan was made in 1948–49 by a

[2] "Stabilized Reflation," *Economic Forum,* 1:186–193 (Spring 1933); *Storage and Stability* (New York and London: McGraw-Hill, 1937); *How to Stop Deflation* (London: Search Publishing Co., 1932).

[3] Frank D. Graham, *Social Goals and Economic Institutions* (Princeton: Princeton University Press, 1942), pp. 94–119; F. A. Hayek, "A Commodity Reserve Currency," *Economic Journal,* 53:176–184 (June–September 1943); A. G. Hart, "L'étalon monétaire et la stabilisation économique," *Économie Appliquée,* 7:133–159 (January–June 1954); W. T. M. Beale, Jr., M. T. Kennedy, and W. J. Winn, "Commodity Reserve Currency: A Critique," *Journal of Political Economy,* 50:579–594 (August 1942); Milton Friedman, "Commodity-Reserve Currency," *Journal of Political Economy,* 59:203–232 (June 1951), reprinted in Friedman's *Essays in Positive Economics* (Chicago: University of Chicago Press, 1953), pp. 204–250; J. M. Keynes, "The Objective of International Price Stability," *Economic Journal,* 53:185–187 (June–September 1943).

group from the Food Research Institute of Stanford University, headed by Merrill K. Bennett.[4] On the whole their conclusions were favorable, especially in preferring our idea to the international single-commodity agreements which have been in operation and under discussion. On the financing side, however, their expert E. S. Shaw definitely preferred orthodox borrowing methods to the creation of commodity-backed money.

In 1953 a special committee of experts of the United Nations, of which Professor Goudriaan was chairman, published a report entitled *Commodity Trade and Economic Development.*[5] Not surprisingly, perhaps, the unanimous report gave extended and, on the whole, favorable attention to the commodity-reserve idea. This report was followed by Commodity Policy Study No. 10 of the Food and Agriculture Organization, entitled *Functions of a World Food Reserve—Scope and Limitations,* published in Rome in 1956. The study took a noncommittal view of the net merits of our plan and concluded, on page 28, that "it would be difficult to regard the adoption of such composite stabilization proposals as being within the realm of practical politics at this stage (though further studies on the many outstanding questions might profitably be pursued)."

The most recent comprehensive discussion of our scheme appears in *Commodity Reserve Currency,* by Dr. Elmer M. Harmon.[6] Dr. Harmon is highly favorable to the idea but adds a suggestion of his own concerning desirable variations

[4] Merrill K. Bennett *et al., International Commodity Stockpiling as an Economic Stabilizer* (Stanford: Stanford University Press, 1949).

[5] United Nations Publication, sales no. 1954. II. B. 1 (November 1953). In paragraphs 211–220, pp. 64–65, the report raises a number of questions regarding our plan as points for study. Most of these are dealt with below. Professor Goudriaan supplies his answers to the committee's questions in appendix C to the report.

[6] *Commodity Reserve Currency* (New York: Columbia University Press, 1959). An extensive bibliography on our subject appears on pages 131–134.

in the automatic buying and selling levels of the unit. He uses the abbreviation CRC to designate the plan, and I shall do the same.

ECONOMIC DEVELOPMENTS SINCE WORLD WAR II IN RELATION TO THE CRC PLAN

Since Korea, developments in the price level have been contradictory, especially in the United States. Finished goods and services have advanced, giving a picture of continuous inflation, which has only recently been arrested. But industrial raw materials have barely held their own, and agricultural products have declined rather severely. Consequently there have been persistent demands by the underdeveloped, raw-materials-exporting nations in the United Nations and elsewhere for measures to stabilize—really to advance—prices in this sector. A resolution to that effect was introduced by Latin American countries at the recent meeting of the Organization of American States at San Jose.[7] Similarly, five oil-exporting nations have just signed an agreement to cut down production and raise prices of petroleum.[8] Thus it might be said that a plan for stabilizing the level of raw-materials prices should be of considerable interest to the underdeveloped nations as a whole, but rather irrelevant at this moment to the price-level problems of the United States and other advanced countries. This is in contrast with the periods of deep depression in the past, when the collapse of raw-materials prices led to destructive price declines in all sectors of our own economy.

On the other hand, there have been important developments in the area of buffer stocks and protective reserves, which should warrant renewed attention in the United States

[7] Cf. "Latins Caught in Price Squeeze," *New York Times*, September 11, 1960, IV, 4:1.

[8] Cf. "The Outlook," *Wall Street Journal*, October 3, 1960, p. 1.

to these aspects of CRC. Since World War II, and mainly since Korea, the United States has actually created a composite commodity reserve of enormous proportions, differing in many details but not in its major lineaments from that envisaged in our plan. I am tempted to refer to Macaulay's witticism about the British Empire having been created in a fit of absent-mindedness. Our national reserve is divided into two quite dissimilar entities of approximately equal size—about $8½ billion in the agricultural holdings of the Commodity Credit Corporation (CCC) and about $7½ billion in the strategic stockpile and related stocks of metals and other industrial raw materials.[9] The full extent of the government's stockpiling operations in recent years appears in the detailed reports of the Secretary of the Treasury. On June 30, 1952, the total holdings of commodities, supplies, and materials (exclusive of military material) were $1.4 billion. On June 30, 1959, this figure was $21.8 billion, an increase of $20½ billion in 7 years.[10]

The CCC holdings have always been of the involuntary type, accumulated through the operation of price supports; the aim has been to own as little as possible. The strategic stockpile is essentially of the opposite character; the materials in it were acquired because we wanted them for national security. In recent years, however, changes in legislation have converted nearly $2 billion into "excess supply," available for disposal under favorable conditions. In fact there

[9] For agricultural holdings see *Report of the President of the Commodity Credit Corporation, [fiscal] 1960* (Washington: U.S. Department of Agriculture, 1960), p. 1. U.S. President, Civil and Defense Mobilization Office, *Stockpile Report to Congress, July–December 1959* (Washington, 1960), p. iv, shows $6.1 billion of industrial commodities on hand in the strategic stockpile. In addition there were $0.7 billion in the supplemental stockpile and $0.8 billion in Defense Production Act inventories in June 1959. (For the latter figures see table in J. D. Morgan, Jr., "U.S. Strategic Stockpile and Our National Plans," *Commercial and Financial Chronicle,* May 26, 1960, p. 18.)

[10] *Report of U.S. Secretary of the Treasury,* June 30, 1959 (Washington: Government Printing Office, 1960), table 115, p. 682.

have been some operations in and out of the strategic stockpile of a stabilizing nature; currently a gradual sale of coconut-oil holdings is proposed in order to relieve a shortage due to drought.

Recent political thinking is moving in the direction of a specifically designated "national food reserve." This would move part of the extremely awkward CCC stocks into a politically more palatable situation. In his presidential campaign Vice President Nixon advocated such a step as part of his solution of the farm problem.[11] The commodity-reserve plan aims to establish a self-financing reserve of both agricultural and industrial raw materials, available for national protection as well as for other purposes. We shall consider in a moment the consequences of transferring to a regularized commodity-reserve system a substantial part of our two presently highly disparate stockpiles.

The case for raw-materials reserves has made some progress also on the international scene. In the United Nations there has been a continuous campaign for a world food reserve.[12] In the United States Senate we have had bills (such as Senate Resolution 86 in 1956) calling for the United States to cooperate with the United Nations in forming and operating an international food and raw materials reserve. Its stated purposes are similar to the benefits claimed for our CRC plan. More recently, both President Eisenhower and Vice President Nixon espoused a "Food for Peace" program to transfer part of our surplus stocks to needy nations. One purpose of such transfers would presumably be to assist underdeveloped countries to establish their own national food reserves, for use in case of famine and other emergencies; another would be to raise the living standards of

[11] See, e.g., *Wall Street Journal*, September 19, 1960, p. 8.

[12] Cf. General Assembly Resolutions 827 (IX) 1954, 1025 (XI) 1957, 1491 (XV) 1960.

undernourished peoples directly. I shall discuss below the relation of our proposal to such objectives and to the problems involved in attaining them.

To present a more concrete picture of how the proposal could conceivably operate in practice, I should like to make one of two assumptions. The first is that a domestic CRC plan would actually have been in operation during the past seven years and have absorbed the commodities otherwise heavily accumulating in the present stockpiles. The alternative assumption is that the plan would be put into effect now by transfer of appropriate amounts of various commodities from our two main reserves. (For simplicity, we shall exclude commodities not in these stockpiles.) On one assumption or the other, a composite commodity reserve would exist or be created, consisting of, say, a half year's production or imports of some 14 basic raw materials. These would be corn, cotton, grain sorghums, tobacco, wheat, aluminum, copper, lead, manganese, nickel, rubber, silk, tin, and zinc. (Important commodities not in this assumed list but likely to be included in an actual unit would be coffee, hides, rice, sugar, and wool, and possibly coal, wood pulp, petroleum, and pig iron.)[18] The assumed reserve would be worth about $7 billion at current prices. Only about $2 billion worth of products, mainly wheat, would still remain in the hands of the CCC; and about $6 billion worth would remain in the industrial-materials stockpiles. (Evidently we now have much larger stockpiles of industrial materials, in terms of months' consumption, than we do of farm products.)

Corresponding to the stockpile held under the plan, some $7 billion worth of commodity-reserve certificates could be created. The simplest way of dealing with them would be to

[18] For sample commodity units, see my *Storage and Stability*, p. 57, *World Commodities and World Currency*, pp. 44–45, and Bennett *et al.*, *International Commodity Stockpiling*, p. 191.

use them to retire United States government obligations now held by the Federal Reserve banks. The note and deposit liabilities of the Reserve banks would be virtually unchanged. The government would save, say, $250 million a year in interest; but it would lose the same amount in transferred profits of the Federal Reserve banks,[14] since their interest income would be correspondingly less. Strangely enough, therefore, the creation of a large self-financed commodity reserve would have made no difference at all to the federal budget or to the present money and credit structure. It would have changed only the reported gross and net federal debt and the asset composition of the Federal Reserve banks. If monetary legislation should allow the commodity-reserve certificates to count, along with the present gold certificates, in the reserve base held against Federal Reserve note and deposit liabilities, then the credit expansion *potential* would be greatly increased. But any actual credit effects would remain, as now, at the discretion of Congress and of the Federal Reserve authorities.

How is it possible that a seemingly radical change in our monetary structure would have apparently so insignificant an effect? The explanation is that, as far as the past eight years are concerned, we have already had the important monetary and other consequences of a commodity-reserve system in this country, as a result of government price-support and stockpiling policies. The years from 1951 to 1959 were ones of almost continuous prosperity and expansion for this country, unaccompanied by the severe price declines that in the past have inspired this proposal and alternative ones. The large stockpile acquisitions may have contributed quite a bit to this continued prosperity. It is true that the farm

[14] These profits are transferred to the United States under the heading of "interest on Federal Reserve notes." Such payment in 1959 amounted to $910 million.

program has been universally condemned, even by its beneficiaries, even though, after 25 years, we are far from agreement as to what to put in its place. The CRC plan would have acquired farm products on a composite basis, without following so-called parity prices for individual products. I do not claim that this approach would have given us a radically different farm situation than we have. I do think that the underlying principle of agricultural price supports would have been more rational under our proposal, and that it might gradually have won greater acceptance than the CCC operations. In particular, I should like to stress that if the general level of raw materials is appropriately stabilized, the problem of individually weak commodities can be seen more clearly and perhaps dealt with more intelligently. I say "perhaps," because the price-movement disparities of recent years have greatly complicated the current farm problem and placed it more than ever in a political rather than in an economic atmosphere. I shall come back later to this question of the proper handling of weak commodity situations within a generally stabilized price level.

This summary sketch of the plan in assumed operation of course leaves a large number of questions unanswered. Two of the most important are: What would have been the mutual relation between this mechanism of a stable composite purchasing price and CCC operations geared to individual price supports? Would not the transfer of a substantial amount of materials from strategic stockpiles to a two-way reserve mechanism have harmed national defense? I shall deal with these and other issues presently, first considering the monetary and price-level aspects of the plan, next its commodity aspects, and, finally, the implications of an international versus a national or multinational version of the proposal.

A preliminary question must be faced immediately: If operation of the plan during the past eight years would have made so little monetary and economic difference, why bother with it at all? The answer is simple. Conditions in the United States since 1951 have been remarkably stable, except for a persistent slow rise in the general price level. As Richard Selden also has argued,[15] I believe that a good part of this price rise is merely a natural concomitant of a great upswing in business; and it may well be followed by moderate declines if the boom levels off or subsides. A plan to stabilize the aggregate price of a composite commodity unit within a range of 95 to 105 per cent of a chosen level would have been inactive or nearly so during an advance of the 1952–1960 proportions. This means that not only my proposal but also any other of the same type would have little reason for being adopted in the United States if the 1952–1960 economic situation, including further large acquisitions of raw materials for the two government stockpiles, were to continue indefinitely.

The commodity-reserve proposal was conceived basically as a measure for dealing with depression-induced price declines and war-induced price advances. If these are now a thing of the past, our proposal loses much, but not all, of its practical utility for America. I think it would still have broad advantages in the international field, where we have the paradox of the underdeveloped nations suffering at the same time from a general shortage of basic commodities and from the effects of price weakness in those they export. Furthermore, the problem of a rational commodity-reserve policy for the United States would still be with us.

MONETARY ASPECTS OF THE PLAN

From the monetary side the CRC proposal has been presented in two quite different guises. Those interested in

[15] "Cost-Push versus Demand-Pull Inflation, 1955–57," *Journal of Political Economy*, 67:1–20 (February 1959).

monetary reform, notably the late Frank Graham, have advocated the replacement of the gold standard by a commodity-reserve standard, integrated with the adoption of 100 per cent reserve banking. But my own view as to the monetary provisions and implications of the plan has always been more limited. I have advocated only that the commodity units be made self-financing by issuing commodity-reserve currency against them, which would be added to our ten existing forms of money.

In this paper I shall not discuss Frank Graham's thesis,[16] but shall speak only of the monetary aspects of my version of the plan. I should point out here that a good deal of the elaborate critique by Milton Friedman in his 1951 article thus becomes basically irrelevant to our present subject. Friedman makes the corresponding point in a footnote to his paper, stating that the bulk of my writings on commodity-reserves is irrelevant to his purpose.[17] Nonetheless, many portions of Friedman's arguments are relevant enough to invite consideration here.

Whether viewed from the broad angle of Frank Graham or in my own narrower perspective, the monetary aspects of CRC involve price-level effects, effects on the quality of money, effects on the quantity of money and credit, and relative efficiency, convenience, and costs as against other proposals.

Our claims for CRC in the area of price stability have been that it would directly stabilize the market value of the commodity basket; it would diminish fluctuations in other groups of prices and thus contribute toward a satisfactory degree of stability in the general price level; and it would diminish instability in the prices of individual primary products and would help rather than harm other justifiable

[16] *Social Goals and Economic Institutions.*
[17] "Commodity-Reserve Currency," p. 203n (*Essays,* p. 205n).

measures for relieving excessive weakness in single commodities.

No one has seriously doubted that the plan would stabilize the price level of the commodity composite within the appointed limits, as long as the reserves were not exhausted by persistent demand. But the plan has been criticized on the following grounds: it would become inoperative in the event of exhaustion of reserves, especially in wartime; it would create burdensome stocks of commodity units through secular growth; its buying operations would tend to advance the prices of scarce components, and sales would further depress the prices of weak components.

The first objection illustrates a general tendency of criticisms of an economic proposal to concentrate on single trees and to forget their relation to the forest. It is true that even substantial reserves could be completely drawn out in the event of war. But is this an imperfection of the plan? Yes, as against a perfect mechanism, if there is such a thing. No, as against alternative monetary measures for stabilizing prices. The very conditions which would exhaust even a medium-sized commodity reserve would make it impossible to control prices by ordinary fiscal and monetary policies. We would have to resort to the usual government price-fixing efforts, supported by appeals to patriotism. These extraneous measures would be more effective under a CRC plan, since the pinch of actual shortage would be lessened. More important than the price effect would be the presence of these large-scale physical resources in a time of acute need. In fact, the actual exhaustion of a large commodity reserve in wartime would be the strongest demonstration of the underlying utility of the plan in terms of national well-being and even of survival. I must speak perforce of a war like the Korean one, since all-out atomic warfare defies discussion.

The second objection is the opposite of the first. Apart

from the real factor of storage costs, there is in theory no more objection to the unlimited growth of *noncommercial* reserves above ground than to the unlimited development of similar reserves below ground. As a practical matter, however, reserves that greatly exceed any possible future use are basically wasteful. There are at least two lines of attack to prevent such undue accumulation of stocks, and I shall discuss these later under the nonmonetary aspects of the scheme. At this point it is relevant to remark that as the commodity reserve grows the supply of money grows with it, tending to raise or sustain the price level and thus to limit CRC purchases.

It is useful also to quote here the concluding sentence of the critique of commodity-reserve currency by Beale, Kennedy, and Winn of the University of Pennsylvania: "And, finally, in view of our experience with gold, it is an alarming and disheartening thought that we should embark upon a plan that calls for the storage of not one but a large number of money commodities." [18]

The critics were then alarmed and disheartened by our huge accumulation of gold reserves, which were believed by them and many others to be basically useless. Now some alarm is directed toward the continuous erosion of these reserves. Instead of too much gold there is danger that we may have too little. Economists must have imagination to envisage conditions different from those existing at the moment, for history tells them that changes come frequently and unexpectedly. This statement applies particularly to commodity stocks, which have often in one period appeared a nuisance and not long thereafter proved of very great value indeed.

A matter of general principle and applicability is involved also in a third criticism of the commodity-reserve mech-

[18] "Commodity Reserve Currency: A Critique," p. 594.

anism, namely, that it might require the purchase of some scarce commodities and thus aggravate their scarcity. Any scheme for stabilizing prices on a group basis must be prepared to advance the price of both weak and strong items in its expansionist phase and to depress the price of both subgroups in its contractionist phase. Otherwise, it reduces itself to a valorization mechanism to maintain the prices of weak commodities above their proper relative levels. Any alternative plan for controlling the price level, such as merely to increase or decrease the supply of money and credit, would necessarily act in somewhat the same fashion on both strong and weak components of the economy.

But critics of our direct buying and selling program are especially worried about cases where there is a genuine scarcity of some commodity, due to crop failure, strikes, or the like; and they anticipate dire results from the necessity of adding to the already unsatisfied demand for such a product. It is at this point that a flexible provision in the CRC plan could relieve rather than accentuate this very special problem. True—because temporary—scarcity of a basic commodity is always accompanied by a higher spot than futures price. (On reflection it will be seen that this relationship may well constitute the *definition* of scarcity, as distinguished from merely relative price strength due to secular or cyclical factors.) My version of the plan provides that under such conditions, commodity-unit purchases would include the cheaper futures contract rather than the dearer spot commodity. Of more positive value is the additional provision that under the same conditions the authority would be directed to sell spot holdings and replace them by futures. By so doing it would both gain a financial advantage until the spread is eliminated and relieve the scarcity which occasioned the problem. To the extent that the reserve contained futures contracts instead of the actual commodity, the total currency outstanding against it will be correspondingly lower.[19]

Milton Friedman, to quote a representative critic, considers this provision ingenious and a necessary ingredient in any operating version of the plan. However, he objects that "this device introduces precisely the kind of arbitrary and discretionary element that it is of the greatest importance to exclude from a currency scheme whose major virtue is its automaticity and impersonality." [20] May I be permitted in turn to object to this objection, and many similar ones, on the ground that it confuses flexibility with arbitrary discretion and wrongly assumes that an automatic mechanism must be completely rigid? Actually, there would be no more discretionary element in the substitution of futures for spot commodities than there would be in any other operating rules of the plan. The same would be true of provisions for gradually modifying the composition of the market basket to reflect secular changes in the commodity situation as well as of permitted measures to reduce the cost of storage by arrangements with producers and consumers, and other desirable features of the same character. These should make the mechanism flexible and thereby produce better results; but they all could be used as part of a stipulated procedure without introducing personal and discretionary elements into the plan.

It is undeniable, however, that certain arbitrary decisions must be made in the formulation of the plan itself. Chief of these, of course, is the choice of the dollar value or price level of the market basket. But every comprehensive economic scheme requires preliminary decisions of this character.

Our next important theme relates to the effect of CRC on

[19] See my detailed discussion of this feature in *Storage and Stability*, pp. 70–71 and *passim*.

[20] "Commodity-Reserve Currency," p. 216n (*Essays*, p. 226n).

the prices of things not included in the composite. We have claimed that narrowing the cyclical fluctuations in primary commodities would tend to do the same thing for finished-goods prices and that this would be an important advantage. This consequence is conceded by most critics as to cyclical movements; but they object that, in their *secular* movement, finished-goods prices may advance or decline appreciably, as against a fixed level for raw materials. It is a fact that, since Korea, finished goods have moved steadily upwards, while raw materials as a whole have tended to fall. Had our plan been in operation, it would have done nothing to prevent the 11 per cent rise of the cost of living in the past eight years. Obviously, if we envisage a continuation of the price behavior of this recent period, the plan would have to be considered unnecessary in the sector of raw-materials prices and ineffective in the sector of finished-goods prices.

May I suggest that these relative-price movements since 1951 are basically of a nonrepresentative kind and are not likely to be continued long in the future? In good part they reflect the correction of an opposite movement in favor of raw-materials prices associated with the World War II and Korean inflation. This point may be brought out by a few simple figures: the Bureau of Labor Statistics index of prices for all crude materials shows a decline of about 17 per cent from 1951 to 1959, while in the same period all finished goods rose nearly 8 per cent. This is the divergent movement that concerns us. But if we view the same data over a longer period we find the following: from 1913 to 1939 raw materials rose 2 per cent, while finished goods advanced 16 per cent. Yet from 1939 to 1959 raw materials rose 132 per cent, while finished goods rose somewhat *less*—121 per cent. For the entire 46-year period the difference in favor of finished goods is hardly important, the ratio of their price index to the raw-materials price index rising only 8 per cent from 1913 to 1959.[21]

My own opinion is that the spread between finished-goods and raw-materials prices is not likely to widen secularly at a rapid rate; hence that a price level stabilized in terms of raw materials will generally be stable enough for practical purposes. Let me go farther and suggest that it would be politically impossible to stabilize the general price level if this meant a further steady *decline* in the price of raw materials. In the light of the persistent efforts of producers and producing countries to prevent such price weakness, it must be expected that, under the assumed conditions, various price-propping measures would be greatly extended. Such measures are less likely to be resorted to if raw materials are stabilized while finished goods advance at a slow secular rate. Thus I believe that, assuming *arguendo* such disparate moves in relative prices in the future, a plan such as ours for stabilizing raw materials as a whole would be more practicable than one for stabilizing the prices of finished goods.

Are the commodity-unit operations compatible with separate support schemes for individual items, such as we have had for a generation in many farm products? The answer, technically, is yes. The only practical effect of such schemes is presumably, though not certainly, to create a higher market price for the individual items than would otherwise obtain. This would in no way interfere with CRC operations; it would merely influence the price calculations which determine the current market value of the unit.

[21] Computed from Bureau of Labor Statistics price indexes by stage of processing, in U.S. Bureau of the Census, *Historical Statistics of the United States, Colonial Times to 1957* (Washington: Government Printing Office, 1960), p. 118, and U.S. Bureau of the Census, *Statistical Abstract of the United States: 1960* (Washington: Government Printing Office, 1960), p. 334.

The CRC mechanism should, on the one hand, significantly reduce the need for support plans for individual components and, on the other hand, promote a better rationale for such rescue operations. An individual commodity, such as wheat or tin, should be specially helped only if its price fell quite significantly in relation to the aggregate price of the composite commodity unit, which would be supported at not less than 95 per cent of the standard level defined under the plan. Any support program for an individual commodity would then function as an auxiliary of the main stabilization mechanism. Such auxiliaries would assist rather than hamper CRC operations, since they would narrow the over-all fluctuations with which CRC would have to deal.

Milton Friedman has contended that a stable commodity unit, constructed according to his specifications, would have brought about greater instability in other prices than we had under the gold standard. But this objection proceeds from his quite theoretical concept of the right kind of commodity money. Let me deal with it as part of the following general discussion of the *quality* of currency as related to the CRC plan.

By the quality of a currency I mean its intrinsic value, considered apart from its value established by mere custom and authority or by management of the economy. The intrinsic value of a currency has had, and perhaps will have, great practical importance to its holders. During the monetary depreciations of my own lifetime enormous advantages have accrued to holders of gold coin throughout the world, and even to those in many countries who owned silver coins—such as French silver francs—as against those who held nonconvertible paper money or deposits. Conceivably, similar advantages may again accrue in the future to hoarders of gold, in spite of its somewhat dubious nonmonetary value. But free and unquestioned convertibility of paper money and deposits into gold vanished from most of the earth a quarter-century ago. Nor is it likely to return to the United States very soon, though this step has its strong advocates. As every one knows, we have had since 1934 an ambiguous and potentially variable relationship between our money and gold. Before World War II it was widely felt that gold's value of $35 per ounce was derived chiefly from our Treasury's buying policy, that is, from its convertibility into our paper money at $35 per ounce.[22] But, conversely, the inflation psychology generated in recent years could conceivably lead to heavy hoarding of gold if that were again made legal.

One important advantage of a well-supplied CRC system is that full-scale convertibility of all forms of money, including demand deposits, into the commodity base could be established and undoubtedly maintained, except under conditions of major war. On the one hand, we could start with a substantial reserve, derived mainly from our two existing stockpiles. On the other hand, large-scale hoarding in the ordinary sense could scarcely take place in the commodities themselves because of the inconvenience and expense of storage. They would be drawn out of the reserve only for use and not for hoarding. Furthermore, since all forms of currency would continue to be made legally interchangeable, there would be no point for would-be hoarders to favor stashing away commodity-reserve certificates, even if these were put into circulation—which I do not advocate, at least not at the outset.

It is on this basis that we claim that CRC would improve the quality of our monetary system: it would establish a direct and viable relation between our money and useful commodities, a relation both more meaningful and less vulnerable to interruption than the one formerly and presently existing between our money and gold. To achieve this per-

[22] Cf. F. D. Graham and C. R. Whittlesey, *The Golden Avalanche* (Princeton: Princeton University Press, 1939).

haps modest result it would not be necessary to disturb our money and credit structure in any way. The CR certificates would be an addition to our monetary system, in somewhat analogous fashion to the addition of our silver certificates. It is my contention that the commodity certificates would have more intrinsic value, more general economic utility, and therefore much more of a *raison d'être* than our hotly attacked and equally warmly defended silver certificates. These statements apply whether the CRC certificates were held by the Federal Reserve banks exclusively or circulated in the hands of the public.

Critics of the proposal attack the quality of CR money on various grounds, mainly asserting that the unit would fail to represent perfectly the composite of goods and services purchased by our citizens. Along these lines it is claimed even by some who favor the plan that it would have to be adopted separately by each interested country, because each would want to set up a commodity unit differing from others'. Even my coinventor, Goudriaan, has been suspicious of my proposal for substituting futures contracts for spot commodities on the ground that this will impair somewhat the uniform quality of CR money.[23] Milton Friedman's similarly based objections to this feature have already been mentioned.

Virtually all these criticisms rest, I believe, on a misconception of the monetary role of commodity reserves. If we reflect on the matter, we shall see that a high degree of precision in the composition of the commodity unit is neither possible nor important to its monetary quality. The market basket behind a dollar certificate is not supposed to contain exactly what every housewife buys in the market for each of her dollars. There is, of course, no such thing. The unit's purpose is served if it is reasonably representative of the raw

[23] Professor Goudriaan expressed this view at a conference of the Committee of Experts, which I attended.

materials universe, in the same way as the various weighted indexes of spot or futures markets, such as Moody's or Dow-Jones, reflect the general position of raw materials. The real purpose of making our calculations as reasonable and as accurate as possible is to deal fairly with the various raw-materials producers who will be benefited by the plan. From the consumer's standpoint, the only matter of moment is that his money should be backed by and ultimately exchangeable for important and useful commodities at a stable rate. It is not difficult to convince an unprejudiced person of the superiority, in this respect, of a suitably constructed commodity composite over the single and doubtfully useful metal, gold. I submit that this is all we need demand of a commodity unit from the standpoint of its intrinsic value.

Advocates of a managed fiat money claim that its quality would be better than that of CR currency because their money would buy a constant amount of all commodities, while ours would acquire only a constant basket of raw materials. I submit that there is a confusion here between the quality or intrinsic nature of the currency unit and the results claimed to be achieved by fiscal and monetary management. The value of fiat money depends entirely on the success of the managers in maintaining its purchasing power. Since it has no intrinsic value there is no real basis for comparing its quality with that of CR money.

As is well known, advocates of achieving price stability through fiscal and monetary controls believe that this objective can be obtained more effectively and conveniently through their own means rather than through the buying and selling mechanism of CRC. Many economists, myself included, doubt whether increasing and decreasing the supply of money and credit and running a federal deficit or surplus can be counted on to maintain a stable price level. In comparing such a proposal with our own in the field of price stability, I may point out that the CRC plan acts directly on prices by buying and selling goods, while controls act indirectly by giving the economy more or less money to use. Secondly, the CRC plan has a *double* countercyclical effect: to check a decline, it both reduces the commodity supply and puts money in the hands of producers, and vice versa, to check an advance. It is for the reader and others to judge whether fiat-money management can really do so good a job as to render commodity-backed currency unnecessary, and therefore unduly expensive, for attaining our price-level and monetary objectives.

Let me return to Milton Friedman's contention that a theoretical commodity unit would have had a destabilizing rather than stabilizing effect on the general price level in the past. This statement is based entirely on his own commodity unit, restricted to metals and metal products, and has no application whatever to the composites recommended in my books or by the Food Research Institute.[24] He excludes each and every agricultural product by the sweeping statement that "the impossibility of controlling the output of agricultural crops over short periods and the dependence of agricultural output on the erratic forces determining growing conditions make them undesirable components of the bundle."[25] He does not explain why it is undesirable to exclude commodities with potentially fluctuating production. He ignores the fact that in the past the actual output of metals has fluctuated much more widely than that of crops as a whole, since the former has often been greatly curtailed in periods of bad business. Friedman cites some figures, based in part on the long-term price indexes of Warren and Pearson, to show that general prices varied more as against a metal and metal-products base than they did against gold. (This

[24] See note 13, above.
[25] "Commodity-Reserve Currency," p. 231 (*Essays*, p. 247).

was due entirely to the great fall in the metal category between 1800 and 1910; in the past half century even Friedman's base would have served reasonably well.) But his own reference data show that the fluctuations of all prices in terms of a combined farm-products and metals base would have been quite narrow over the past 100 years. (See table in Appendix II.)

I should add that Friedman excludes fuels as well as foods and fibers from his commodity unit on the ground that oil and coal are too expensive to store. The fact is that huge stocks of coal and oil[26] are constantly carried by both producers and consumers under physical arrangements that make their storage costs and losses comparatively small—much less, I am sure, than the cost of stockpiling the more vulnerable farm products. My more recent studies of storage costs, based on data now available from the CCC, the FAO, and the Strategic Stockpile,[27] lead me to reaffirm my original estimate, made in 1937,[28] of an approximate over-all annual storage expense of about 3 per cent of total value. Individual agricultural components, such as wheat, cost up to a maximum of 6 per cent, but the nonagricultural staples can be handled for much less than 3 per cent.

Let me conclude this section by asking what would be the effects on the credit structure of the buying and selling operations of a CRC system. Obviously, it would be expansionary when the reserve is buying and creating additional money and restrictive when it is selling. It is not to be assumed, however, that these changes would dominate or

[26] Cf. *Storage and Stability*, p. 252n.

[27] See United Nations Food and Agriculture Organization, *National Food Reserve Policies in Underdeveloped Countries*, Commodity Policy Study No. 11 (Rome, 1958), pp. 67–70; U.S. President, Civil and Defense Mobilization Office, *Stockpile Report to Congress, July–December 1959*, p. 8.

[28] *Storage and Stabilty*, p. 108. Cf. *World Commodities and World Currency*, app. iii.

necessarily control the credit structure. The Federal Reserve would still have available all of its instruments for controlling credit, and it would be able to use them either to reinforce or to offset the effects of CRC operations, should either seem appropriate.

The important points here are that (a) the normal effects of CRC operations would be in a countercyclical and therefore desirable direction, and (b), in the unlikely case that monetary policy would want to counteract such effects, as by maintaining credit ease in the face of a rising price level, the Federal Reserve would have ample power to bring that about. As an analogy I might remark that, within wide limits, the Federal Reserve is now able to offset the credit-contracting influences of our loss of gold.

COMMODITY-RESERVOIR ASPECTS OF THE PLAN

As already mentioned, the purely monetary aspects of the CRC scheme have always been subordinate in my thinking to its potential benefits in the difficult area of commodity surpluses. The plan could operate without monetizing the composite reserves. They could be financed by borrowing money, and this alternative was in fact recommended in the Food Research Institute study. My preference for the currency provision does not come from any burning desire to reform our monetary system, but simply to the great fiscal and political advantage of a self-financing mechanism, once it has overcome the handicap of novelty. Furthermore, I am persuaded that the other economic effects of monetization as against borrowing would be favorable on balance.

My main discussion here will consider the broad uses of the commodity reservoir to help achieve balanced expansion and to build up living standards throughout the world. But first a brief section on the use of the commodity reserve for defense requirements.

To my claim that the commodity-unit reservoir would be invaluable in times of war, critics have objected that its composition would be quite different from that of a defense reserve. Let me reply that in wartime virtually all the basic commodities in our reserve would be needed for military and civilian use, and, furthermore, that defense-stockpile needs not provided for in the commodity units would be acquired and held separately, as at present. It is, of course, absurd to imply that a huge store of goods would be unsatisfactory in time of need because it might not meet each need in its exact proportion.

Defense-stockpile requirements that are met by our commodity-unit holdings would *not* have to be duplicated in a separate military stock. It would only be necessary to provide that in time of reduction of the units (by sale at the 105 per cent price level), items needed for defense would be sold and transferred to the military reserve instead of in the open market. The higher price ruling for such commodities would be of no importance, since in effect one department of the government would be paying it to another. In this way, conceivably, all or part of the $1.5 billion of strategic-stockpile items that we earlier assumed would have been acquired by the CR operation could be returned to the strategic stockpile, if necessary.

We all know that commodity reserves are potentially of great value for a number of purposes, but at the same time they can have bad effects on business. We know that natural resources underground are always a major asset, yet these same resources above ground and ready for sale seem often a major liability. We know that in theory there is no such thing as general overproduction; when it seems to exist, as in a depression, it is really a case of general underconsumption. However, under those conditions it is difficult to put both the purchasing power and the desire to consume in the same hands. The United States has reached the point where it is willing to give generously of its burdensome surpluses to aid needy nations—not entirely out of altruism, we must recognize. But even here we face the nettlesome problem of interference with established channels of commercial trade. These challenges seem to be growing in urgency in the restless world of today, because everywhere people are less willing than heretofore to accept the paradox of want in the midst of actual or potential plenty. Finally, alongside the grim spectre of atomic annihilation, a second spectre haunts many serious-minded men—that of the population upsurge, which may create enormous new pressures on the world's resources before the century's end.

The commodity-reserve proposal could be quite helpful, I maintain, in this perplexing area of present-day economics. It would not present complete solutions for these problems, but would offer two cardinal points of great value. First, it would provide an initial stage of mobilization of surplus resources in a form where they were prevented from doing harm. Secondly, it would give our statesmen and economists ample time and breathing space to determine practicable means of using these resources for beneficial ends.

Let me outline here a possible approach to the use of the CRC plan to aid the various buffer-stock and food-reserve objectives that have been making increasing claims on the world's attention. As the FAO has carefully pointed out, a buffer stock for price-stabilization purposes is quite a different matter from a food reserve to meet famine needs or to raise nutritional standards.[29] A stabilization reserve can be financially self-supporting, or nearly so; it is ordinarily self-replenishing in the course of a complete business cycle. A world food reserve, or food and industrial-raw-material re-

[29] See its *Functions of a World Food Reserve—Scope and Limitations*, Commodity Policy Study No. 10, *passim*, and esp. para. 82, pp. 18–19.

serve, for the benefit of needy nations, is largely eleemosynary in character; it operates mainly through gifts or loans on noncommercial terms. However, this does not mean that the two kinds of reserves are mutually opposed, nor even that they must in all cases be physically separated. It does mean that quite different provisions must be made for the use of reserves for relief and development on the one hand and for buffer-stock operations on the other.

In my thinking I envisage a CRC scheme operated, on its money side, by an agency of the International Monetary Fund, or a similar plan set up in the United States and possibly in a few other developed nations. I imagine that during a period of peace (or even of cold war) the reserve would have a tendency to grow secularly. Presumably, it would expand at the rate of, say, 3 per cent a year from any assumed normal figure, merely to keep pace with the growth of our economy. Let us assume, moreover, as many critics seem to do, that under peace conditions the fixed 95 per cent buying level would stimulate general production of the unit commodities to such an extent as to create more than an ordinary secular increase in the reserve. Under these conditions of so-called "mounting surpluses" we would have two possible alternatives, either of which would be quite feasible.

(1) To reduce the buying level in accordance with a definite formula which will limit the maximum size of the reserve to some desired figure. Such a formula, under the name of "the Tangent Kicker," has been worked out and recommended by Dr. Harmon is his recent book.[30] A somewhat different technique along the same lines was recommended in the Food Research Institute study.[31]

(2) To transfer excess reserves from the CRC system to

[30] *Commodity Reserve Currency*, pp. 47–53.

[31] Bennett *et al.*, *International Commodity Stockpiling as an Economic Stabilizer*, pp. 84–85.

a relief and development reserve system, to be made available to needy countries on a donation or special-loan basis. (Some years ago Colin Clark suggested that such loans of basic commodities be made without interest charges and be repayable at a fairly long date.) These transfers would require a corresponding reduction in the money claims against the CRC system, which is another way of saying that the countries who really owned the reservoir would have to reduce their money claims to the extent of the excess donated to less fortunate nations. At bottom this is the procedure envisaged in the "Food for Peace" proposals of Eisenhower and Nixon, though the lack of a federal balance sheet would obscure the financial results of such gifts. The procedure could and should be extended to industrial raw materials in surplus supply, as defined, since these too would be of vital assistance in building up underdeveloped nations.

AN INTERNATIONAL CRC MECHANISM

In the foregoing discussion I have not made clear-cut distinctions between the operation of the plan on a national and an international level. In my view the differences in terms of mechanics need be only minor in character. The composition of an international commodity unit would undoubtedly differ from that of a United States index, but it is my firm belief, already expressed, that such differences would be of little basic importance. Consequently, the adoption of an international commodity unit would be equivalent to the adoption of as many similar national units by the nations participating in the plan.

The really important difference relates to the treatment in the United States of locally price-supported commodities, such as wheat, corn, and cotton. With an international mechanism the purchase and sales would be made at world prices, below those ruling in this country. If the United States continued its support operations, it would have to subsidize sales to the international commodity reserve in the same way as it now subsidizes exports of cotton and wheat at world prices. On the other hand, world prices established as a result of international commodity agreements would necessarily govern commodity-reserve operations as they do all others.

Let me in conclusion sketch out my conception of an international CRC mechanism broadly organized to carry out the various functions already suggested in this paper.

There would be a single international commodity unit, certificates for which would be freely exchangeable among central banks at a gold-parity value, and otherwise dealt with on the same basis as gold. The plan would be administered by an international agency, perhaps a subsidiary of the International Monetary Fund. To the extent that a nation held commodity-unit certificates, it could require that all or part of the corresponding commodities be stored within its borders, thus constituting part of its defense reserves.

International commodity agreements and national price-support plans would be limited to "needy" commodities; their support levels would be kept below that corresponding to the buying level for the unit as a whole.

The rate of growth of the commodity reserve would be the prime indicator of the capacity of wealthier nations to assist underdeveloped countries by gifts and noncommercial loans of commodities. This could be done in various ways. One mechanical approach would provide for the automatic transfer of commodity units, in excess of a given maximum, to a separate international relief and development agency. Owning nations would contribute for retirement a corresponding total of commodity-reserve certificates. The relief and development agency would employ these commodities for beneficial purposes in accordance with directions and safeguards set forth in its charter.

A mechanism such as this would, I submit, make a powerful contribution to prosperous expansion in the world. It would stimulate balanced production and at the same time safeguard the world's markets against disastrous oversupply. It would protect us at once against depressed price levels and against inflation resulting from a shortage of goods. It would give a rational embodiment to our attack on two of the outstanding international economic problems of this century: the instability of prices of basic raw materials, and the use of the world's surplus wealth to aid economically substandard nations.

APPENDIX I

HITHERTO UNPUBLISHED LETTER OF LORD KEYNES TO BENJAMIN GRAHAM ON COMMODITY STOCKPILES AND PRICE STABILITY *

December 31, 1943

Benjamin Graham Esq.

Dear Mr. Graham:

The articles of yourself and Professor [Frank D.] Graham † make me feel that it was a great mistake for one, who, being occupied on official work, has no leisure except to write briefly on one particular point without the full background of his thought and is not free to publish the more detailed work he has actually been doing on the subject behind the scenes, to write for publication at all. For the result, as your article shows, is to lead to a wild misconception of one's opinions. And nothing is more futile than public controversy about what one has *not* said and does *not* mean.

(1) You say I "imply strongly that any mechanism aiming at a stable price-level is in itself undesirable". I said no such thing, and it is the exact opposite of what I believe. After all, I was one of the pioneers (along with yourself) in advocating buffer stocks for this very purpose, and there is no-one in the world who has so spent more time than I have in that last two years trying to carry this policy into fruition.

My point was an entirely different one. I was pointing out

* This letter is published by permission of Professor R. F. Kahn of King's College, Cambridge.

† Keynes refers to manuscript articles submitted to the *Economic Journal.* Frank D. Graham's was later published as "Keynes *vs.* Hayek on a Commodity Reserve Currency," in volume 54 (December 1944), pp. 422–429.

that a currency stable in terms of a composite commodity, whilst serving certain objects, either did not achieve stable national prices or postulated stable efficiency-wages without having the power to impose them. That was my *only* contention in that brief note.* I ought to have made it clear that I was thinking primarily of the long-term. The avoidance of short-term fluctuations is another matter; though I am not clear about the advantages (in the short-term) of stabilizing a composite commodity as compared with those of stabilizing individual commodities. For the latter is a better means of stabilizing the national income of individual raw-material producing countries.

(2) You restate my argument as meaning that "full employment can be maintained only while money-wages are rising faster than efficiency". Here again I said no such thing, and it is the opposite of what I believe. If money-wages rise faster than efficiency, this aggravates the difficulty of maintaining full employment, and, so far from being a condition of full employment, it is one of the main obstacles which a full employment policy has to overcome.

My point was an entirely different one. Some people over here are accustomed to argue that the fear of unemployment and the recurrent experience of it are the only means by which, in past practice, Trade Unions have been prevented from overdoing their wage-raising pressure. I hope this is not true. I said in my article that, the most aware we were of this risk, the more likely we should be to find a way round other than totalitarianism. But I recognised the reality of the risk.

(3) This leads me to what was intended to be my central point. The task of keeping efficiency-wages reasonably stable (I am sure they will creep up steadily in spite of our best efforts) is a political rather than an economic problem. In my country it is quite essential that it should not be

* "The Objective of International Price Stability," *Economic Journal,* 53:185–187 (June–September 1943).

> handled in obedience to the dictates of an international currency system (which will be identified in labour circles with international bankers). From this point of view, the legal stabilization of national currencies in terms of a composite commodity would be just as dangerous and objectionable in operation as in terms of gold. That was the point I was concerned to establish. And if my article is to be discussed, that is the only relevant point to raise.

On the use of buffer stocks as a means of stabilizing short-term commodity prices you and I are ardent crusaders on the same side, so do not let a falsely conceived controversy arise between us.

Yours very truly,

(signed) KEYNES

APPENDIX II

RELATION BETWEEN WHOLESALE PRICE LEVELS OF "ALL COMMODITIES" AND OF A COMPOSITE OF FARM PRODUCTS AND METALS AND METAL PRODUCTS AT SELECTED INTERVALS, 1860–1960

Year	(1) All commodities	(2) Farm products	(3) Metals and metal products	(4) Composite[a] of (2) and (3)	(5) Ratio of (4) to (1)
			1910–1914 = 100		
1860	93	77	149	101	109
1870	135	112	200	141	105
1880	100	80	166	109	109
1890	82	71	123	88	108
			1926 = 100		
1890	56.2	50.4	105.3	69	122
1900	56.1	50.5	98.0	66	118
1910	70.4	74.3	85.2	78	111
1920	154.4	150.7	149.4	150	97
1930	86.4	88.3	92.1	90	104
1932	64.8	48.2	80.2	59	91
1940	78.6	67.7	95.8	77	98
1950	161.5	170.4	173.6	171	106
			1947–1949 = 100		
1950	103.1	97.5	110.3	102	99
June 1960	119.5	89.0	153.8	111	93

Source: U.S. Bureau of the Census, *Historical Statistics of the United States, Colonial Times to 1957* (Washington: Government Printing Office, 1960), pp. 115–117, and Bureau of Labor Statistics indexes reprinted in the *Federal Reserve Bulletin.*

[a] Giving two-thirds weight to farm products and one-third weight to metals and metal products.

· VIII ·

SHOULD THERE BE AN INDEPENDENT MONETARY AUTHORITY?

MILTON FRIEDMAN

THE TEXT for this paper, to paraphrase the famous remark attributed to Poincaré, is, "Money is too important to be left to the central bankers." The problem that suggests this text is the one of what kind of arrangements to set up in a free society for the control of monetary policy. The believer in a free society—a "liberal" in the original meaning of the word, but unfortunately not in the meaning that is now current in this country—is fundamentally fearful of concentrated power. His objective is to preserve the maximum degree of freedom for each individual separately that is compatible with one man's freedom not interfering with other men's freedom. He believes that this objective requires power to be dispersed, that it be prevented from accumulating in any one person or group of people.

The need for dispersal of power raises an especially difficult problem in the field of money. There is widespread agreement that government must have some responsibility for monetary matters. There is also widespread recognition that control over money can be a potent tool for controlling and shaping the economy. Its potency is dramatized in Lenin's famous dictum that the most effective way to destroy a society is to destroy its money. It is exemplified in more pedestrian fashion by the extent to which control over money has always been a potent means of exacting taxes from the populace at large, very often without the explicit agreement of the legislature. This has been true from early times, when monarchs clipped coins and adopted similar expedients, to the present, with our more subtle and sophisticated modern techniques for turning the printing press or simply altering book entries.

The problem is to establish institutional arrangements that will enable government to exercise responsibility for money, yet will at the same time limit the power thereby given to government and prevent the power from being used in ways that will tend to weaken rather than strengthen a free society. Three kinds of solutions have developed or have been suggested. One is an automatic commodity standard, a monetary standard which in principle requires no governmental control. A second is the control of monetary policies by an "independent" central bank. A third is the control of monetary policies by rules that are legislated in advance by the legislature, are binding upon the monetary authority, and greatly limit its initiative. This paper discusses these three alternatives with rather more attention to the solution through a central bank.

A COMMODITY STANDARD

Historically, the device that has evolved most frequently in many different places and over the course of centuries is a commodity standard, that is, the use as money of some physical commodity such as gold, silver, brass, or tin, or cigarettes, cognac, or various other commodities. If money consisted wholly of a physical commodity of this type, in principle there would be no need for control by the government at all. The amount of money in society would depend on the cost of producing the monetary commodity rather than on other things. Changes in the amount of money would depend on changes in the technical conditions of producing the monetary commodity and on changes in the demand for money.

This is an ideal that animates many believers in an automatic gold standard. In point of fact, however, as the system developed it deviated very far from this simple pattern, which required no governmental intervention. Historically, a commodity standard—such as a gold standard or a silver standard—was accompanied by the development of alternative forms of money as well, of fiduciary money of one kind or another, ostensibly convertible into the monetary commodity on fixed terms. There was a very good reason for this development. The fundamental defect of a commodity standard, from the point of view of the society as a whole, is that it requires the use of real resources to add to the stock of money. People must work hard to dig something out of the ground in one place—to dig gold out of the ground in South Africa—in order to rebury it in Fort Knox, or some similar place. The necessity of using real resources for the operation of a commodity standard establishes a strong incentive for people to find ways to achieve the same result without employing these resources. If people will accept as money pieces of paper on which is printed "I promise to pay so much of the standard commodity," these pieces of paper can perform the same functions as the physical pieces of gold or silver, and they require very much less in resources to produce. This point, which I have discussed at somewhat greater length elsewhere,[1] seems to me the fundamental difficulty of a commodity standard.

If an automatic commodity standard were feasible, it would provide an excellent solution to the liberal dilemma of how to get a stable monetary framework without the

[1] *A Program for Monetary Stability* (New York: Fordham University Press, 1959), pp. 4–8.

danger of irresponsible exercise of monetary powers. A full commodity standard, for example, an honest-to-goodness gold standard in which 100 per cent of the money consisted literally of gold, widely supported by a public imbued with the mythology of a gold standard and the belief that it is immoral and improper for government to interfere with its operation, would provide an effective control against governmental tinkering with the currency and against irresponsible monetary action. Under such a standard, any monetary powers of government would be very minor in scope.

But such an automatic system has historically never proved feasible. It has always tended to develop in the direction of a mixed system containing fiduciary elements such as bank notes, bank deposits, or government notes in addition to the monetary commodity. And once fiduciary elements have been introduced, it has proved difficult to avoid government control over them, even when they were initially issued by private individuals. The reason is basically the difficulty of preventing counterfeiting or its economic equivalent. Fiduciary money consists of a contract to pay standard money. It so happens that there tends to be a long interval between the making of such a contract and its realization, which enhances the difficulty of enforcing the contract to pay the standard money and hence also the temptation to issue fraudulent contracts. In addition, once fiduciary elements have been introduced, the temptation for government itself to issue fiduciary money is almost irresistible. As a result of these forces, commodity standards have tended in practice to become mixed standards involving extensive intervention by the state, which leaves the problem of how intervention is to be controlled.

Despite the great amount of talk by many people in favor of the gold standard, almost no one today literally desires to see an honest-to-goodness full gold standard in operation. People who say they want a gold standard are almost invariably talking about the present kind of standard, or the kind of standard that was maintained in the 1930's, in which there is a small amount of gold in existence, held by the central monetary authority as "backing"—to use that very misleading term—for fiduciary money, and with the same authority, a central bank or other government bureau, managing the gold standard. Even during the so-called "great days" of the gold standard of the nineteenth century, when the Bank of England was supposedly running the gold standard skillfully, the monetary system was far from a fully automatic gold standard. It was even then a highly managed standard. And certainly the situation is now more extreme. Country after country has adopted the view that government has responsibility for internal stability. This development, plus the invention by Schacht of the widespread direct control of foreign exchange transactions, has meant that few if any countries are willing today to let the gold standard operate even as quasi-automatically as it did in the nineteenth century.

Most countries in the world currently behave asymmetrically with respect to the gold standard. They are willing to allow gold to flow in and even to inflate somewhat in response, but almost none is willing either to let gold flow out to any large extent or to adjust to the outflow by allowing or forcing internal prices to decline. Instead, they are very likely to take measures such as exchange controls, import restrictions, and the like.

My conclusion is that an automatic commodity standard is neither a feasible nor a desirable solution to the problem of establishing monetary arrangements for a free society. It is not desirable because it would involve a large cost in the form of resources used to produce the monetary commodity. It is not feasible because the mythology and beliefs required to make it effective do not exist.

AN INDEPENDENT CENTRAL BANK

A second device that has evolved and for which there is considerable support is a so-called "independent" monetary authority—a central bank—to control monetary policy and to keep it from being the football of political manipulation. The widespread belief in an independent central bank clearly rests on the acceptance—in some cases the highly reluctant acceptance—of the view I have just been expressing about a commodity standard, namely, that a fully automatic commodity standard is not a feasible way to achieve the objective of a monetary structure that is both stable and free from irresponsible governmental tinkering.

The device of an independent central bank embodies the very appealing idea that it is essential to prevent monetary policy from being a day-to-day plaything at the mercy of every whim of the current political authorities. The device is rationalized by assimilating it to a species of constitutionalism. The argument that is implicit in the views of proponents of an independent central bank—so far as I know, these views have never been fully spelled out—is that control over money is an essential function of a government comparable to the exercise of legislative or judicial or administrative powers. In all of these, it is important to distinguish between the basic structure and day-to-day operation within that structure. In our form of government, this distinction is made between the constitutional rules which set down a series of basic prescriptions and proscriptions for the legislative, judicial, and executive authorities and the detailed operation of the several authorities under these general rules. Similarly, the argument implicit in the defense of an independent central bank is that the monetary structure needs a kind of a monetary constitution, which takes the form of rules establishing and limiting the central bank as to the powers that it is given, its reserve requirements, and so on. Beyond this, the argument goes, it is desirable to let the central bank have authority largely coordinate with that of the legislature, the executive, and the judiciary to carry out the general constitutional mandate on a day-to-day basis.

In recent times, the threat of extension of government control into widening areas of economic activity has often come through proposals involving monetary expansion. Central bankers have generally been "sound money men," at least verbally, which is to say, they have tended to attach great importance to stability of the exchange rate, maintenance of convertibility of the nation's currency into other currencies and into gold, and prevention of inflation. They have therefore tended to oppose many of the proposals for extending the scope of government. This coincidence of their views in these respects with those of people like myself, who regard narrowly limited government as a requisite for a free society, is the source of much of the sympathy on the part of this group, whom I shall call "new liberals," for the notion of an independent central bank. As a practical matter, the central bankers seem more likely to impose restrictions on irresponsible monetary power than the legislative authority itself.

A first step in discussing this notion critically is to examine the meaning of the "independence" of a central bank. There is a trivial meaning that cannot be the source of dispute about the desirability of independence. In any kind of a bureaucracy, it is desirable to delegate particular functions to particular agencies. The Bureau of Internal Revenue can be described as an independent bureau within the Treasury Department. Outside the regular government departments, there are separate administrative organizations, such as the

Bureau of the Budget. This kind of independence of monetary policy would exist if, within the central administrative hierarchy, there were a separate organization charged with monetary policy which was subordinate to the chief executive or officer, though it might be more or less independent in routine decisions. For our purposes, this seems to me a trivial meaning of independence, and not the meaning fundamentally involved in the argument for or against an independent central bank. This is simply a question of expediency and of the best way to organize an administrative hierarchy.

A more basic meaning is the one suggested above—that a central bank should be an independent branch of government coordinate with the legislative, executive, and judicial branches, and with its actions subject to interpretation by the judiciary. Perhaps the most extreme form of this kind of independence in practice, and the form that comes closest to the ideal type envisaged by proponents of an independent central bank, has been achieved in those historical instances where an organization that was initially entirely private and not formally part of the government at all has served as a central bank. The leading example, of course, is the Bank of England, which developed out of a strictly private bank and was not owned by or formally a part of the government until after World War II. If such a private organization strictly outside the regular political channels could not function as a central monetary authority, this form of independence would call for the establishment of a central bank through a constitutional provision which would be subject to change only by constitutional amendment. The bank would accordingly not be subject to direct control by the legislature. This is the meaning I shall assign to independence in discussing further whether an independent central bank is a desirable resolution of the problem of achieving responsible control over monetary policy.

It seems to me highly dubious that the United States, or

for that matter any other country, has in practice ever had an independent central bank in this fullest sense of the term. Even when central banks have supposedly been fully independent, they have exercised their independence only so long as there has been no real conflict between them and the rest of the government. Whenever there has been a serious conflict, as in time of war, between the interests of the fiscal authorities in raising funds and of the monetary authorities in maintaining convertibility into specie, the bank has almost invariably given way, rather than the fiscal authority. To judge by experience, even those central banks that have been nominally independent in the fullest sense of the term have in fact been closely linked to the executive authority.

But of course this does not dispose of the matter. The ideal is seldom fully realized. Suppose we could have an independent central bank in the sense of a coordinate constitutionally established, separate organization. Would it be desirable to do so? I think not, for both political and economic reasons.

The political objections are perhaps more obvious than the economic ones. Is it really tolerable in a democracy to have so much power concentrated in a body free from any kind of direct, effective political control? What I have called the "new liberal" often characterizes his position as involving belief in the rule of law rather than of men. It is hard to reconcile such a view with the approval of an independent central bank in any meaningful way. True, it is impossible to dispense fully with the rule of men. No law can be specified so precisely as to avoid problems of interpretation or to cover explicitly every possible case. But the kind of limited discretion left by even the best of laws in the hands of those administering them is a far cry indeed from the kind of far-reaching powers that the laws establishing central banks generally place in the hands of a small number of men.

I was myself most fully persuaded that it would be politically intolerable to have an "independent" central bank by the memoirs of Emile Moreau, the governor of the Bank of France during the period from about 1926 to 1928, the period when France established a new parity for the franc and returned to gold. Moreau was appointed governor of the Bank of France in 1926, not long before Poincaré became premier after violent fluctuations in the exchange value of the franc and serious accompanying internal disturbances and governmental financial difficulties. Moreau's memoirs were edited and brought out in book form some years ago by Jacques Rueff, who was the leading figure in the recent French monetary reform.[2]

The book is fascinating on many counts. The particular respect that is most relevant for our present purpose is the picture that Moreau paints of Montagu Norman, governor of the Bank of England, on the one hand, and of Hjalmar Schacht, at that time governor of the Bank of Germany, on the other; they were unquestionably two of the three outstanding central bankers of the modern era, Benjamin Strong of the United States being the third. Moreau describes the views that these two European central bankers had of their functions and their roles, and implies their attitude toward other groups. The impression left with me—though it is by no means clear that Moreau drew the same conclusions from what he wrote, and it is certain that he would have expressed himself more temperately—is that Norman and Schacht were contemptuous both of the masses—of "vulgar" democracy—and of the classes—of the, to them, equally vulgar plutocracy. They viewed themselves as exercising control in the interests of both groups but free from the pressures of either. In Norman's view, if the major central bankers of the world would only cooperate with one another—

[2] Emile Moreau, *Souvenirs d'un gouverneur de la Banque de France* (Paris: Génin, [1954]).

and he had in mind not only himself and Schacht but also Moreau and Benjamin Strong—they could jointly wield enough power to control the basic economic destinies of the Western world in accordance with rational ends and objectives rather than with the irrational processes of either parliamentary democracy or laissez-faire capitalism. Though of course stated in obviously benevolent terms of doing the "right thing" and avoiding distrust and uncertainty, the implicit doctrine is clearly thoroughly dictatorial and totalitarian.

It is not hard to see how Schacht could later be one of the major creators of the kind of far-reaching economic planning and control that developed in Germany. Schacht's creation of extensive direct control of foreign exchange transactions is one of the few really new economic inventions of modern times. In the older literature, when people spoke of a currency as being inconvertible, they meant that it was not convertible into gold or silver or some other money at a fixed rate. To the best of my knowledge, it is only after 1934 that inconvertibility came to mean what we currently take it to mean: that it is illegal for one man to convert paper money of one country into paper money of another country at any terms he can arrange with another person.[3]

[3] Another feature of Moreau's book that is most fascinating but rather off the main track of the present discussion is the story it tells of the changing relations between the French and British central banks. At the beginning, with France in desperate straits seeking to stabilize its currency, Norman was contemptuous of France and regarded it as very much of a junior partner. Through the accident that the French currency was revalued at a level that stimulated gold imports, France started to accumulate gold reserves and sterling reserves and gradually came into the position where at any time Moreau could have forced the British off gold by withdrawing the funds he had on deposit at the Bank of England. The result was that Norman changed from being a proud boss and very much the senior partner to being almost a suppliant at the mercy of Moreau. Aside from the human drama, it emphasizes how important it is whether the rate of exchange is fixed 5 per cent too low or 5 per cent too high. Britain went back on gold in 1925 at a price of gold in terms of the pound that was probably something like 5 or

I turn now to the economic or technical aspects of an independent central bank. Clearly there are political objections to giving the group in charge of a central bank so much power independent of direct political controls, but, it has been argued, there are economic or technical grounds why it is nevertheless essential to do so. In judging this statement, much depends on the amount of leeway that the general rule governing the central bank gives to it. I have been describing an independent central bank as if it could or would be given a good deal of separate power, as clearly is currently the case. Of course, the whole notion of independence could be rendered merely a matter of words if in fact the constitutional provision setting up the bank established the limits of its authority very narrowly and controlled very closely the policies that it could follow.

In the nineteenth century, when wide support for independent central banks developed, the governing objective of the central bank was the maintenance of exchange stability. Central banks tended to develop in countries that professed to have commodity currencies, which is to say had a fixed price for the commodity serving as the monetary standard in terms of the nominal money of the country. For two countries on the same standard, this meant a fixed rate of exchange between the corresponding national currencies. In consequence, the maintenance of such fixed rates had to be the proximate aim of the central bank if it was to achieve its major aim of keeping its currency convertible into standard money. The Bank of England, for example, was narrowly limited in what it could do by the necessity of keeping England on gold.

10 per cent too low, and France went back *de facto* at the end of 1926 and *de jure* in mid-1928 at a price of gold in terms of francs that was 5 or 10 per cent too high. This difference meant the difference between the French being at the mercy of the British and the British being at the mercy of the French.

In the same way, in the United States when the Federal Reserve System was established in 1913, it never entered into the minds of the people who were establishing it that the System would really have much effective control internally in ordinary times. The Reserve System was established when the gold standard ruled supreme, and when it was taken for granted that the major factor determining the policy of the System, and hence the behavior of the stock of money in this country, would be the necessity of maintaining external equilibrium with the currencies of other countries. So long as the maintenance of a fixed exchange rate between one country's currency and the currencies of other countries was the overriding objective of policy, the amount of leeway available to the central bank was narrowly limited. It had some leeway with respect to minor movements of a short-term character, but it ultimately had to respond to the balance of payments.

The situation has changed drastically in this respect in the course of the past few decades. In the United States, which is of most immediate concern to us, the Reserve System had hardly started operations before the fundamental conditions taken for granted when it was established had changed radically. During World War I, most of the countries of the world went off gold. The United States technically remained on gold, but the gold standard on which it remained was very different from the one that had prevailed earlier. After the end of World War I, although other countries of the world gradually re-established something they called the gold standard, the gold standard never again played the role which it had before. Prior to World War I, the United States was effectively a minor factor in the total world economy, and the necessity of maintaining external stability dominated our behavior. After the war, we had become a major factor to which other countries had to adjust. We held a very large fraction of the world's gold. Many countries never went back on gold, and those that did went back in a much diluted form. So never again has there been anything like the close domination of day-to-day policy by the gold standard that prevailed prior to 1914. Under these circumstances, "independence" of the central bank has become something meaningful, and not merely a technicality.

One defect of an independent central bank in such a situation is that it almost inevitably involves dispersal of responsibility. If we examine the monetary system in terms not of nominal institutional organization but of the economic functions performed, we find that the central bank is hardly ever the only authority in the government that has essential monetary powers. Before the Federal Reserve System was established, the Treasury exercised essential monetary powers. It operated like a central bank, and at times a very effective central bank. More recently, from 1933 to 1941, the Federal Reserve System was almost entirely passive. Such monetary actions as were taken were taken predominantly by the Treasury. The Treasury engaged in open-market operations in its debt-management operations of buying and selling securities. It created and destroyed money in its gold and silver purchases and sales. The Exchange Stabilization Fund was established and gave the Treasury yet another device for engaging in open-market operations. When the Treasury sterilized and desterilized gold, it was engaging in monetary actions. In practice, therefore, even if something called an independent central bank is established and given exclusive power over a limited range of monetary matters, in particular over the printing of pieces of paper or the making of book entries called money (Federal Reserve notes and Federal Reserve deposits), there remain other governmental authorities, particularly the fiscal authority collecting taxes and dispersing funds and managing the debt, which also have a good deal of monetary power.

If one wanted to have the substance and not merely the form of an independent monetary authority, it would be necessary to concentrate all debt-management powers as well as all powers to create and destroy governmentally issued money in the central bank. As a matter of technical efficiency, this might well be desirable. Our present division of responsibility for debt management between the Federal Reserve and the Treasury is very inefficient. It would be much more efficient if the Federal Reserve did all of the borrowing and all of the managing of the debt, and the Treasury, when it had a deficit, financed it by getting money from the Federal Reserve System, and when it had a surplus, handed the excess over to the Federal Reserve System. But while such an arrangement might be tolerable if the Federal Reserve System were part of the same administrative hierarchy as the Treasury, it is almost inconceivable that it would be if the central bank were thoroughly independent. Certainly no government to date has been willing to put that much power in the hands of a central bank even when the bank has been only partly independent. But so long as these powers are separated, there is dispersal of responsibility, with each group separately regarding the other group as responsible for what is happening and with no one willing to accept responsibility.

In the past few years, I have read through the annual reports of the Federal Reserve System from 1913 to date, seriatim. One of the few amusing dividends from that ordeal was seeing the cyclical pattern that shows up in the potency that the authorities attribute to monetary policy. In years when things are going well, the reports emphasize that monetary policy is an exceedingly potent weapon and that the favorable course of events is largely a result of the skillful handling of this delicate instrument by the monetary authority. In years of depression, on the other hand, the reports emphasize that monetary policy is but one of many tools of economic policy, that its power is highly limited, and that it was only the skillful handling of such limited powers as were available that averted disaster. This is an example of the effect of the dispersal of responsibility among different authorities, with the likely result that no one assumes or is assigned the final responsibility.

Another defect of the conduct of monetary policy through an independent central bank that has a good deal of leeway and power is the extent to which policy is thereby made highly dependent on personalities. In studying the history of American monetary policy, I have been struck by the extraordinary importance of accidents of personality.

At the end of World War I, the governor of the Federal Reserve System was W. P. G. Harding. Governor Harding was, I am sure, a thoroughly reputable and competent citizen, but he had a very limited understanding of monetary affairs, and even less backbone. Almost every student of the period is agreed that the great mistake of the Reserve System in postwar monetary policy was to permit the money stock to expand very rapidly in 1919 and then to step very hard on the brakes in 1920. This policy was almost surely responsible for both the sharp postwar rise in prices and the sharp subsequent decline. It is amusing to read Harding's answer in his memoirs to criticism that was later made of the policies followed. He does not question that alternative policies might well have been preferable for the economy as a whole, but emphasizes the Treasury's desire to float securities at a reasonable rate of interest, and calls attention to a then-existing law under which the Treasury could replace the head of the Reserve System. Essentially he was saying the same thing that I heard another member of the Reserve Board say shortly after World War II when the bond-support program was in question. In response to the view expressed by some of my colleagues and myself that the bond-support program should be dropped, he largely agreed but said, "Do you want us to lose our jobs?"

The importance of personality is strikingly revealed by the contrast between Harding's behavior and that of Emile Moreau in France under much more difficult circumstances. Moreau formally had no independence whatsoever from the central government. He was named by the premier, and could be discharged at any time by the premier. But when he was asked by the premier to provide the Treasury with funds in a manner that he considered inappropriate and undesirable, he flatly refused to do so. Of course, what happened was that Moreau was not discharged, that he did not do what the premier had asked him to, and that stabilization was rather more successful. I cite this contrast neither to praise Moreau nor to blame Harding, but simply to illustrate my main point, namely, the extent to which a system of this kind is really a system of rule by men and not by law and is extraordinarily dependent on the particular personalities involved.

Another occasion in United States history which strikingly illustrates this point is our experience from 1929 to 1933. Without doubt, the most serious mistake in the history of the Reserve System was its mismanagement of monetary matters during those years. And this mismanagement, like that after World War I, can very largely be attributed to accidents of personality. Benjamin Strong, governor of the Federal Reserve Bank of New York from its inception, was the dominant figure in the Reserve System until his death at a rather early age in 1928. His death was followed by a shift of power in the system from New York to Washington. The people in Washington at the time happened to be fairly mediocre. Moreover, they had always played a secondary role, were not in intimate touch with the financial world, and had no background of long experience in meeting day-to-day emergencies. Further, the chairmanship changed hands just prior to the shift of power and again in mid-1931. Consequently, in the emergencies that came in 1929, 1930, and 1931, particularly in the fall of 1930, when the Bank of United States failed in New York as part of a dramatic series of bank failures, the Federal Reserve System acted timorously and passively. There is little doubt that Strong would have acted very differently. If he had still been governor, the result would almost surely have been to nip the wave of bank failures in the bud and to prevent the drastic monetary deflation that followed.

A similar situation prevails today. The actions of the Reserve System depend on whether there are a few persons in the System who exert intellectual leadership, and on who these people are; its actions depend not only on the people who are nominally the heads of the System but also on such matters as the fate of particular economic advisers.

So far, I have listed two main technical defects of an independent central bank from an economic point of view: first, dispersal of responsibility, which promotes shirking responsibility in times of uncertainty and difficulty, and second, an extraordinary dependence on personalities, which fosters instability arising from accidental shifts in the particular people and the character of the people who are in charge of the system.

A third technical defect is that an independent central bank will almost inevitably give undue emphasis to the point of view of bankers. It is exceedingly important to distinguish two quite different problems that tend to be confused: the problem of credit policy and the problem of monetary policy. In our kind of monetary or banking system, money tends to be created as an incident in the extension of credit, yet conceptually the creation of money and the extension of credit are quite distinct. A monetary system could be utterly unrelated to any credit instruments whatsoever; for example, this would be true of a completely automatic commodity standard, using only the monetary commodity itself or warehouse receipts for the commodity as money. Historically, the connection between money and credit has varied widely from time to time and from place to place. It is therefore essential to distinguish policy issues connected with interest rates and conditions on the credit market from policy issues connected with changes in the aggregate stock of money, while recognizing, of course, that measures taken to affect the one set of variables may also affect the other, and that monetary measures may have credit effects as well as monetary effects proper.

It so happens that central-bank action is but one of many forces affecting the credit market. As we and other countries have seen time and again, a central bank may be able to determine the rate of interest on a narrow range of securities, such as the rate of interest on a particular category of government bonds, though even that only within limits and only at the expense of completely giving up control over the total stock of money. A central bank has never been able to determine, at all closely, rates of interest in any broader or more fundamental sense. Postwar experience in country after country that has embarked on a cheap-money policy has strikingly demonstrated that the forces which determine rates of interest broadly conceived—rates of return on equities, on real property, on corporate securities—are far too strong and widespread for the central bank to dominate. It must sooner or later yield to them, and generally rather soon.

The central bank is in a very different position in determining the quantity of money. Under systems such as that in the United States today, the central bank can make the amount of money anything it wishes. It may, of course, choose to accept some other objective and give up its power over the money supply in order to try to keep "the" or "a" rate of interest fixed, to keep "free reserves" at a particular level, or to achieve some other objective. But if it wishes, it can exercise complete control over the stock of money.

This difference between the position of the central bank in the credit markets and in determining the money supply tends to be obfuscated by the close connection between the central bank and the banking community. In the United States, for example, the Reserve banks technically are owned by their member banks. One result is that the general views of the banking community exercise a strong influence on the central bank and, since the banking community is concerned primarily with the credit market, central banks are led to put altogether too much emphasis on the credit effects of their policies and too little emphasis on the monetary effects of their policies.

In recent times, this emphasis has been attributed to the effects of the Keynesian Revolution and its treatment of changes in the stock of money as operating primarily through the liquidity preference function on the interest rate. But this is only a particular form of a more general and ancient tendency. The real-bills doctrine, which dates back a century and more, exemplifies the same kind of confusion between the credit and the monetary effects of monetary policy. The banking and currency controversy in Britain in the early nineteenth century is a related example. The central bank emphasized its concern with conditions in the credit market. It denied that the quantity of money it was creating was in any way an important consideration in determining price levels or the like, or that it had any discretion about how much money to create. Much the same arguments are heard today.

The three defects I have outlined constitute a strong technical argument against an independent central bank. Combined with the political argument, the case against a fully independent central bank is strong indeed.

LEGISLATED RULES

If this conclusion is valid, if we cannot achieve our objectives by giving wide discretion to independent experts, how else can we establish a monetary system that is stable, free from irresponsible governmental tinkering, and incapable of being used as a source of power to threaten economic and political freedom? A third possibility is to try to achieve a government of law instead of men literally by legislating rules for the conduct of monetary policy. The enactment of such rules would enable the public to exercise control over monetary policy through its political authorities, while at the same time preventing monetary policy from being subject to the day-to-day whim of political authorities.

The argument for legislating rules for monetary policy has much in common with a topic that seems at first altogether different, namely, the Bill of Rights to the Constitution. Whenever anyone suggests the desirability of a legislative rule for control over money, the stereotyped answer is that it makes little sense to tie the monetary authority's hands in this way because the authority, if it wants to, can always do of its own volition what the rule would require it to do, and, in addition, has other alternatives; hence "surely," it is said, it can do better than the rule. An alternative version of the same argument applies to the legislature. If the legislature is willing to adopt the rule, it is said, surely it will also be willing to legislate the "right" policy in each specific case. How then, it is said, does the adoption of the rule provide any protection against irresponsible political action?

The same argument could apply with only minor verbal changes to the first amendment to the Constitution and, equally, to the entire Bill of Rights. Is it not absurd, one might say, to have a general proscription of interference with free speech? Why not take up each case separately and treat it on its own merits? Is this not the counterpart to the usual argument in monetary policy that it is undesirable to tie the hands of the monetary authority in advance; that it should be left free to treat each case on its merits as it comes up? Why is not the argument equally valid for speech? One man wants to stand up on a street corner and advocate birth control; another, communism; a third, vegetarianism; and so on, ad infinitum. Why not enact a law affirming or denying each the right to spread his particular views? Or, alternatively, why not give the power to decide the issue to an administrative agency? It is immediately clear that if we were to take up each case separately, a majority would almost surely vote to deny free speech in most cases and perhaps even in every case. A vote on whether Mr. X should spread birth control propaganda would almost surely yield a majority saying "no"; and so would one on communism. The vegetarian might perhaps get by, although even that is by no means a foregone conclusion.

But now suppose all these cases were grouped together in one bundle, and the populace at large was asked to vote for them as a whole: to vote whether free speech should be denied in all cases or permitted in all alike. It is perfectly conceivable, if not highly probable, that an overwhelming majority would vote for free speech; that, acting on the bundle as a whole, the people would vote exactly the opposite to the way they would have voted on each case separately. Why? One reason is that each person feels much more strongly about being deprived of his right to free speech when he is in a minority than he feels about depriving somebody else of the right to free speech when he is in the majority. In consequence, when he votes on the bundle as a whole, he gives much more weight to the infrequent denial of free speech to himself when he is in the minority than to the frequent denial of free speech to others. Another reason, and one that is more directly relevant to monetary policy, is that if the bundle is viewed as a whole, it becomes clear that the policy followed has cumulative effects that tend neither to be recognized nor taken into account when each case is voted on separately. When a vote is taken on whether Mr. Jones may speak on the corner, it is not clearly affected by favorable effects of an announced general policy of free speech, and an affirmative vote will not produce these effects. In voting on the specific case, it is only peripherally relevant that a society in which people are not free to speak on the corner without special legislation is a society in which the development of new ideas, experimentation, change, and the like are all hampered in a great variety of ways. That these ways are obvious to all is due to our good fortune of having lived in a society that did adopt the self-denying ordinance of not considering each case of speech separately.

Exactly the same considerations apply in the monetary area. If each case is considered on its merits, the wrong decision is likely to be made in a large fraction of cases because the decision-makers are examining only a limited area and are not taking into account the cumulative consequences of the policy as a whole. On the other hand, if a general rule is adopted for a group of cases as a bundle, the existence of that rule has favorable effects on people's attitudes and beliefs and expectations that would not follow even from the discretionary adoption of precisely the same policy on a series of separate occasions.

Of course, the general rule need not be explicitly written down or legislated. Unwritten constitutional limitations supported unthinkingly by the bulk of the people may be as effective in determining decisions in individual cases as a written constitution. The analogy in monetary affairs is the mythology of gold, referred to earlier as a necessary ingredient of a gold standard if it is to serve as an effective bulwark against discretionary authority.

If a rule is to be legislated, what rule should it be? The rule that has most frequently been suggested by people of a generally "new liberal" persuasion is a price-level rule; namely, a legislative direction to the monetary authorities that they maintain a stable price level. I think this is the wrong kind of rule. It is the wrong kind of rule because the objectives it specifies are ones that the monetary authorities do not have the clear and direct power to achieve by their own actions. It consequently raises the earlier problem of dispersing responsibilities and leaving the authorities too much leeway. There is unquestionably a close connection between monetary actions and the price level. But the connection is not so close, so invariable, or so direct that the objective of achieving a stable price level is an appropriate guide to the day-to-day activities of the authorities.

The issue of what rule to adopt is one that I have considered at some length elsewhere.[4] Accordingly, I will limit myself here to stating my conclusion. In the present state of our knowledge, it seems to me desirable to state the rule in terms of the behavior of the stock of money. My choice at the moment would be a legislated rule instructing the monetary authority to achieve a specified rate of growth in the stock of money. For this purpose, I would define the stock of money as including currency outside commercial banks plus all deposits of commercial banks. I would specify that the Reserve System should see to it that the total stock of money so defined rises month by month, and indeed, so far as possible, day by day, at an annual rate of X per cent, where X is some number between 3 and 5. The precise definition of

[4] *A Program for Monetary Stability*, pp. 77–99.

money adopted and the precise rate of growth chosen make far less difference than the definite choice of a particular definition and a particular rate of growth.

I should like to emphasize that I do not regard this proposal as a be-all and end-all of monetary management, as a rule which is somehow to be written in tablets of gold and enshrined for all future time. It seems to me to be the rule that offers the greatest promise of achieving a reasonable degree of monetary stability in the light of our present knowledge. I would hope that as we operated with it, as we learned more about monetary matters, we might be able to devise still better rules which would achieve still better results. However, the main point of this paper is not so much to discuss the content of these or alternative rules as to suggest that the device of legislating a rule about the stock of money can effectively achieve what an independent central bank is designed to achieve but cannot. Such a rule seems to me the only feasible device currently available for converting monetary policy into a pillar of a free society rather than a threat to its foundations.

· IX ·

THE NECESSARY AND THE DESIRABLE RANGE OF DISCRETION TO BE ALLOWED TO A MONETARY AUTHORITY

JACOB VINER

I UNDERTAKE in this paper to explore the extent to which it is possible and desirable to limit the discretionary activity of a monetary authority by subjecting it, by statute or otherwise, to conform in its operations to a precise rule. I take for granted that some limitations of consequence in the monetary field can be effectively imposed on a monetary authority in the form of an obligation to follow an explicit code of general "principles," and more explicitly, in the negative form of prohibition, from pursuing some specified goals and from engaging in some specified types of activity. Beyond this it does not seem possible to limit the discretion of a monetary authority unless one can impose on it adherence to a single rule which is fairly simple, objective, and operationally workable. Otherwise, "discretion" can be freely exercised by variable interpretation of an ambiguous or elastic rule or by choosing between alternative rules when adherence to both simultaneously is or can be made to seem impossible.

Advocacy of replacement of "authorities" by "rules" is usually associated with a strong belief in the desirability of "economic freedom," and this is conspicuously the case in academic discussion of monetary policy. There is no inherent association, however, logical or historical, between freedom from governmental restraint and the issue as to whether when governmental restraint is present and perhaps is inevitable it is preferable that the restraint should be applied through the imposition of a rigid rule or through the exercise of discretionary authority.

In the monetary field advocates of economic freedom have in the past demanded freedom from both rules and discretionary authority with respect to the minting of coin, the issue of paper money, and the creation of deposits transferable by check. The limitation of the creation of money to government, or the regulation of its private creation, instead of leaving it free to be determined by the accidents of gold or silver mining, or by market competition in the banking industry, is already a major interference by government with free enterprise. Depending on the character of the rule and on the quality and objectives of the discretionary authority, the rule can be an instrument of tyranny, and discretion can be the means whereby economic freedom is promoted to the utmost extent possible consistent with respect for other values. As between the tyranny of an oppressive rule and the misery which could result from an authority which by using its discretionary power to do nothing permits anarchy to reign, even the zealots for economic freedom might find that the choice lay between comparable evils.

The enthusiasm of "liberals" for rules in preference to other modes of economic regulation nevertheless has an obvious and logical source; a government limited to operating through simple and inflexible rules would inevitably be a government tightly limited in the scale and range of its operations. Whether this is in itself desirable or undesirable is an appropriate matter for reasoned debate, or for expression of one's value judgments, prejudices, and emotions. In any case, it is a matter with which I have no concern for present purposes,[1] and my special concern here is with the narrower question of the suitability of "rules" as the major instrument of monetary regulation. I will assume throughout that where there is discretionary authority it will be exercised in accordance with some set of publicly approved principles and by men with the measure of good faith, intelligence, judgment, and skill which it is reasonable to expect them to possess.

I concede at once to rules certain advantages in principle over discretionary authority as rival instruments for the execution of public policy. On purely a priori grounds, not needing to extend beyond the obligation to avoid self-contradictory argument, it can be said for an unambiguous rule, provided it is enforceable and enforced, that it is a complete protection within the area of its immediate subject matter against arbitrary, malicious, capricious, stupid, clumsy, or other manipulation of that subject matter by an "authority." It can be said for a rule rigid through time, if it works and is counted on to work, that it provides absolute certainty and predictability, with respect to the behavior prescribed by the rule. It can also be said for—or against—limitation of government to the choice between action by imposition of rules or inaction that it will in all probability choose inaction more often than if discretionary action by itself and by its agencies were an adopted or permitted alternative. These are all considerations of substantial weight.

On the other hand, it can be said that within the area of

[1] I have recently presented my views on the logical flaws of some "libertarian" argument in "The Intellectual History of Laissez Faire," *Journal of Law and Economics,* 3:45–69 (1960), and in "Hayek on Freedom and Coercion," *Southern Economic Journal,* 27:230–236 (1961). I intend in the near future to subject to similar examination the arguments commonly used by the "interventionists" and "planners." I have no interest and see no profit, however, in attempting to reach a definite position with respect to the merits of the two positions in the general, abstracted from particular conjunctures of time, place, and circumstance, and my biases, insofar as I am aware of them, are perhaps equally strong against what seem to me extreme positions in either direction.

its application a rule *ipso facto* shuts out the possibility of adaptation of regulation by well-intentioned, wise, and skillful exercise of discretionary authority to the relevant differences in circumstance. A rule doubtfully or irregularly enforced, and a rule subject at any time to revision, may involve less certainty and predictability than a control operated by a discretionary authority which follows a known set of principles. The particular certainty which the best rule conceivable provides, moreover, may be a certainty which no one in his right mind would want, and may involve the accentuation of uncertainties in a wide range of other matters. A particular rule may accomplish its objective, but it may have undesired side-effects which will drive the government, in order to cope with them, to widen the range of its other activities, whether in a discretionary manner or by adopting additional rules. It may even be a general principle that the attempt to deal by simple rules with complex phenomena will lead to a proliferation of rules, or of authorities, or of rules *and* authorities. Even, therefore, if we accept the minimization of interference by government with the economic behavior of its citizens as a major objective, to substitute rules for discretionary authority can be to move away from rather than towards "economic freedom."

Even if it were conceded, therefore, that, where the objective consequences would be the same, regulation by rule would involve less impairment of economic freedom than regulation by discretionary methods, this would not suffice to settle the general issue in favor of rules. Particular freedoms, moreover, precious values though they may be, need to be limited and qualified so that they may be fitted into a complex value system in which there is conflict and rivalry of values.

There are in consequence of all these factors important limitations on the extent to which it is operationally practicable and psychologically and politically feasible to substitute rule by rule for government by discretionary authority. In the economic field important rules affecting important social issues have in fact been extremely scarce, and to the extent that they have had a substantial degree of durability this has been largely explicable either by the fact that they evolved into taboos, or ends in themselves, and were thus removed from the area of open discussion and rational appraisal, or by the tolerance of widespread evasion. The most conspicuous instances of economic rules with a substantial degree of durability were the prohibition of lending at interest and the maintenance of fixed monetary standards in terms of the precious metals. The most enthusiastic advocate of rules can derive little comfort from the availability of these historical precedents. Aside from the questionability of the ends which these rules were in their origin intended to serve and of the suitability of these rules as means to serve their ends, their durability was largely specious. In the case of the prohibition of usury, both widespread evasion and the promulgation of an elaborate set of exemptions or valid "titles" to the charge of interest on loans resulted in unequal and erratic enforcement and in the development of an elaborate, highly discretionary, and unstable casuistry, which made the rule a generator of uncertainty rather than of certainty. In the case of the metallic monetary standard, the degree of certainty and of genuine durability of the rule was made much less in fact than in appearance by discretionary and often arbitrary debasements and devaluations, by illegal corruptions of the legal coinage, by discretionary alterations in the laws and regulations affecting the nonmonetary uses of the precious metals and their export and import, and by the operation of Gresham's law, where more than one precious metal had legal tender privileges. In both instances there was much to be said for the social usefulness of the breaches of the rules which occurred, whether these were legal or illegal.

The obstacles in principle and in practice to the substitution of rules for discretionary authority can be summarized in a compact set of propositions.

(1) If there is plurality of ends and if several ends are in complex and unstable rivalry or conflict with each other, no rule can be devised which will dispense with the need of exercise of flexible discretionary authority.

(2) If there is a single end but plurality of means, the most appropriate combination, in kind and degree, of means to be used will vary with time, circumstances, and available information and insight, and will therefore need to be determined by more or less *ad hoc* judgment rather than be susceptible of determination by a fixed rule.

(3) If authority is diffused among a number of substantially independent agencies, decision-making will need to be carried out by resort to a continuous or intermittent process of negotiation and mutual accommodation, to the exclusion of fixed and stable rules.

(4) Even if there are a single end, a single authority, and a single means, but the end is a quantity of some kind which is a function of several variables, all of which are important and are in unstable relation to each other, there will be no fixed rule available which will be both practicable and appropriate to its objective.

I will now attempt to explore the significance of these rather abstract propositions for the more concrete field of decision-making in the monetary policy area. In this area there are a multiplicity of objectives, a multiplicity of available tools, a multiplicity of authorities, a multiplicity of governmental agencies whose activities infringe on monetary phenomena; these agencies may be substantially independent of external authority and may be unaware of and unconcerned about these impacts. All of this increases the difficulty of the task of formulating and administering monetary policy.

The task would admittedly be facilitated if there could be reduction of the list of objectives, preferably to a single one, reduction of the list of authorities, preferably to a single one, reduction of the list of tools, if it is a long list, and the imposition on other governmental agencies of the requirement that they avoid actions which have undesired monetary impacts.

All of this, however, is easier said than done. Our monetary authorities may perhaps be attempting to serve too wide a range of objectives. Authority in the monetary field may be too widely diffused, as I am certain it is. A host of miscellaneous agencies of the federal government may have mandates from Congress which are inconsistent with our monetary policy, and may within the limits of the discretion allowed to them act irresponsibly with respect to monetary policy.

Things are as they are, however, for historical and constitutional and political reasons, which in many cases carry great weight with Congress and with the public. It is a useful service to speculate on the improvements which could be made in the operation of our monetary system if we could rearrange and reconstruct at will our existing political institutions and our banking and financial system. It is defeatist to confine oneself to the assumption that we must take the existing institutional complex as fixed and unalterable in making policy recommendations. Where between these extremes is the most profitable point from which to start in making one's policy recommendations will be answered differently by different economists, according to their judgment and temperament. I will operate throughout on the assumption that institutional changes are almost always difficult to attain, even when the case in their favor is strong, and that the chances of obtaining a desired improvement in the mode of operation of our monetary system are much greater if the improvement does not involve any substantial change in the institutional framework of our government or of our financial structure.

I will start with a grossly unrealistic model, in which Congress has assigned exclusively to the Federal Reserve the task of promoting price-level stability, has assigned it no other task, and has confined it to the use of a single tool, open-market operations, so that no questions as to choice of authorities, choice of goals, or choice of tools can arise. I will assume also that whatever happens in the nongovernmental economy and whatever Congress or other agencies of the government may do, there will always be some pattern of open-market operations which will in form and degree suffice to prevent a significant deviation, either short-run and long-run, or only long-run, from the desired price level. Unless it is a fact, and a believed fact, that there is a simple and stable relation between a particular pattern and degree of open-market operations and the general course of prices, the Federal Reserve will still not be able to operate on the basis of a rule, but will have to exercise discretion as to when, in what degree, and in what direction to carry out open market operations, and also as to what securities and in what relative proportions to buy or sell.

There would also remain the question as to how to define the "price level" and how to obtain a reasonably precise measure of its behavior, so defined. Some "authority" would have to decide this, and it could make its decision only by exercising a substantial degree of "discretion," which would inevitably involve some measure of judgment and some measure of arbitrariness. Let this problem be resolved, or evaded, by the assumption that Congress prescribes the "price level" which is to be stabilized and the precise procedure which is to be followed in measuring it. Further, let it be assumed that a constitutional amendment authorizes Congress to make decisions which neither that Congress nor its successors shall have the power, for a stated and substantial period of time, to change. This would relieve the Federal Reserve of the necessity of exercising discretion in the definition of its single goal. There would still remain the need, however, of deciding the pattern and degree of open-market operations required to maintain a stable price level. No one, as far as I know, has ever claimed that the relation to the price level of the scale of open-market operations of a given pattern, or with a pattern changeable at will, has been, is, or could be simple enough and stable enough to make it possible to find a quantitative rule of open-market operations which could be counted on to maintain approximate stability in the price level, either in the cyclical short run or in the long run. Even, therefore, if price stability were the sole goal and if the Federal Reserve were the sole monetary authority and open-market operations the sole tool it was permitted to use, we would still not have escaped from the necessity of leaving to the discretionary judgment of the Federal Reserve the decision at least of the scale of its open-market obligations.

If with price stabilization as the sole goal it is not possible, analytically or on the basis of past experience, to frame a rule prescribing the scale of open-market operations which could be expected to serve that goal with a tolerable degree of approximation, is any other suitable rule available? Professor Milton Friedman claims that a suitable rule is available as far as long-run stabilization of the price level is concerned—provided a number of important changes are made in the structure and functions of our monetary institutions. The monetary authority should so conduct open-market operations as to result in a constant monthly rate of increase in the stock of money, the rate to be either 3 or 4 per cent, depending on whether "money" is defined as including or excluding time deposits.

Friedman acknowledges that "there is little to be said in theory for the rule that the money supply should grow at a constant rate,"[2] does not indicate what that "little" consists of, and does not seriously expound what can be said "in theory" against commitment to a constant rate of growth in money supply in a world which in most of its economic respects, and perhaps in all, has not grown at a constant rate in the past and offers no ground for expectation that it will do so in the future, near or far. He is concerned, and rightly so, about the ill-behavior of the money supply in the past as judged by any arguable standards, and is concerned, and rightly so, lest its future behavior be as bad as in the past, or at least be not considerably better. What he claims on behalf of his proposed rule is that it is objective, unambiguous, precise, and therefore would leave no significant scope for the exercise of discretion to the monetary authority as far as the supply of money was concerned, that if it had been followed over the past century, or since 1920, our monetary system would have worked much better than it has in fact, and that if it had been in effect since 1948, it would have worked about as well as it has in fact.

I raise no question about the validity of Friedman's statistical report of what our past experience has been because I am neither informed nor competent enough to do so, and because I have great respect for his statistical skill, and also because the statistical record does not seem to me to be of much relevance for the present issue. We are asked to prescribe for the future, and not for a distant past. If we look to past experience for guidance, as we of course should, the most relevant period is the period since 1951, after the Korean War and after the Treasury-Federal Reserve "Accord" of 1951, which restored to the Federal Reserve the power to

[2] *A Program for Monetary Stability* (New York: Fordham University Press, 1959), p. 98.

use its controls in support of price stabilization. It seems to me that our experience during this period was by Friedman's own standards superior to what his rule would have achieved. With the gains which one can reasonably expect time to bring in available statistical data, skills, and insights, the Federal Reserve will be able to perform even better in the future, if it is given adequate authority.

Friedman presents stabilization of the price level as the single appropriate and practicable objective of monetary policy and stabilization of the rate of growth of the money supply merely as a means, though presumably the only effective one available, of attaining that end. The question arises: Why could not the Federal Reserve be given, as the "rule" to follow, the maintenance of the stock of money at whatever level appears necessary to keep stable a particular index number of prices? Friedman raises against this the "technical problem" of choice of a particular index number. But the technical problem of definition of "money" is at least as difficult. If it is the case that different reputable index numbers of prices vary substantially in their behavior through time and that choice between them is difficult, acceptance of the rule that the rate of increase in the money supply should be kept constant at some specified rate becomes the equivalent not of accepting a stable price level as the goal of monetary policy but of accepting whatever price-level trend the rule would happen to produce. The rule thus becomes the end, and the original end is more or less abandoned.

As far as cyclical price movements are concerned, Friedman explicitly abandons price stabilization as a practicable goal. "The link between price changes and monetary changes over short periods is too loose and too imperfectly known to make [short-run] price level stability an objective and reasonably unambiguous guide to policy." [3] To justify faith in a

[3] *A Program for Monetary Stability*, p. 87.

close enough linkage of secular price-level changes to money-supply changes to qualify the money-supply rule as a satisfactory rule for long-run price-level stabilization, he appeals to the statistical record, as he has presented it, both of the behavior of the money supply and of the behavior of the price level as reflected in a particular series of index numbers. Without raising any question about either his money-supply data or his price-level data, I reject that faith on the basis of another article of faith which I hold, but which I concede is not fashionable today in the profession. I believe that the nature of the economic universe is such, and the degree of mutual independence of the money supply and the price level is so substantial as far as logic by itself can determine, that any empirical constancy of relations that is discovered must be suspected of being either fortuitous or the consequence of the particular selection of series, from among those available, subjected to comparison, and that routine extrapolation into the future of such constancy of relations is consequently a highly hazardous basis for prediction. I suggest also that even if we accept an empirical constancy of relations discovered in the past as demonstrating a logical relation in that period, the introduction into the economic universe of a specific rule of behavior for the money supply would constitute an alteration of potential significance in the nature of that universe, and that we must not take for granted that the relation of the price level to the supply of money will be even approximately the same after such a rule is adopted and effectively enforced as it was before. The transformation of a hitherto unpredictable economic variable to one which everyone can predict with certainty is almost certain to have some effect, though one unpredictable in advance, on the pattern of its relations to other economic variables.

Friedman's proposed 3 per cent constant-rate-of-growth-of-the-money-supply rule is compounded of two elements: the assumption, or prediction, of a secular rate of growth of the economy at 2 per cent per annum and of a secular rate of shift of 1 per cent per annum from demand deposits to bank and non-bank time deposits, based on the average experience of the past ten years. This second element is a recognition that the impact of a given stock of "money" on the price level depends upon its velocity of use, and that shifts from one kind of "money" to another, or from money to near-money, will tend to affect the velocity of use of the money supply. It seems to me inadequate recognition, however, of the potential variability in extent and kind of these shifts through time, and to give too much weight to a particular average rate of shift as between an arbitrarily restricted range of the moneys and near-moneys in one decade of past history whose peculiarities of circumstance may not be repeated in any succeeding decade. Here once more an improbable constancy is being projected into the future.

To prescribe a formula which makes a stated percentage of allowance for the influence on the velocity of the stock of money, however defined, of shifts in the relative proportions of money and of one kind of near-money is to predict in effect the net results on velocity of a wide range of unpredictable changes. Such are changes in the relative proportions of currency, demand deposits freely drawable by depositors, "demand deposits" which are required to be maintained as a condition of the grant of loans or as compensation for services rendered, and time deposits with commercial or noncommercial banks or with non-banks. Such also are shifts in the holdings of deposits as between different categories of depositors with different patterns of rate of use of their deposits. Such also are changes in the relative proportions of securities and other more or less liquid assets held by the public to their holdings of money, and shifts in the maturity pattern of these securities. Such also are changes in subjective appraisal by the public of the degree of liquidity of their assets, induced by changes in interest rates, or by changes in the character or in the mode of operation of financial institutions or in the mechanics of payment transfers.

For purposes of academic theorizing, one is free to assume that in the absence of special information these various factors will be mutually offsetting, or will have net effects on the velocity of "money," defined in a particular way, corresponding to their average effects over some preceding period more or less arbitrarily selected. The only logical basis for such assumptions, however, even for purposes of theoretical analysis, rests on convenience and the absence of superior alternatives. But what is under consideration here is not theorizing for its own sake but the adoption of a rule of practice. Staking our future on present prophesying seems a high price to pay for escaping from the bondage of a discretionary authority, especially if one considers how dismal has been the past record of success and failure in economic prophesying on the basis of the projection into the future of past trends.

The choice in practice, of course, need not be between, on the one hand, the grant to the monetary authority of complete discretion, subject presumably to a Congressional mandate to follow some specified general principle or principles, and, on the other hand, its subjection to a precise rule not subject to change, even if it obviously was working badly. Congress could, for example, require the Federal Reserve each year to bring into being such rate of increase (or decrease) in the stock of money, as specifically defined, as in the judgment of the Federal Reserve would if it had prevailed in the preceding five-year period have resulted in a secularly stable price level during that period. This would not require the Federal Reserve to engage in forecasting, would call for annual adjustment of the planned rate of increase in the stock of money in strict conformity with the price-stabilization goal, and would at least weaken any tendency of the price-level trend to deviate cumulatively from stability. This more flexible rule would have the advantage also over a more rigid one that by lessening the risk of a marked discrepancy between the goal of the rule and its actual results it would increase its acceptability and durability. Since the public interest is presumed to be in price stability and in the behavior of the stock of money only as it bears on price stability, substitution of the flexible for the rigid rule would give the public a greater measure of certainty with respect to something it cares about, the trend of the price level, at the cost of introducing a measure of uncertainty about something it cares nothing about for its own sake.

I have been assuming so far that the Federal Reserve has only one goal: stabilization of the price level. This is, of course, not the case. The Federal Reserve states its principal functions to be those of fostering price level stability, high-level employment, and economic growth. It also acknowledges as a subordinate function the damping of cyclical instability, and it at times talks and operates as if it had some additional, though minor, functions. It presents these functions as not of its own choosing but as dictated to it by Congressional mandate and by its understanding of the intent of Congress.

If the Federal Reserve had a single objective, let us say secular price-level stability, the possibility of finding a precise rule or a simple set of rules which would serve this objective with an acceptable degree of efficiency would, other things being equal, be at a maximum. This would be equally true if it were a fact, and were believed to be a fact, that maintaining price-level stability was all that it was feasible to do in the monetary field to promote high-level employment and economic growth. If, however, it is a fact, and recognized by the Federal Reserve to be a fact, that the causal relations between the behavior of the price level, the level of employment, and the rate of economic growth are, as I believe them to be, highly complex, unstable through time, and in large measure unpredictable, there would seem to be only two alternatives open: either to plead uncertainty as to what the effect of its actions would be as a justification for not taking any action specifically directed towards promoting high-level employment and economic growth, or to use its best judgment each time that a decision of some sort is called for as to the relative weight to be given to the three objectives and as to the effect on the three objectives of any specific action available to it. The first would mean, in effect, abandonment by the Federal Reserve of these goals as part of its responsibilities. The second would mean that the Federal Reserve had no choice but to use its authority in a discretionary manner.

This states somewhat too sharply the issue between accepting plural goals and accepting only a single goal. All three goals could be *nationally* accepted, but with the Federal Reserve being assigned responsibility only for the maintenance of price-level stability and with other agencies being assigned the specific tasks of promoting high-level employment and economic growth by the use of other than monetary measures. If the other agencies thereby exercised an influence on the price level which was from the point of view of price-level stabilization wrong in direction or in degree, it would be the duty of the Federal Reserve, in fullfillment of its own obligation, to take compensatory measures with respect to the money supply. If it should prove in practice that there was basic incompatibility between the goals such that a satisfactory level of employment and a satisfactory rate of economic growth required—or seemed to require—some degree of inflation, the decision would have to be made somewhere as to which goal or goals must be given precedence, and wherever the decision was made, "discretion" would have to be exercised both in reaching that decision and in carrying it into effect.

A fourth goal has as a result of the developments of the past few years been brought into the forefront of official and public consciousness: the goal of restoring equilibrium in the American balance of payments, or of maintaining the present dollar price of gold. As in the case of the level of employment and of the rate of growth of the American economy, there could be basic incompatibility between the balance-of-payments-equilibrium goal and the stable-price-level goal. It is, moreover, a characteristic of the stable dollar price of gold as a goal which is perhaps unique to it that the virtues that it possesses or that are claimed for it are such that they vanish if there are recurrent casual, seasonal, or cyclical intermissions in its fulfillment. Like Caesar's wife, the gold standard in any of its variants, to accomplish its purposes, must remain above suspicion of its integrity, without dispensation even for momentary deviations. If there is conflict between the fixed dollar price of gold and the price-level-stabilization goals, or between the former and a rule adopted in the service of the latter, one or the other must give way, and in the absence of a rule for breaking rules I do not see how that can be brought about in an orderly way, except through the decision-making of a discretionary authority.

The price-stabilization goal could itself be regarded as a sort of multiple goal if what was sought was not merely secular stability but also cyclical stability. Friedman's rule disregards this latter goal, except as the maintenance of a constant monthly rate of increase of the money supply might as an incidental by-product make a greater contribution to cyclical price stability than would any other available procedure for regulating the money supply. Friedman in fact claims that our understanding of the cycle is so meager and the lags between the taking of corrective measures in the monetary field and their impact on the economy so long and so uncertainly known that we are justified in concluding that deviations from the rule of maintaining a constant monthly rate of increase of the money supply which are intended to lessen cyclical instability would more often hinder than help. I hold in low regard the state of my knowledge with respect to the intricacies of the business cycle, and therefore cheerfully hand this problem over to the experts. I cannot, however, exorcise from my mind the question as to whether Friedman's verdict that attempts to dampen the business cycle by use of countercyclical monetary measures would tend rather to accentuate it would remain unaltered if such attempts did not necessarily involve departure from a fixed rule of constant growth in the money supply. I venture also to suggest that the "announcement effects" of countercyclical monetary actions may be important, and that the lags associated with them may be very short.

It seems to me that from all this one must conclude that even if a simple rule were practicable if there was only a single objective of monetary policy, plurality of goals makes resort to discretionary management unavoidable. It may be demonstrable that some goals are ill-chosen and that the country should abandon them, and that other goals can be best served by other means than monetary controls or can be only damaged, not helped, if the attempt is made to serve them through the control of the money supply. All of this is open to discussion. The more extreme position that interference of an otherwise valid goal with the practicability of resort to a simple rule for the determination of the money supply can ever be a sufficient or even a strong argument for abandonment of that goal appears rational only if one's enthusiasm for simple rules goes beyond mere faith in their efficiency as means to economic ends. The commitment to an ascetic limitation of goals in order to establish the possibility of the substitution of rules for discretionary authorities can be logically supported only on the basis of a personal set of value premises, unlikely to be widely shared.

I readily concede, however, that a monetary authority, in this instance the Federal Reserve, should seek within reason to practice parsimony of goals, and should not permit its decision-making to become confused and its operations cluttered by accepting an unlimited array of goals, ranging from major ones to relatively trivial ones. Multiplicity of goals may serve as a screen, moreover, for not having any well-defined goals, for operating in a haze of uncertain and volatile objectives, and for using as an alibi for failure to operate vigorously in support of major objectives the need to serve other unspecified or trivial objectives. I, for one, would not absolve the Federal Reserve—or the Treasury—from the charge that at times in the past this plea has been used in defense of failure to formulate clear-cut and rational policy.

Multiplicity of agencies with independent powers of control in the monetary field also constitutes a formidable obstacle to resort to simple rules. A more important drawback of multiplicity of agencies is that it can constitute a formidable obstacle to *any* effective pattern of monetary control.

In the United States the degree of decentralization of direct and indirect control over the quantity and velocity of money, as well as of official power to influence the supply of near-moneys and their velocities, is nothing short of fantastic, and is unquestionably without parallel anywhere else in the world. Within the Federal Reserve System, control over the supply of money would on a functional organization chart be shown to be divided among the Board of Governors, the Open Market Committee, and, with respect to the administration of the "discount window" and the determination of discount rates, the twelve district banks. Non-member banks, which hold about 16 per cent of the total bank deposits of the country, are regulated by fifty state agencies. Bank supervision and bank examination, which can so operate as to affect directly the quantity of money, are divided among the Federal Reserve, the Controller of the Currency, the F.D.I.C., and state agencies. Federal debt management, which influences the liquidity of the banking system and of the economy, is a function solely of the Treasury, especially since the adoption by the Federal Reserve of the "bills-only" policy for its open-market operations. (In England the Bank of England is to a large extent the debt manager; it determines what kind of national securities the public shall hold by releasing for public sale varying proportions of its subscriptions to Treasury loan issues as well as by carrying out its open-market transactions in securities of an unlimited range of maturities.) There is also a great mass of credit-creating and velocity- and liquidity-influencing activity which is carried on by private financial institutions other than commercial banks, and over these activities the Federal Reserve has as a rule no direct regulatory power, the one significant exception being its control over margin requirements for lending on securities.

The multiplicity of monetary control agencies in the United States is primarily a historical product, with limited correspondence to the needs of an efficient system of monetary and banking controls. In large part it derives its durability and finds such justification as is available to it in loyalties to "states' rights" and in the special features of a unit-banking system. It is thus partly the result of the existence of a multiplicity of objectives, but it also leads naturally to the multiplying of objectives. Multiplicity of tools or instrumentalities of control is also in part a by-product of the multiplicity of agencies. It should be said, however, that the degree of diffusion of control is much greater in appearance than in reality. Within the Federal Reserve System there has been a strong trend toward effective concentration of power in the Board of Governors, even when the formal allocation of power has been left unaltered. As between the Federal Reserve and other agencies there is a substantial amount of formal and informal coordination of policies. The banking resources of the country are quantitatively overwhelmingly within the Federal Reserve System and are thus subject to control, although this exaggerates the degree of control over the banking system as a whole which the Federal Reserve can exercise. As long as entry into and surrender of membership in the Federal Reserve System is at the free will of the individual banks, the Federal Reserve has to give consideration, in applying restrictive control measures, lest they lead to transfers of banks from Federal Reserve membership to non-member state-bank status.

I would in general approve of any move toward concentration of regulatory power over credit-creating agencies, both within the Federal Reserve itself and with respect to the banking system as a whole. But as long as decentralization of authority persists in anything like its present dimensions, the impracticality of regulating the national money supply by means of a simple and rigid rule is for this reason alone complete and unqualified.

The multiplicity of tools used by official agencies which have as their purpose influencing the national supply of money, its velocity, and the liquidity of the economy, or which, while having other primary objectives, have or can have significant influence, direct or indirect, on the quantity of money or its velocity, or on the general liquidity of the economy, provides a further obstacle to the resort to a rigid rule for control of the money supply, especially if price stabilization is accepted as a major goal. Within the Federal Reserve System, the tools available include open-market operations, changes in reserve requirements, changes in the discount rate, the administration of the discount window, changes in the rigor of bank supervision and examination, and the use of selective credit controls. Outside the Federal Reserve System, but within the federal orbit, there are Treasury management of its debt and its cash balance procedures, fiscal policy, the lending, guaranteeing, and credit-insurance activities of federal agencies, and the possible interventions of the President and of Congress. There are also the instruments of control of the state regulatory agencies, which may differ in mode of operation or even in kind from the related federal ones. I am sure that I have failed to make my list of tools used, or available for potential use on a stand-by basis, long as it is, a complete one.

This multiplicity of tools is, I have no doubt, excessive and an obstacle to the efficient pursuit of the major objectives of monetary control. It is, however, in large part a by-product of the multiplicity of authorities and the plurality of objectives. Without concentration of monetary authority and some measure of reduction of the range of objectives for which the controlling agencies are assigned responsibility, the possibility of substantially reducing the number of tools is small. Multiplicity of tools is obviously a barrier to operation by simple rule, since it creates the necessity at all times of discretionary choice as to which tools shall be used and in what proportions.

It does not follow, however, that even if there were a single authority, say, the Federal Reserve, and a single objective, the ideal would be a single tool, unless operation by a simple rule is made the single objective, and perhaps not even then. On the number of tools which should be used, Friedman says: "Retaining defective instruments of control which interfere with the operation of more efficient instruments does not mean retaining power any more than a marksman's ability to hit a distant target with a rifle would be enhanced by requiring him to shoot a blunderbuss at the same time with his left hand." [4]

Quite true. But I can easily picture the Federal Reserve replying that it has more than one target, that it has several hands, none of them left hands, that all its rifles are good instruments for their respective purposes, and that it is sometimes desirable to shoot at more than one target at a time, or to shoot at a single target with more than one rifle.

The Federal Reserve insists on its need of a wide range of tools, but not apparently as wide as is now available to it for use, and, as far as I know, it is not desirous of acquiring the authority to use the many new tools which the younger central banks have invented and are using to their own satisfaction. It does not approve of the use of the discount window as a means of regulating either the stock of money or its velocity, and makes use of it chiefly as a means of supervision over individual banks, to soften the impact of its credit-restriction moves on individual banks which are particularly hard hit thereby, and to provide "last-resort" money to individual banks or to localities which do not have adequate and quick resort to money-market supplies of cash. As long as we have a unit-banking system, there is genuine need of these services, and their absence in countries with branch-banking systems has little if any relevance. If ours was a branch-banking system on a national scale, all of the banks could reasonably be expected either not to need external facilities to meet such exigencies or to have adequate connections with private money-market institutions to be assured of adequate facilities for meeting them without recourse to the Federal Reserve.

[4] *A Program for Monetary Stability*, p. 51.

The Federal Reserve also finds merit in *changes* in the rediscount rate as a "signaling" device and of occasional use of the discount window to ease adjustment to change in reserve requirements. I see no advantage, however, in signaling in an obscure manner which will be differently interpreted by various sections of the public over signaling in language which is clear and unambiguous to all whenever it takes a restrictive or a relaxing move. In this latter way it would give greater leverage to the "announcement effect" of its moves, and thus lessen the lag between the action and its effect on the economy. I have never been able to see what advantage the Federal Reserve, or the public, derives from permitting all its moves to be surrounded by an aura of mystery, instead of endeavoring to make the objectives of such moves at least as clear to the public as they are to itself. If the Federal Reserve made its changes in reserve requirements more frequent and smaller, as would seem to me to be preferable on other grounds as well if the purpose of such changes was to serve as a flexible instrument of monetary control supplementing open-market operations, there would not be obvious need to lessen their impact through the discount window. I see no other need for rediscounting than that associated with the prevalence of unit banking, which involves the existence of small banks with limited resources and limited access to money-market facilities and makes more significant local differences in the demand for credit and regional differences in the seasonal pattern of demand for and availability of bank credit. But as long as unit banking continues to prevail, rediscounting facilities are needed and should be retained; and their operation as an attraction to small banks to enter the Federal Reserve System also deserves consideration.

If confined to these purposes, rediscounting would always be limited in its over-all dimensions. It is ordinarily so limited in fact. Only a small fraction of the member banks ever rediscount, and only a still smaller fraction are in debt to the Federal Reserve banks at any one time. With the possible exception of one year, the year-to-year and cyclical fluctuations in the indebtedness of member banks to the Federal Reserve have been too small to have been an appreciable influence, for good or ill, on the size of the national stock of money. The temptation to abuse access to the discount window should be thwarted, however, by making the discount rate always a penalty rate, higher than the prevailing rates charged on commercial loans by banks in the relevant Federal Reserve district.

The Federal Reserve does not hold a brief for the use of bank supervision and examination as an instrument of control of the stock of money or its velocity. It defends its retention of supervisory and examining authority over member banks only as a needed control over the potential aberrations of unit banks, in the interest of depositors, of the solidity of the banking system as a whole, and of the individual banks themselves where they are weak or badly managed.

Under its "bills-only" policy, the Federal Reserve, in effect, abstained from any participation in debt management, whether for purposes of price-level stabilization or for any other purpose. I believe that debt management is probably too serviceable a tool of monetary policy to justify such abstention, although the same purpose could be served if the Treasury would, in the interest of monetary management, seek and accept the advice of the Federal Reserve with respect to the maturity and other terms of its issues, while the Federal Reserve confined its own operations on the debt holdings of the public to purchases and sales of bills only in the open market. In either case, the immediate objective would be that as far as practicable in the light of other considerations changes in the maturity and rate structure of the federal debt should be such as support instead of working against the monetary objectives of the Federal Reserve. The minimum of coordination of Treasury policy and Federal Reserve policy that can reasonably be demanded is that prior to any major issue the Treasury should invite the Federal Reserve to submit to it the monetary-management considerations which should play a part in Treasury decision-making.

I have little to say that is relevant to the issues dealt with in this paper with respect to the much-debated question as to whether selective controls of lending operations by banks or non-bank financial institutions should be used. From the point of view of monetary management alone, the case for their use rests on the belief that some important classes of loan operations have a wider amplitude of cyclical fluctuation than other classes, so that they constitute "strategic" sectors for control; that the cyclical pattern of these fluctuations, if left uncontrolled, increases the difficulty of damping the cycle through indirect monetary control over banking operations in general; and that selective direct controls take hold more quickly and therefore have shorter lags in their effects than over-all indirect monetary controls. It is here that the issue of "economic freedom" is most widely raised, and I think most justifiably, in connection with discussion of the appropriate tools for monetary and credit control. The behavior of the stock market during the late 1920's, for which "mass mania" would not be too derogatory a label, suggests at least that there is something to be said against the proposition that the aggregate of atomistically motivated economic decisions of the public at large in a strategic sector should always be accepted by Congress, or by individuals acting in their political role as voters, or by a monetary authority, or by philosophers and economists, as valid collective or social decisions, and should therefore not be interfered with. This raises some questions of practice rather than of principle: If selective controls are to be sanctioned, should they be used as routine measures or only as stand-by power to be applied only in emergencies? Or if their purpose is to serve as a tool of monetary management, should only the decisions as to their mode of use be assigned to the monetary authority, or should it also operate and administer the controls? Presentation of the issues involved suffices for present purposes, and what I would recommend as the appropriate answers in any given situation I neither clearly foresee nor see much reason why anyone, including myself, should regard as a matter of consequence. But they would have to be discretionary decisions.

I am not attempting to write a monetary-management manual, and I am using the availability of a variety of alternative tools of monetary control only as providing illustrative material both for the obstacles which the necessity of choice between tools and of choice as to the combinations in kind and degree in which they are to be used presents to resort to a simple rule. It should suffice for present purposes, therefore, if I conclude my discussion of the problem always present to the Federal Reserve of making the proper choice between the tools which it is authorized to use by a glance at the problems presented by the availability as major instruments of monetary control of both open-market operations and changes in reserve requirements for member banks.

In the modern world at large a wide range of methods of changing reserve requirements in the interest of monetary management is employed or has been proposed. I have been wrongly charged with—or credited with—the invention and advocacy of one particular method: the application of reserve ratio requirements to the cash-to-assets ratio, with different minimum ratios applied for different categories of assets, thus facilitating "selective controls" of credit. Other methods which are used or have been proposed are: variable special deposits with central banks, on which interest is paid; minimum reserve ratios of cash to deposits which rise or fall automatically as the volume of deposits rises or falls; and minimum "liquidity" ratios, where cash and near-moneys are lumped together as reserve assets and compared with the volume of deposits. In the United States the minimum ratio required of cash against demand deposits is the sole important tool of monetary control falling within this class.

The only question I will discuss here is: What are the advantages in the availability to the Federal Reserve of the choice between the use of open-market operations and changes in reserve requirements as against its being restricted to the use of open-market operations?

If, as has happened in the past but is not relevant now and is unlikely to be relevant in the foreseeable future, the Federal Reserve at a time of inflationary pressure is not in possession of sufficient securities of an appropriate kind to conduct large-scale open-market selling operations, availability of a substitute method of reducing the cash holdings of the member banks would be essential. This need not be, however, the power to raise reserve requirements. One alternative would be for the Federal Reserve to borrow from the market or, what amounts to the same thing, to sell its own debentures.

A change in reserve requirements has an immediate impact on the entire Federal Reserve bank membership, whereas the impact of open-market operations is at first concentrated on the great financial centers and its spread through the economy as a whole may be slow. This would ordinarily be regarded as a point in favor of the use of changes in reserve requirements rather than of open-market operations as the instrument of control.

The incidence of the cost of restrictive control operations differs as between open-market operations and changes in reserve requirements. The former affect member and non-member banks alike, other things being equal, whereas the latter put member banks at a competitive disadvantage as compared to non-member banks. Open-market sales reduce the revenues of the Federal Reserve Banks and purchases increase them, whereas changes in reserve requirements do not directly affect their income. Open-market sales affect the market status of federal securities for operations of corresponding scale more than a rise in minimum reserve requirements.

If at a time when restrictive action is indicated the member banks have surplus reserves, increases in reserve requirements will make it possible for the Federal Reserve to make the member banks illiquid without recourse to massive open-market sales.

Appraisals of the significance of these differences in the mode of operation of the two tools will differ from person to person, and perhaps from time to time, as circumstances change. From the point of view of the Federal Reserve, I have no doubt that it welcomes the availability of choice between the two tools, and that it can cite advantages arising from such availability which I have overlooked. The Federal Reserve claims that at the appropriate times recourse to changes in reserve-ratio requirements provides a more conspicuous indication to the banks and the public of Federal Reserve objectives or appraisal of the situation than would open-market operations. I am not sure, however, that this would be true if the open-market operations and the changes in reserve requirements were of corresponding dimensions, and that this judgment is not based on a misreading of past experience resulting from the fact that the Federal Reserve carries on its open-market operations in small doses, whereas its changes in reserve requirements are infrequent and greater in their scale. In any case, it seems to me that the

Federal Reserve can indicate its intentions and its appraisal of an existing situation more clearly and less ambiguously if it uses ordinary language as its means of transmitting information to the public instead of symbolic acts whose significance will be variously interpreted even by experts—and perhaps also by itself.

With respect to the activities which have impacts on the monetary field of federal agencies other than Congress, the Federal Reserve, or the Treasury, the ideal situation from the single point of view of monetary management would be that the Federal Reserve should have some kind of veto power over operations of those agencies which go counter to its objectives. This is, however, impracticable, and the best that can be hoped for is that these other agencies should be instructed by the President or by Congress that as far as is consistent with the performance of the functions assigned to them they should endeavor to avoid acts which do not conform to Federal Reserve policy. Beyond this, the Federal Reserve must accept as part of the facts of life the activities of these agencies which make more difficult its attainment of its own objectives and must endeavor to offset these activities by appropriate measures of its own, in accordance with its best judgment. This also applies to the activities of Congress and the Treasury, although these can be of great enough dimensions to make impossible the full achievement of the Federal Reserve's goals.

I have argued that the nature of economic process, the plurality of goals, the plurality of authorities, the plurality of tools, all of these operate to make impracticable the conduct of monetary management in conformity with a "rule." Consideration of monetary management from the point of view of the possibility of reducing its operations to conformity to the requirements of a single rule has the merit, however, of forcing a re-examination of the validity of its objectives, of the possibility of concentrating authority, and of the inadvisability of extending indefinitely the range of tools used by the controlling agencies. This by-product of the advocacy of reducing monetary management to the application of a single rule can be of great service to the better understanding of how monetary problems can be best handled. But with respect to the issue as between a rule and a discretionary monetary authority, I must close as I began, but now in Aristotle's words rather than my own, substituting only "monetary policy" where Aristotle says "morality":

> Monetary policy lives on details, like all that is practicable and real. Its rules are like the rule of lead of the Lesbians which follows all the turns and contours. Of things which are indeterminate, the rule also needs to be indeterminate.

· X ·

100 PER CENT RESERVE BANKING

GEORGE S. TOLLEY

CHANGES in bank reserve requirements to combat economic fluctuations have received wide attention, but there has been almost no consideration of the long-term level of reserves, except by advocates of 100 per cent reserves.

The following discussion will first review the conditions leading to early proposals for 100 per cent reserves and the main arguments that were advanced for the proposals. The remainder of the discussion will attempt to look in more depth at issues now of major importance, thirty years after the proposals first received wide attention. The first issue concerns the extent to which higher long-term levels of reserves can contribute to battling business fluctuations. The second issue concerns whether or not to pay interest on reserves. The third issue concerns effects of higher reserve requirements on location of financial intermediation.

The primary aim of the discussion is to show what consequences need to be taken into account in formulating policies related to bank reserves. A specific set of policies will be tentatively recommended.

GENESIS OF 100 PER CENT RESERVE PROPOSALS

Stimulus for the idea that fractional-reserve banking should be abolished was provided by experience from 1930 to 1933. During this period more than one third of the banks were forced to suspend payments, even apart from closings on publicly proclaimed bank holidays. People deciding to try to hold their money in the form of coin and paper instead of deposits contributed to the suspensions. Fear of bank failure made them take this action, which in turn made failure more likely. The assets offsetting most of the deposit liabilities of the banks were loans and investments which could be liquidated to raise coin and paper money only with delay, if indeed that could be accomplished at all.

The attempt by people to hold more coin and paper money reduced the total amount of required reserves available to banks. This contributed to the decline in the money supply over and above the relatively small decline due directly to bank failures. The government was the only ultimate source of the additional coin and paper money wanted by the public. In obtaining the coin and paper, the member banks drew down their reserve accounts at the district Federal Reserve banks. Since member banks had to carry only a fraction of a dollar of required reserves for every dollar of deposit liabilities, the public's decision to hold more coin and paper was bound to lead to a contraction of the total money supply unless the loss in member bank reserves could be restored.

Whether or not the Federal Reserve could reasonably have been expected to follow more vigorous policies in supplying reserves to banks, the record remains that the money supply declined substantially. The possibility and profitability of restoring reserves through rediscounting depended on terms acceptable to the Federal Reserve, and even on the most favorable terms commercial banks were hesitant to go into debt when times were so bad. The volume of rediscounting was actually less in the period from 1930 to 1933 than in the twenties. Another way to replenish the member-bank reserves was for the Federal Reserve banks to buy government obligations, so that when the payments cleared the member banks would find that they had larger reserve balances on account with the Federal Reserve banks. The increase in Federal Reserve security holdings from 1930 to 1933 did provide a significant offset to the drain on reserves. However, it was not sufficient to prevent contraction by more than 20 per cent in the total money supply.

Reserve base, money supply, velocity, and gross national product, 1930–1933

(Dollar amounts in billions)

Year	Total reserve base[a]	Concept I: Money supply[b]	Concept I: Velocity[c]	Concept II: Money supply[d]	Concept II: Velocity[c]	Gross national product[e]
1930	$6.6	$25.0	3.6	$54.1	1.7	$90.0
1933	7.7	19.2	2.9	40.8	1.4	55.8
Change	+17%	–23%	–20%	–25%	–18%	–40%

[a] Money in circulation plus member-bank reserves, June 30 figures. Source: *Banking and Monetary Statistics* (Washington: Board of Governors of the Federal Reserve System, 1943), pp. 375–376.

[b] Demand deposits adjusted plus currency outside banks, June 30 figures. Source: *Banking and Monetary Statistics*, p. 34.

[c] Gross national product divided by money supply.

[d] Same as [b], except that total time deposits are also included.

[e] Source: *National Income and Product of the United States, 1929–1950* (Washington: Department of Commerce, 1951), p. 150.

While coin and paper increased by $1 billion, demand and time deposits held by the public decreased about $15 billion. The accompanying table indicates that the decline in gross national product was associated with a slightly greater decline in the money supply than in the velocity of money. If there had been 100 per cent reserves, an increase of the magnitude that occurred in funds available to support the money supply would almost certainly have increased the money supply instead of letting it contract.

For economists who believed in the efficacy of monetary measures, the 1930–1933 experience was convincing evidence that structural reorganization was needed to permit better control of the money supply. Independently, proposals for 100 per cent reserve banking were formulated by Simons, Fisher, Currie, Bostrom, and others.[1] The essence of the proposals was that each dollar of deposit money should be backed by a dollar of reserves instead of a fraction of a dollar. Corresponding to deposit liabilities, there would be only reserves on the asset side of balance sheets instead primarily of loans and investments, as under the prevailing fractional-reserve banking.

As a prelude to considering the 100 per cent reserve proposals in a more modern setting, the main issues that emerged in the thirties may be reviewed. One advantage listed for the proposals was that the likelihood of bank failure would be diminished. Knowing that deposits were backed entirely by reserves readily convertible into coin and paper, people would have little reason to start runs on banks, and runs would create no particular problem even if they occurred. On the other hand, against this advantage there was a need to evaluate the argument that less radical measures such as deposit insurance can have virtually the same effect on public confidence.

As a second advantage of 100 per cent reserves, changes in the public's decisions about the proportion of money they want to hold as coin and paper would not lead to changes in the total money supply. If a dollar of reserves was used to pay out coin and paper money, there would still be reserves for all remaining deposits with no forced multiple contraction of deposits. Against this advantage, counterarguments to be

[1] For a discussion and further references on these proposals, see Albert G. Hart, "The 'Chicago Plan' of Banking Reform," *Review of Economic Studies,* 2:104–116 (1935).

weighed were that (1) with deposit insurance there would be little reason for cyclical shifts between deposits and paper money such as raised problems in the Great Depression, and (2) even though the Federal Reserve authorities may not have always done so in the past, they could undertake open-market operations to counteract the effects of any such cyclical shifts on member-bank reserve accounts.

A third advantage claimed for 100 per cent reserve banking was that it would put control of the money supply more directly in the hands of the Federal Reserve System. From the point of view of present-day desirability, this is the most important consideration that has been mentioned. Under the prevailing system, the banks and their short-term borrowers have a great deal of influence in determining changes in the money supply. This is undoubtedly a greater source of instability in the money supply nowadays than the shifts between deposits and coin and paper money discussed above. Perhaps the main question to be considered in relation to the advantage of having better control over the money supply is how important the advantage is. This involves a long-debated issue: To what extent is control of the money supply effective or desirable in combating economic fluctuations? The relation of 100 per cent reserves to economic stabilization policies will be considered more fully later in this discussion.

A fourth advantage often given in favor of 100 per cent reserves was related to the fact that the Federal Reserve banks would have to acquire securities in order for the member-bank reserve accounts to expand. A transition to 100 per cent reserves could in effect retire a great deal of government debt. Presumably, since the Federal Reserve banks are quasi-public agents, *either* interest might be suspended on the increased holdings of government securities they would acquire, *or*—what would come to about the same thing—any large profits made by the Federal Reserve banks could be turned back to the United States Treasury.[2] So the net effect would be as if this debt were retired. On the other hand, arguments can be made in favor of paying interest on reserves. This would require the Federal Reserve to pay out income received on its securities, nullifying the debt-retirement effect. Choice between these alternatives involves interrelated problems concerning bank earnings, service charges on deposits, and the question of who would take over financial intermediary functions of banks. These problems will be considered later in this discussion.

The first two of the above advantages—lowered risk of bank failures and mitigation of effects of shifts toward hand-to-hand currency in times of low confidence—lost force with establishment of the Federal Deposit Insurance Corporation, which insures every deposit up to $10,000. Since the introduction of deposit insurance, bank failures have been practically nil.

The third and fourth advantages listed above remain to be considered more fully. Present-day consideration of these advantages needs to differ from that of the thirties for several reasons. The existence of the greatly enlarged national debt that came about as a result of World War II makes it more tempting today to resort to higher reserves as a means of reducing the national debt. Even more important, at the time the original proposals were made, avoiding depression was perhaps the prime concern of the nation. Recently, prime concern has shifted from avoiding depression to avoiding inflation and promoting growth and national defense. It will be argued below that this changed environment makes the attaining of government revenues with as few deleterious effects as possible a major consideration. In particular, this consideration militates against paying interest on reserves.

Refinements in thinking by monetary economists since the

[2] When the Federal Reserve acquired large amounts of government securities during World War II, the latter arrangement was adopted.

thirties can contribute to a discussion of bank reserves. Interest elasticity of demand for money is a concept which has received much attention in the intervening years. The advantage of achieving a low interest elasticity of demand for transactions money is the basis for suggesting below that reserve requirements might be abolished for time deposits and raised very high for demand deposits. Another topic of increasing interest to economists in recent years is the role of financial institutions other than banks. This helps to emphasize more than was done in the early discussion of 100 per cent reserves that consideration needs to be given to the effects of higher reserves on lending functions of banks. A result in the following discussion is to suggest the possibility of transferring liability for the money supply completely to the Federal Reserve, so that banks could retain their traditional lending functions. It will be argued that rearrangements of financial intermediation activities accompanying higher reserves would thereby be minimized.

With this brief preview, we may proceed to a fuller presentation of the analysis leading to the suggestions just mentioned.

RESPONSE TO ECONOMIC CHANGE WITH HIGHER RESERVES

Achieving better control of the money supply is the main motivation of present-day advocates of 100 per cent reserves. Under present fractional-reserve banking, if business conditions worsen, demand will decline for the kinds of loans banks are accustomed to accepting. The banks are likely to let their loans run down, so that deposit money is extinguished on the liability side. Profitability considerations militate against the resulting excess reserves, which can be reduced most easily by letting borrowings from the Federal Reserve banks run down.[3] If this is not sufficient to get rid of the excess reserves,

[3] This pattern of loan retardation and contraction of member-bank borrowings at the Federal Reserve is evident for the recession years of 1954,

securities—most often government obligations—can be purchased from the public. These purchases put upward pressure on Treasury security prices.[4] While this makes for over-all credit ease, the fact that the money supply contracts during most recessions without significant changes in excess reserves[5] seems to imply inescapably that the Federal Reserve at times is holding less securities than it would in the absence of recession. If so, it is actually retarding instead of contributing to the credit ease and allowing the recessionary forces to reduce the amount of reserves it supplies to the banking system.

Under most variants of 100 per cent reserve banking, there would be a greater separation between lending activities and money creation than at present. Since the assets offsetting deposit money would consist entirely of reserves, lending now done by banks would have to be carried on by institutions that issued non-money liabilities. When demand for business loans declined during a business recession, these institutions might find—as old loans were paid off and fewer new loans were made—that their deposit balances were accumulating. The loan repayments might still be used to extinguish deposit money if the lending institutions were in debt to the Federal Reserve. Liquidation of rediscounts would tend automatically to decrease the indebtedness to the Federal Reserve banks, simultaneously reducing reserve funds and the money supply by equal amounts. However, the process might be inhibited by the necessity with 100 per cent reserves of having larger changes in indebtedness than

---

1958, and 1960, from the *Federal Reserve Chart Book on Financial and Business Statistics* (Washington: Board of Governors of the Federal Reserve System, April 1961), pp. 3, 4, 9.

[4] These relations of bank holdings of government securities to the level of business activity are analyzed by Robert H. Parks, "Portfolio Operations of Commercial Banks and the Level of Treasury Security Prices," *Journal of Finance*, 14:52–66 (March 1959).

[5] See *Federal Reserve Chart Book*, pp. 4, 6.

at present in order to produce a given movement of the money supply. Large changes in its own accounts might prompt the Federal Reserve to take counteractive measures sooner against privately initiated movements in the money supply than is done now. These considerations indicate that 100 per cent reserves would put Federal Reserve operations in closer relation to the money supply, even if rediscounting were continued.

It is not surprising that 100 per cent reserve schemes have been linked with proposals to abolish rediscounting. Then the only way the money supply could change would be through open-market operations. The initiative for such operations is less directly lodged with short-term business lenders and borrowers. As loans declined during a recession, barring deflationary open-market operations, the lending institutions would find themselves accumulating deposits. They would most likely exchange all or part of these deposits for securities. The deposits would stay with the public, either passing into the hands of persons who would put them back into the income flow or ending up in inactive balances, where at least they would have a salutory effect on liquidity.

The precise effect of higher average reserves on business fluctuations depends on the contracyclical policies that accompany the higher reserves. Proposals for 100 per cent reserves have been linked recently with proposals to have the quantity of money increase at a fixed rate.[6] The quantity of money would then be prevented from varying in response to business disturbances.

With 100 per cent reserves, if the rule of a fixed rate of increase of money supply were not followed, the Federal Reserve could still find itself making deflationary open-market operations in times of recession. Especially if policies

[6] See Milton Friedman, *A Program for Monetary Stability* (New York: Fordham University Press, 1959), esp. pp. 100–101.

were geared to levels of interest rates deemed appropriate or to maintaining a given degree of credit ease, the Federal Reserve might find itself succumbing to the increased demand for securities during recessions on the part of lending institutions. When payment for these securities cleared, the quantity of money would run down, that is, bank reserves and deposits held by the public would decline by equal amounts. Note that this chain of events could occur even if the recession were foreseen and the Federal Reserve allowed bond prices to rise to some extent. The real issue is whether the magnitude of the Federal Reserve's efforts would be great enough to prevent its having a loss of securities. Experience suggests the loss might not be prevented.

However, with 100 per cent reserves endogenous changes in the money supply of the kind just described would probably be smaller than under the present fractional-reserve system. At present, if we illustratively assume that reserve requirements for demand deposits are 15 per cent, 85 per cent of change in a member bank's deposit liabilities can occur as a direct consequence of the bank's own portfolio policy. In a recession, bank portfolio policy results in a more or less automatic concomitant decline in loans and deposit liabilities. Even barring the possibility of the bank's accumulating excess reserves, the Federal Reserve has only to acquiesce to the extent of allowing member-bank reserves to vary 15 per cent as much as the change in deposits. Furthermore, with rediscounting a bank may achieve the desired change in reserves by initiating a change in borrowings at the Federal Reserve to which the latter may acquiesce passively.

A conclusion is that, even in the absence of a rule of increasing the quantity of money at a fixed rate, 100 per cent reserves could make a contribution to combating business fluctuations. While the foregoing illustrations are all given in terms of downside recessionary movements, similar reasoning would also hold for the upside. Following a rule of a fixed rate of increase in the money supply would of course tend to completely eliminate the positive correlation observed in the past between money and business conditions, and the above reasoning suggests that even without such a rule 100 per cent reserves would at least reduce the positive correlation. This is the same as saying that, under either of the foregoing arrangements, monetary policy would be more combative against business declines and expansions at the time they were occurring than is the case under present arrangements. It should be emphasized that this does not guarantee unequivocally that 100 per cent reserves, with or without a rule of fixed rate of increase of the money supply, would be more successful in damping fluctuations. The lagged effects of the policies during downswings might conceivably be such as to reinforce the upswing, and vice versa. In the absence of further objective study, my tentative feeling is that complicated lag effects of this kind would not predominate in the real world. The illustrations given above suggest that under either of the alternatives to present arrangements being considered, financial institutions would find themselves becoming more liquid during downswings and less liquid during upswings than at present. One hypothesis is that if they are going to respond at all to the liquidity change they will do so rather quickly. Delay in response is likely to be due to the assumption on their part that the liquidity change is too small or too temporary to merit a change in portfolio criteria (standards for loans made or securities purchased). It seems doubtful that, if the assumption of temporariness is questioned at some later date, an explicit decision will be made to act as if the change were not temporary just when conditions are about to reverse—or perhaps already have reversed—so as to fulfill the original expectation of temporariness. Only a modicum of correct information about business conditions would be required to reach the right decision in this regard.

While myriad complicated possibilities can be visualized, the hypothesis suggests that the lags relevant in this analysis may not be so complicated, after all. Acceptance of the hypothesis supports the conclusion that adoption of 100 per cent reserves would be likely to reduce business fluctuations.

Up to this point, the discussion has been in terms of higher reserves without specifying anything about possibly paying interest on reserves or about effects of higher reserves on financial intermediation. These issues will be considered more fully later. In the meantime, they need to be anticipated here to the extent of allowing consideration of their relation to response to economic change with higher reserves.

Higher reserves would most likely be associated with acquisition of government bonds by the Federal Reserve. To some extent the government bonds for the increased reserves could be obtained as a result of the banks' reducing their own holdings of government bonds. However, a point would eventually be reached where substantially higher reserves could be achieved only at the expense of such assets as private-sector loans and investments. The banks might create new non-deposit liabilities to offset private loans and investments, using the proceeds to acquire reserves. Or the banks might divest themselves of the loans and investments. Most likely in the latter case, new non-deposit liabilities would be created too. These would be created by the financial institutions acquiring the loans and investments. In either case, after the banks' supply of government securities had been drawn down, an effect of going to higher levels of reserves would be to withdraw government bonds from the non-bank public and at the same time to supply the non-bank public with about an equal amount of new debt instruments which would be the liabilities of banks or of other private financial institutions. To the extent that the new debt instruments were similar to the withdrawn bonds, the total supply of different kinds of debt instruments would not be changed much. It is difficult to do more than guess about the form of the new debt instruments. My guess is that, especially if the banks were the issuing institutions, the new instruments would tend to be somewhat better substitutes for money than the withdrawn government bonds. They might well be essentially interest-bearing deposits not subject to check. Perhaps the main point is that the total supply of different kinds of debt instruments might not change much, but to the extent there was a shift in the direction of closer money substitutes—such as those just mentioned—the stabilization problems about to be considered would be accentuated.

Consider as an extreme example a situation where time deposits were perfect substitutes for near-moneys and demand deposits were held to a minimum that enabled each firm or household to make its check payments. Then with cyclical declines in income, if the money supply (defined to include time deposits) did not decline as much as national income, we might expect a shift into time deposits or near-moneys away from demand deposits. Therefore we would observe declines in velocity accompanied by shifts toward time deposits. The main effect of increasing the supply of money would be to add a little bit to the large stock of near-moneys. Suppose, on the other hand, that money was defined as excluding time deposits. Then, barring changes in customary pay periods, the only possible final outcome would be to raise money income. If demand deposits were used only for recurring payments, it is difficult to visualize any result whereby income would not rise.

If there were 100 per cent reserves for time deposits without payment of interest on the reserves, banks would be at a competitive disadvantage, as compared to other institutions whose liabilities were near-moneys. The other institutions could offer more interest on their near-moneys than the banks could on time deposits because they would have earning assets instead of reserves on the asset side of their balance sheets. Depositors would have no reason to hold time deposits, and we would therefore expect to see their extinction in favor of near-moneys not having the required reserves.

Requirement of 100 per cent reserves on demand deposits would not raise the same problems. If pay periods and other arrangements in transactions were completely fixed, there would have to be a one-to-one correspondence between changes in national income and in the money supply defined as demand deposits plus currency. Failure to pay interest on reserves would confront depositors with an increased cost of holding money because banks would have less earnings on their assets and would therefore have to pay less interest to their depositors (or charge higher service charges where these were levied). In practice there might be some economizing of demand deposits with the higher costs of holding them; for example, shorter pay periods might tend to emerge. But substitutes for accounts subject to check are limited. Taking account of the fact that at present demand deposits are not held as exclusively for current transactions as the above example assumes, a higher cost of holding demand deposits—though it would force an initial substitution toward time deposits and near-moneys—might have the good effect for stabilization purposes of making a sharper distinction in people's holdings between the circulating medium and other debt instruments. Then control of the former could be more effective in combating economic fluctuations.

A possibility that may be tentatively suggested is to drop all reserve requirements on time deposits and require 100 per cent reserves for demand deposits. If no interest were paid on commercial-bank reserve deposits, the acquisition of reserves by the Federal Reserve would be equivalent to a great deal of debt retirement. As will be brought out more fully later, increments to Federal Reserve holdings are tantamount to the proceeds from an implied tax on deposits. If interest were paid, there would of course be no debt-retirement effect, since there would be no interest saving. If interest were not paid on the demand-deposit reserves, the possibility just mentioned might substantially enhance stabilization of the economy. It would also raise a great deal of revenue initially and give increments of revenue with yearly growth in demand deposits. Against these advantages is the disadvantage that a tax on deposits distorts resource allocation. The nature of the misallocation will be discussed presently. In weighing these considerations, it should be noted that virtually every tax has some undesirable effects. Given the fact that taxes are needed to help fight inflation, to undertake education and other investments for growth and national defense, the gains from the deposit tax might outweigh the resource allocation costs. It would be desirable to have estimates of the loss in product associated with the tax in order to weigh the pros and cons.

TO PAY OR NOT TO PAY INTEREST ON RESERVES

As reserve requirements are raised, banks' total income from assets is reduced because the banks are forced to replace earning assets with reserves. They will have a decline in revenue not offset by decline of expenses. If resources in banking are being paid roughly what they could earn elsewhere, the banks will eventually have to make up for the lost income or go out of business. They can be expected to offer less attractive terms to the holders of deposit liabilities. Interest paid on deposits may be expected to go down and possibly become negative, taking the form of service charges. For deposits that already have service charges, the charges can be expected to increase.

Meanwhile the Federal Reserve also experiences income changes. It was noted earlier that to raise required reserve ratios without enforcing contraction of the money supply implies that reserve accounts must increase. This is most likely to be accomplished through open-market purchases by the Federal Reserve. Thus, corresponding to the commercial banks' decrease in earning assets is an increase in holdings of earning assets by the Federal Reserve.

Elsewhere I have said that required reserve ratios impose a tax on deposits.[7] The tax manifests itself in the loss of commercial-bank income on the displaced assets, accompanied by the simultaneous rise in revenues flowing into the Federal Reserve. Under present arrangements, almost all increases in Federal Reserve earnings are turned over to the Treasury.

The nature of the tax may be clarified by contrasting present arrangements with a strict gold standard. If a dollar of gold had to be held for every dollar of checking-account money, banks would need to bill depositors for the full costs of servicing accounts in order to be able to stay in business. However, under present arrangements the amount of deposit money is many times greater than the gold stock. Competition makes banks tend to offer terms on deposits equal to what the banks earn on their assets, less expenses, including costs of servicing the deposits.

Assuming that the difference between return on bank earning assets and terms offered to depositors is competitively determined by cost considerations, an estimate can be obtained of the yearly cost of providing bank-account services. Note first that the return on bank earning assets has been on the order of 2½ per cent of the value of deposits in recent years. Second, the banks pay depositors about zero (an aver-

[7] See my "Providing for Growth of the Money Supply," *Journal of Political Economy*, 65:465–485 (1957).

age between interest received on time deposits and service costs paid on demand deposits). The bank service cost estimate is a residual return to factors of production in banking, 2½ per cent minus zero, or 2½ per cent.

Present required reserves appear to impose a yearly tax of perhaps ½ per cent of the value of deposits. This is an estimate of the increase in earnings of banks, as a per cent of deposits, if banks earned on reserves what they do on earning assets. If it were not for required reserve ratios, the commercial banks could hold additional earning assets and earn 3 per cent of the value of their deposit liabilities and—since servicing costs appear to be 2½ per cent—could pass on ½ per cent to the depositors instead of passing on about zero, as at present.

The foregoing figures are crude estimates from earlier research.[8] While I believe that these tell a large part of the story, some refinements will now be considered that may help lay groundwork for making more accurate estimates.

The analysis just reviewed assumed that the incidence of higher reserves would be entirely on deposit holding. In fact, raising required reserves probably lowers earnings of factors of production in banking so that not all of the effect of higher reserves is passed on to depositors. That is, one effect is probably to reduce bank shareholders' earnings and to create tendencies to provide less remuneration to persons specialized to the banking business. This would be associated with the probable lag in upward adjustment of costs paid by depositors. Where service charges are levied, these would not be raised instantaneously; and where interest is paid on deposits, the rate would be adjusted downward only gradually. Lapses from perfect competition in banking could allow these short-run effects to last in some measure permanently.

There might be some tendency for rates of interest on

[8] *Ibid.*, pp. 477–481.

assets of banks to rise. This would accompany the divesting of assets in order to acquire the reserves. The rise in interest rate would provide another avenue for making up the loss in income due to higher reserves. The previous analysis assumed there would be no effect on interest rates of assets. For highly marketable securities held by banks the previous assumption may be good, but extremely high required reserve ratios might begin to cut into the ability of banks to make short-term business loans, raising rates on them at least until alternative sources of supply developed. Clearly, these effects would depend in part on the precise variant of higher reserves adopted. Under the variant to be suggested in the next section, such effects would be minimal, since that variant is designed to enable banks to continue to follow their traditional portfolio practices. Moreover, the interest-rate effects just noted probably apply to extreme rises in required reserves. For modest rises, the effects may be much less because there may be largely a substitution of reserves for other non-earning or low-earning cash assets. The foregoing calculations may for this reason overestimate the present tax on deposits.

Thus far in this section we have reasoned on the assumption that the present arrangements of paying no interest on reserves would be continued. With higher reserves, the government would have increased revenues from the earnings on assets it acquires. It is these earnings that are the manifestations of proceeds from the tax already mentioned. Zero profit to the Federal Reserve in connection with money-creation, which would be in the direction of a resource-allocation optimum whereby depositors bore only resource costs of money-creation, would be achieved by using the proceeds from the increased earnings to pay the banks for service costs and letting any residual deficit or surplus earnings accrue to depositors in the form of charges or interest payments according to whether the residual was a deficit or a surplus in earnings.

Following a policy of zero profit in money-creation would tend to nullify the effect of reserve requirements on costs of holding money. With low reserves the banks would be holding offsetting earning assets which, after subtraction of service costs, would tend to accrue to depositors because of banking competition. With high reserves, the banks would not have so many earning assets, but the Federal Reserve would now have acquired government bonds in connection with the increase in reserves. If earnings on the bonds were paid out, they would help to make up the loss in earnings of the banks.

If banks and the government held exactly the same kinds of assets, the increased government earnings with higher required reserves would exactly offset the banks' loss, which with perfect competition would leave the depositors' position unchanged. However, one qualification is that the Federal Reserve does not hold just the same kinds of assets as commercial banks. To the extent that banks divested themselves of short-term government securities and the Federal Reserve acquired the same securities, as might be the direct or short-run effect of a modest rise in reserve requirements, then clearly the increase in Federal Reserve earnings would be exactly equal to the banks' decreases in earnings. For somewhat larger increases in reserves, and allowing a longer time for the banks and the Federal Reserve to adjust their portfolios, the Federal Reserve might end up with acquisitions of assets with higher earnings than the banks divested themselves of. The Federal Reserve might, for instance, tend to end up with long-term government securities, whereas the adjustment of the banks might be, as noted earlier, to make offsetting dimunitions of cash assets, with little or no earnings. But for extreme changes in reserve requirements, such as going toward 100 per cent reserves, the point would probably come where the banks would have to divest themselves of mortgages and business loans with substantially higher earnings than the long-term government securities which the Federal Reserve would acquire if it stuck to its traditional portfolio policy.

What are the implications of the fact, discussed in the previous paragraph, that the banks and the Federal Reserve follow different portfolio policies and so would differ in the amount of earnings they could pass on to depositors? In effect, with substantially higher required reserves, the assets offsetting the money supply would be long-term government securities, which earn less than the present offset to the money supply. Therefore, with higher reserves, even if the Federal Reserve paid out the interest earnings on its assets offsetting the money supply, the cost to depositors of holding money could be expected to rise; that is, interest paid on deposits would have to fall, or service charges, where levied, would have to rise. Meanwhile, the liabilities offsetting the assets that formerly offset the money supply could be paid the earnings that were formerly paid to money holders. These liabilities would be substitutes for money, and a conjecture already noted in the preceding section is that they would most likely be close substitutes for money, such as savings-and-loan-type liabilities. So the return on holding money might go down (or the cost up), and the return on money substitutes would go up. We would expect the aggregate amount of money to decline and the aggregate amount of other types of liabilities to rise. But as long as the alternative liabilities were prohibited from being used for transactions purposes, limits to this type of substitution might be reached rather quickly.

The various refinements that have been considered in this section are relevant to discussion of effects of reserve policy in the face of growth of the money supply that has received recent attention.[9] The refinements point to considerations to be taken account of in trying to make precise estimates of effects on bank earnings and other consequences of changing reserve policies. However, when all is said and done, the refinements do not seem to alter the underlying issues involved in choosing the optimum level of reserves and in deciding whether or not to pay interest on these reserves. These issues, as discussed at the close of the preceding section, concern resource allocation in the use of money, sharpness of distinction between circulating medium and other assets, and revenue-raising possibilities of not paying interest on reserves.

BANK RESERVES AND FINANCIAL INTERMEDIATION

Suppose the aim were to raise the average level of reserves with the least dislocation of present institutional arrangements. Legally, all that would be necessary would be to give the Federal Reserve authority to raise reserve requirements without limitation. To prevent the money supply from being unduly affected, Federal Reserve security purchases could be geared to the rise in reserve requirements. In this way, member-bank reserves would be made to grow just enough so that commercial-bank deposit liabilities would not have to undergo deflationary contraction.

In 1960, demand deposits subject to reserve requirements were about $100 billion, against which required reserves were about $15 billion, and time deposits subject to reserve requirements were about $55 billion, against which reserves were about $2.5 billion. Thus, to institute 100 per cent reserves against demand deposits would require purchase by

[9] See, for instance, Joint Economic Committee, *Staff Report on Employment, Growth and Price Levels* (Washington: Government Printing Office, 1959), chap. 9.

the Federal Reserve of about $85 billion in securities, and to include both demand and time deposits would necessitate purchases of about $135 billion. The purchases would be somewhat greater if all commercial banks were brought into the Federal Reserve System, as would probably become necessary. These figures compare with a total of government securities of about $200 billion held in the private sector (outside the Federal Reserve banks, federal government agencies, and trust funds). There would exist enough debt, therefore, so that the Federal Reserve could adhere to its portfolio policy of dealing principally in government securities.

As the reserve requirements began to be raised, with the money supply maintained by open-market purchases, there would be two related side effects having to do with financial intermediation. First, the drain on holdings of government securities throughout the economy would cause these holders to look for good substitutes for the government securities. Second, the banks, as they experienced a rise in reserves with relatively fixed deposit liabilities, would lose their traditional earning assets.

The persons giving up government securities would be demanding about as many securities as the banks were releasing, but many of the released assets—particularly mortgages and business loans—would be less liquid than government securities.

Adjustments would involve changes in the location of financial intermediation functions. Few today consider seriously Henry Simons' scheme to abolish intermediation and let banks become brokers for bringing wealth holders and borrowers together to deal directly with one another. In the absence of such a scheme, as the banks ceased to hold business loans, a growth of other intermediaries could be expected. Personnel concerned with making loans would not be needed by banks, and they would tend to go to work for intermediaries where the growth was occurring. Possibly the main growth would be in savings-and-loan-type institutions, including some that specialized in short-term business loans. The growing institutions would issue liabilities or equities that might be good portfolio substitutes for the withdrawn government securities. The issues might in fact be all too liquid, and legal steps if necessary would be in order to keep them from being subject to check withdrawal or otherwise being used for transactions purposes. The end result of the adjustments might be a structure of portfolios much the same as before the rise in reserves, except that the added supply of liabilities and equities of non-bank intermediaries would replace the withdrawn government securities.

Meanwhile, the banks—having lost their traditional earning assets—would have to find other sources of income. Service charges would have to be raised on deposits unless the Federal Reserve decided to pay interest on the member-bank reserves.

Are there arrangements permitting banks to remain lending institutions that would impose less financial readjusting than described above? Consider first some "halfway-house" proposals. Few initial adjustments would occur under an alternative sometimes mentioned whereby 100 per cent requirements would be initiated by making a gift to the banks of the needed reserves. The Federal Reserve banks would have an increase in their liabilities and a corresponding decline in equity. Since the Federal Reserve banks are quasi-public institutions whose actions are presumably taken in view of the economy at large rather than in view of their own balance sheet, their decline in equity would need have no practical significance. The rise in assets of the commercial banks would be matched by a rise in their equity position. However, their earnings would not be affected by the gift, provided no interest were paid on the gratuitous reserves.

If this proposal were adopted, the real adjustments would take place gradually as the money supply changed after date of initiation. The proposal seems identical in its effects to one that is less extreme from a bookkeeping standpoint. Reserve requirements for the amount of deposits in existence on a given date of initiation would be those prevailing on that date. Any deposits in excess of this would have a 100 per cent reserve requirement.

These proposals represent a halfway house because even without inflation the money supply could be expected to double in less than twenty years. Within this period the banks' earning assets per dollar of deposits would be more than halved, leading to the kinds of effects on location of intermediation and bank service charges described previously. There would be an asymptotic approach to virtual 100 per cent reserves. Starting from a position where demand deposits have reserve requirements of 15 per cent, and assuming growth of the money supply at 4 per cent per year, the result would be 75 per cent reserves by the end of 30 years, and 95 per cent reserves by the end of 50 years. There seems no particular reason to believe that this represents an optimal rate of transition. Another drawback is that potential banks would be at a disadvantage over existing ones, since new banks would have to carry 100 per cent reserves on all deposits.

The gradual rise in service charges, as banks ceased to acquire their traditional earning assets with deposit growth, could be avoided by paying interest on any increases in reserves after the data of initiation. However, it does not appear possible under any variants of the foregoing proposals to avoid the gradual transfer of intermediation to institutions issuing non-bank liabilities.

With 100 per cent reserves, if the commercial banks were to continue to intermediate, they would have to relinquish their money-creation function. Their deposit liabilities would be transferred to someone else, whoever this someone might be. To replace the deposits on the liability side of bank balance sheets, the banks would issue securities which would provide the wherewithal to compensate whoever took over the deposit liabilities.

An early proposal was that commercial-bank deposits should be transferred to the post offices. The banks would issue debentures which would be held as assets by the post offices and would replace the deposits as liabilities of the banks. The banks could then continue to hold the assets to which they are accustomed, carrying on their usual lending activities. One shortcoming of this proposal is that it would involve changes in the way the public handles its money. This might be an obstacle to acceptance of the proposal and would surely increase problems of transition. Another shortcoming is that the government would become the chief creditor of the commercial banks. This might make for difficulty in setting the interest to be paid on the debentures and leave the government open to the charge of either subsidizing or exploiting the banks by the terms accepted on the debentures. Over time there might be a tendency for the government as a creditor to interfere with the lending policies of the banks. Conversely, there would probably be pressure from the banks to vary the amount of debentures according to the demand for loans. This would be particularly true if the method of varying the money supply after date of initiation involved dealings in the debentures. If the government succumbed to bank pressures regarding the amount of debentures, it would be relinquishing the control over the money supply which is one of the main aims of a 100 per cent reserve plan.

The following suggestion appears to avoid the shortcomings just noted. Let the deposit liabilities of the commercial banks be transferred to the Federal Reserve banks. If "reserves" are defined in the usual way, as Federal Reserve liabilities connected with deposit money, there would be 100 per cent reserves in the sense that deposit money and reserves would be identical.

The physical arrangements in the use of money could be continued as at present, located in the commercial banks with servicing expenses paid for on a contract basis by the Federal Reserve banks. This would have the advantage of involving no change in the public's money arrangements, and the problems of transition might be limited mainly to those of accounting, costing, and contract-writing—all of which seem easily surmountable.[10]

In order to prevent the government from becoming the chief creditor of the banks, bank shares or bonds could be marketed to the public. The banks would pay the proceeds to the Federal Reserve in exchange for the latter's taking over liability for the banks' deposits. The Federal Reserve would in turn use the proceeds to add to its government-

[10] Friedman has made a similar proposal, except that liability for deposits would remain with private institutions. His proposal would "require our present commercial banks to divide themselves into two separate institutions. One would be a pure depositary institution, a literal warehouse for money . . . The other institution that would be formed would be an investment trust or brokerage firm . . . Since it would have no power to create or destroy money, monetary considerations would not demand any special control over its activities" (*A Program for Monetary Stability*, pp. 69–70).

After completing my analysis I found that Angell had proposed a plan even more similar to the one being discussed in the text. He proposed "first, the conversion of the present demand deposit liabilities of the commercial banks into similar liabilities of the United States, but backed 100 per cent by currency and administered by the commercial banks as agents; second, the grant to the United States of a lien on the commercial banks' assets equal to the liabilities thus taken over; third, the conversion of the present time and savings deposits of the commercial banks into negotiable serial obligations of varying maturities; and fourth, the virtual stabilization (apart from a relatively slow secular shift) of the total supply of circulating money." See James W. Angell, "The 100 Per Cent Reserve Plan," *Quarterly Journal of Economics*, 50:34 (November 1935).

bond holdings. A way of avoiding the possible chaos of all the banks issuing securities hit or miss would be for the Treasury to market the bank securities to the public in the course of debt-refunding operations. To make them similar to Treasury issues, the bank securities might carry a government-insurance feature. A roughly similar maturity composition might also be maintained. If the public found the bank securities reasonably good substitutes for the maturing government issues, the transition might be made as quickly as issues came due. The rapidity of transition would be dictated by experience with the marketability of the bank securities. The operations would involve the technicality of the commercial banks issuing their securities to the Federal Reserve banks in exchange for the shift of deposit liabilities. Then there would be the further technicality that the Federal Reserve would transfer the bank securities to the Treasury in exchange for government bonds. The latter exchange would be essentially a meaningless intragovernment type of transfer, since the Federal Reserve turns most of its earnings back to the Treasury. These technical exchanges could be made to happen in one day if desired. Finally, the Treasury would market the bank securities to raise funds to pay off maturing government bonds in the hands of the public. The end result would be to reduce the government debt in the hands of the public by an amount equivalent to the new bank issues.

Even though the bank issues were passing through government hands, there would not likely be charges of either subsidizing or exploiting the banks. As the issues were sold to the public, market valuation would quickly be established. During the short time it held the bank issues, the government would attempt to make neither profit nor loss on them.

The suggestion that has been outlined to transfer liability for deposit money to the Federal Reserve is designed to achieve 100 per cent reserves with as little disruption of present arrangements as possible. It has already been noted that commercial banks would continue as investors and lenders, in line with their traditional asset structure. Depositors would continue as customers of commercial banks, and the man in the street would not necessarily be aware of the transition except as he might read about it on the financial page. Suppose a person in Atlanta wrote a check to someone in Philadelphia. Physically, the same events would ensue as at present, but they would have a different legal interpretation. When the check was taken for deposit to a commercial bank in Philadelphia, the credit to the depositor's account would be in the name of the Federal Reserve rather than of the commercial bank, as at present. The Federal Reserve would immediately turn the check over to the commercial bank where it had been deposited and debit that bank's account accordingly. The bank would receive payment on the check when during the clearing process it was honored by a commercial bank in Atlanta. The Atlanta bank would in effect turn the check over to the Federal Reserve, which would simultaneously credit the bank's account and debit the account of the customer who originally wrote the check.

A principal change if the suggestion were followed might be that the commercial banks would no longer need to carry as many cash assets against the contingency of large-scale deposit withdrawals. Large withdrawals would make no essential difference to their operations. The new securities issued by the commercial banks to replace their liability for deposits —the bank shares and bonds referred to earlier—would not be instantaneously callable and so would presumably permit their assets to be less heavily weighted toward liquidity than at present. Adjustments in the direction of less bank liquidity could be avoided by legal primary and secondary reserve requirements against the deposits being serviced by a bank. However, might it not be more desirable to let the liquidity adjustments take place? A commercial bank could make part payment for being divested of its deposit liabilities by drawing down its existing reserve accounts with the Federal Reserve, so that fewer new bank securities would have to be issued. If a bank still had unneeded liquidity after drawing down reserve accounts, remaining cash assets could be shifted in the direction of higher yielding assets. Alternatively, the bank might prefer to use some of the remaining cash assets to further reduce the amount of the new securities outstanding.

The added flexibility, including opportunity to shift toward higher-yielding assets, could help win acceptance of the entire proposal by the banking community. This is a possibly important consideration, since the commercial banks might tend to be chief fomentors of opposition to 100 per cent reserves.

The policy variant that has been proposed would, unlike many variants, continue present physical arrangements in the use of money and allow the commercial banks to carry on their traditional intermediary functions. The suggestion would divest them of liability responsibility for the money supply and leave them only as lending institutions. Many previous suggestions have done the opposite, that is, have reduced banks' lending functions and left them with legal liability for the money supply.

POLICY CONCLUSIONS

Higher bank reserve requirements would help to separate money-creation from the lending business. Largely for this reason, it has been argued above that with higher reserves Federal Reserve policy would be likely to be more effective in combating business fluctuations. The analysis suggests to me that the desirable long-run policy is to go in the direction of 100 per cent reserve banking. What priority this action should receive on the list of things that need to be done is another question. This depends on how great a contribution more effective monetary policies can be in contributing to economic stability and on other broad considerations not taken up in the above discussion. The analysis does not necessarily suggest that lack of 100 per cent reserves is a really pressing national problem.

A sensible once-for-all change in monetary arrangements would be to have the Federal Reserve take over liability for the deposits of commercial banks. The ease of transition from present fractional-reserve banking makes this change particularly attractive. Abolishing reserve requirements on time deposits and imposing 100 per cent requirements on demand deposits would be helpful in differentiating the circulating medium from other assets.

Because the nation's pressing problems include finding the revenues to finance increased levels of government spending, a case can be made for the tax on deposits represented by not paying interest on reserves. The real alternative to this procedure may be inflation, worse taxes elsewhere, or foregoing of desirable or even urgently needed expenditures. Therefore, the gains may be worth the deleterious effects on resource allocation in the use of money.

· XI ·

SOUND MONEY—WHY NEEDED AND HOW OBTAINABLE

WILLFORD I. KING

THOUSANDS of years ago, when civilization and production first advanced to the stage where trade attained some importance, men found it necessary to establish definite *standards* of weight and volume—standards remaining unchanged decade after decade. Today, in all fields except money, such fixity of standards is taken for granted. For example, who would ever consider varying from year to year the size of a bushel or gallon or pound or gram? But in the United States, no other measure is used by so many people and so frequently as is the dollar—and this is the one measure that we have never standardized. In this respect, we are as primitive as the tribes in which trade played such a minor role that no necessity for standardizing weights or volumes had made itself apparent.

What have been some of the effects on the welfare of the people of the United States of this failure to standardize the value of our money unit? Let us first consider a case in which the dollar's purchasing power moved up sharply, or in other words, in which the price level declined markedly.

SOME EFFECTS OF A RISE IN THE VALUE OF THE DOLLAR

Between 1872 and 1896, the general index of wholesale prices in this country declined almost exactly 50 per cent, or, on the average, by almost 3 per cent a year.[1] Now whenever such a decline in the prices of farm and factory products occurs, debts, interest payments, and taxes due from farmers and manufacturers to creditors and government do *not* likewise fall. It is also true that wage rates, being widely governed by custom or by union contracts, are very "sticky" and decline but little. Therefore the net incomes of farmers and factory owners shrink. Furthermore, employers, not being able to cut wage rates, are compelled to lay off their less efficient workers, unemployment mounts, and many of those becoming idle suffer severely from poverty. Because of these factors, a large part of the period from 1873 to 1896 was characterized by "hard times," culminating in a major depression in 1893–94.

FREE SILVER VERSUS THE GOLD STANDARD

This situation brought on the notable campaign of William Jennings Bryan for increasing the money supply by restoring "the free and unlimited coinage of silver," a privilege which had been abolished by Congress two decades previously by legislation that Bryan referred to as "The Crime of '73." His opponent, William McKinley, contended that free coinage of silver would lead to inflation, that "sound money" was essential, and that the one dependable way to keep money sound was to keep the money unit permanently redeemable on demand in a fixed weight of gold. As you all know, McKinley won the Presidency, and redeemability of the dollar in a fixed weight of gold was reaffirmed as the law of the land. Did this consolidation of the gold standard actually stabilize the price level?

[1] See the Warren and Pearson index in U.S. Bureau of the Census, *Historical Statistics of the United States, 1789–1945* (Washington: Government Printing Office, 1949), p. 231. The 3 per cent figure takes account of the effect of compounding.

The answer is clear. The Snyder-Tucker general price index ran up from 79 in 1900 to 193 in 1920, fell to 158 in 1922, rose to 179 in 1929, and dropped to 132 in 1932—all while our nation was on the gold standard.[2] Evidently that standard completely failed to stabilize the purchasing power of the dollar. Why? An important part of the answer is that gold is a marketable commodity, and, as is true of other commodities, its value fluctuates with its supply and with the demand for it.

THE GOLD-RESERVE PROBLEM

The existing legal status of gold, which gives foreign authorities the privilege of demanding and receiving at any time, at the expense of the United States Treasury, an ounce of gold in exchange for $35 of our money, is a hangover from the old gold-standard legislation. Since, in these days of relative gold scarcity and hence of rising prices for the yellow metal, this privilege tends to cause our nation trouble, it should be canceled. If indications should develop that a dollar-redemption policy would facilitate our foreign trade, our Treasury might readily arrange to have stocks of gold and silver constantly available for sale in leading cities abroad. The prices charged would be variable, perhaps being based on the average open-market prices of gold and silver in New York during the latest calendar quarter. A commission would be included which would be large enough to cover operating expenses. Actually, I attach little importance to this idea. The main thing is to free our Treasury from the burden of pegging the price of gold at a constant figure. Such gold-pegging is at best irrelevant and at worst an obstacle to stabilizing the purchasing power of the dollar.

[2] *Ibid.* The Snyder-Tucker index measures the price fluctuations of currently produced goods and services and also of existing property, including securities.

GENERAL PRICE DROPS AND RECESSIONS

That general price declines and recessions tend to go hand in hand is well illustrated by the fact that, between 1920 and 1921, the general wholesale price index dropped 37 per cent, according to data of the United States Bureau of Labor Statistics, and employment in manufacturing declined 31 per cent. Similarly, in the next downward cycle movement—one running from 1929 to early 1933—the wholesale price index fell 37 per cent, while factory employment volume tumbled 45 per cent.[8]

In the absence of adequate experimentation, one is not justified in drawing any positive conclusions concerning the feasibility of reducing the severity of depressions by the use of appropriate monetary action on the part of the federal government. However, in view of the previously mentioned association of falling prices and slumping business, it seems highly probable that if, whenever the advent of a wave of pessimism caused business activity and prices to start downward together, the federal monetary authorities acted vigorously to support the price level, the prospective recession would either be checked or at least have its degree of severity decidedly lessened. The experiment is certainly worth trying, for depressions bring hardship to millions of worthy people.

SOME EFFECTS OF A SHRINKAGE IN THE VALUE OF THE DOLLAR

In considering the untoward effects of dollar-value instability, we have thus far confined our attention to the ills resulting from *falling* price levels—from enlargement in the value of the dollar. However, as it happens, the prevailing tendency within the lifetimes of the majority of us has been

[8] *Statistical Abstract of the United States, 1934* (Washington: Government Printing Office, 1934), pp. 284 and 304.

for the price level to rise. Has this decline in the purchasing power of the dollar been large enough to be of real significance? Official government figures give the answer. Between 1939 and August 1960, the consumer price index of the Bureau of Labor Statistics more than doubled, advancing 113 per cent; in other words, the dollar has lost 53 per cent of its purchasing power over consumer goods and services. Creditors who, over this entire time period, have held long-term obligations payable in fixed amounts of dollars have lost more than half of the real value of these assets and of the income due on them. Such losses receive far less attention in dramatic headlines than do robberies and embezzlements, but they are far greater in amount.

But someone may suggest that what creditors lose in this way their debtors gain, so that the net effect on the nation is zero. It would be equally true—and equally unsatisfying—to suggest that stealing is not antisocial, since the losses of the victims are completely offset by the gains of the thieves. That this conclusion would be the opposite of that arrived at by leaders of thought throughout the ages is evidenced by the ethical laws of all religions and the statute laws of all civilized nations.

Thinkers everywhere have noted the fact that, except for occasional gains resulting from inventive genius, practically all economic advancement is the product of thrift and resulting capital accumulation, and hence that it is socially desirable to penalize practices discouraging saving and hindering the productive use of property. How this general principle works out in practice is illustrated by the following example.

While taxes are burdensome in the United States, it fortunately still remains true that the typical resident continues to have disposal over the major part of his income and the privilege of deciding what fraction of this part, if any, he will save. His desires for current conveniences and luxuries commonly far exceed any amount left over after paying for taxes and necessities. The amount and form of investment of any saving he may do depend partly upon the size of the reward which he believes to be obtainable. He may consider buying a corporation bond yielding 4½ per cent. But if he concludes that shrinkage in the value of the dollar is likely to reduce his real income from it by more than one half, his enthusiasm for such an investment is not likely to be great. If millions of potential investors in corporate obligations arrive at similar conclusions, the amount of capital which corporations can raise by issuing bonds or notes is curtailed, and the rate of growth of industrial output may be reduced. It follows that failure on the part of the federal government to prevent deterioration in the purchasing power of the dollar injures the public in general and hence is a weakness the elimination of which should be favored by all good citizens.

Now let us consider another situation which illustrates the fact that shrinkage in the purchasing power of the dollar has produced results conflicting both with our code of ethics and with our economic welfare. Consider, for example, a man who, in his productive years, accumulated a sizable amount of property. He died; and his widow, seeking maximum safety, sold such assets as were marketable and put the proceeds into a savings bank at the going rate of interest. But during the 21-year period from 1939 to 1960, the dollar's shrinkage in value was 53 per cent, or an average of over 3 per cent a year. So the widow's loss in real capital at least equaled her interest receipts. When she spent these receipts, she was, probably unwittingly, using up her capital. Perhaps she also inherited a pension or an annuity from her late husband. Its purchasing power was shrinking at a rate averaging over 3 per cent yearly. The widow's assets and income were shrinking much as if they had been subjected piecemeal to outright confiscation.

The next question to be considered is the nature and origin of the forces which have produced these antisocial results.

WHY THE DOLLAR-VALUE SHRINKAGE IN THE LAST TWO DECADES?

If the typical well-educated citizen is asked what has caused this long-continued rise in the price level, he is likely to reply without hesitancy, "Inflation, of course." This glib answer is, by itself, usually sufficient to prove that the person giving it is unfamiliar either with the basic principles of monetary economics or with the historical facts.

The equation of exchange presented by Irving Fisher in his monumental treatise *The Purchasing Power of Money* (New York: Macmillan, 1911) included symbols for the quantities and velocities of currency and demand deposits taken separately. To simplify and shorten the equation, I have long used the symbol M'' to represent the average amount of circulating medium, including both currency and demand deposits, and V'' to cover their combined annual rate of turnover, or velocity of circulation. In my condensed form, just as in Fisher's original equation, P equals the general price level, and T the total volume of trade for the year, so the equation may be expressed either as $M''V'' = PT$ or as $P = M''V''/T$.

The figures appearing in the accompanying table represent the results of my computations with data for the years 1939 to 1959. What, if anything, do these figures show concerning the forces responsible for the marked rise in the price level in the period under consideration? To what extent was inflation a factor?

Before answering this question, we must be sure that we

Estimates of the terms in the equation of exchange (each expressed as index numbers on the base 1939) and significant ratios derived therefrom[a] (United States: 1939–1959).

Year	Circulating medium[b] (M'')	Velocity of circulation[c] (V'')	Payments volume[d] ($M''V''$ or PT)	Physical volume of trade[e] (T)	General price level[f] (P)	Index of inflation or deflation (M''/T)
1939	1.000	1.000	1.000	1.000	1.000	1.000
1940	1.140	0.919	1.048	1.076	0.974	1.059
1941	1.348	0.947	1.276	1.202	1.062	1.121
1942	1.658	0.898	1.489	1.295	1.150	1.280
1943	2.275	0.797	1.813	1.450	1.250	1.569
1944	2.822	0.720	2.032	1.532	1.326	1.842
1945	3.308	0.663	2.192	1.562	1.404	2.118
1946	3.375	0.693	2.340	1.553	1.507	2.173
1947	3.194	0.791	2.525	1.533	1.647	2.083
1948	3.219	0.868	2.794	1.569	1.781	2.052
1949	3.199	0.854	2.731	1.535	1.779	2.084
1950	3.329	0.933	3.106	1.691	1.837	1.969
1951	3.544	0.986	3.494	1.729	2.021	2.050
1952	3.746	1.001	3.751	1.784	2.103	2.100
1953	3.807	1.045	3.980	1.857	2.143	2.050
1954	3.875	1.099	4.257	1.898	2.243	2.042
1955	4.023	1.134	4.564	2.023	2.255	1.989
1956	3.991	1.231	4.912	2.115	2.323	1.887
1957	4.017	1.305	5.244	2.125	2.397	1.890
1958	4.057	1.311	5.320	2.121	2.462	1.913
1959	4.181	1.415	5.929	2.280	2.566	1.834

[a] All ratios in this table are based upon data appearing in the *Federal Reserve Bulletin* or the *U.S. Survey of Current Business*.

[b] Includes demand deposits and money outside banks.

[c] Payments volume divided by circulating medium.

[d] Derived from the sum of reported bank debits, wages and salaries paid, retail sales of nondurable goods, local transit revenues, and personal expenditures for housing, personal service, and recreation.

[e] An average of relatives weighted respectively as follows: physical volume of sales at wholesale, 65; at retail, 100; of farm products, 40; units of securities, 22; physical production in mining and manufacturing, 60; transportation and electric services, 27; construction, 20; hours worked, 80.

[f] A weighted average of price-relatives given the following weights: wholesale, 70; retail, 105; securities, 19; freight, 8; wages and salaries, 80.

define that term appropriately. As the Committee on Economic Accord, made up of about a hundred leading economists, long ago indicated, it is illogical to apply the term "inflation" either to a rise in the price level or to a mere enlargement of the quantity of circulating medium. Correctly used, that term signifies that M'', the aggregate of currency and demand deposits, is increasing *faster* than T, the volume of trade—in other words, that the ratio M''/T is growing larger. The facts for the period we are considering are shown quantitatively by the figures appearing in the last column of the table. They bring out very definitely the fact that while inflation was rampant in the period from 1939 to 1946, in the years since the latter date, the Treasury and the Federal Reserve have cooperated so effectively in preventing inflation that the index has sagged from 2.173 in 1946 to 1.834 in 1959. This 13-year period was, therefore, characterized by mild *de*flation! Nevertheless, between 1946 and 1959, P, my comprehensive index of the general price level (taking account not only of wholesale and retail prices but also of freight rates, wages and salaries, and security prices), moved up from 1.507 to 2.566, or by 70 per cent. What was responsible for this advance? Reference to the third column of the table gives the answer. V'', the velocity of circulation of our media of exchange, rose from 0.693 in 1946 to 1.415 in 1959, a growth of 104 per cent. So the real reason that the price level rose was that the average dollar was doing more and more money work. The continued growth of buying on credit plays a part in the explanation. But there is little basis for predicting either a continuation or a reversal of the postwar uptrend in velocity. Policy-makers should remain alert to changing trends.

The facts just presented show that prevention of inflation will not in itself necessarily prevent deterioration in the purchasing power of the money unit. What other procedures are necessary if that ultraimportant goal is to be attained?

MATTERS TO BE CONSIDERED WHEN PREPARING A DOLLAR-STABILIZATION PROGRAM

Since $P = M''V''/T$, the size of P evidently varies directly not only with M'' but also with V'', and inversely with T. Does it not then follow that we cannot hope to attain stability in the value of the dollar unless the federal government exercises effective control over both the rate of turnover of money and the volume of trade?

The answer to this query is a decided "No." Direct regulation either of the volume of trade or of the velocity of circulation of currency and bank deposits would necessitate the abrogation of economic freedom and its replacement by government control of transactions in general. The value of P can be stabilized by regulating the size of any *one* of the three factors on the other side of the equation. Fortunately, controlling M'', the volume of currency and demand deposits, to the extent necessary to stabilize P, thus keeping the dollar's value on a horizontal trend year after year and decade after decade, appears to be perfectly feasible.

However, attainment of this goal would not give the *maximum* social benefit attainable by proper regulation of the size of M''. The symbol P represents a very inclusive index of prices. Included in this aggregate are government services, the real worth of which is not susceptible of numerical measurement, and also vast amounts paid for labor, for stocks of corporations, and for real estate. In a progressing economy, it is to be expected that prices in all three of these latter categories should climb.[4] Therefore, those of

[4] In particular, it seems quite acceptable that rising productivity and real wages should find expression in rising money wages rather than in a falling consumer price index. To aim at the latter would be asking for trouble, especially considering the facts that have been made so familiar in discussions of whether even a stable price level is compatible with sustained high-level employment.

I cannot explore here the problem of a possible tendency for wages to be pushed up faster than average labor productivity, nor do I have space to

us who seek to stabilize the value of the dollar should aim at keeping constant its general command over goods commonly purchased for purposes of consumption. The Bureau of Labor Statistics now provides an excellent index of the average of prices charged consumers. Keeping this index from departing markedly or for any long period of time from a horizontal trend is clearly the proper goal to be sought.

This consumer price index tends to fluctuate materially less than does the index representing P. Manipulating M'', the total volume of circulating medium, will therefore control the former index more readily than would be true of an index P.

We now come to the fundamental question: how must the policies of the federal government be modified if a horizontal trend for the consumption-goods price index is to be maintained?

THE EMERGENCY PROBLEM

Anyone familiar with the behavior of prices in our nation throughout its history knows that the major instances of rapid advances in the indexes have been due to wars. At such times, federal expenses run up by leaps and bounds, while tax receipts do not rise comparably. The usual practice has been to obtain the additional funds needed for war expenses by printing paper money, borrowing from the banks, or both. This procedure boosts M'' and makes the price level move up rapidly.

Since experience to date gives us little reason to hope that we will have no future wars, it seems improbable that permanent stabilization of consumption-goods price averages

justify my judgment that acceptance of creeping price inflation is no answer. Monetary policy is extremely important, but it is not the answer to all economic ills.

can be attained unless and until most of the persons responsible for federal financial policies come to realize a basic truth, namely, that no war can be fought with men, arms, or supplies drawn from the future. All must come from presently existing stocks and from current production. Therefore, all that federal borrowing in time of emergency accomplishes is to postpone the time for deciding which class of taxpayers is ultimately to bear the burden.[5]

When large additional revenues are needed to finance a war or some other grave emergency, the federal government should obtain them by levying excise taxes upon purchases of all goods except basic necessities sufficiently high to cover all needed expenditures. To make sure that such a policy would actually be followed, it might be desirable to enact a constitutional amendment forbidding the federal government to incur any debt payable more than a few months later, and thus compel Congress, not only under ordinary conditions but also in time of emergency, to decide how all government expenses should be *currently* allocated among the various classes of our people. One great advantage of a financial policy that eliminated tendencies toward general price increases, and also generated no pressures for price and wage controls, would be the avoidance of the notorious inefficiencies that such direct controls tend to cause. Clearly, such a policy would not be followed in time of emergency unless preceded by a long and widespread campaign of educating legislators, public officials, and the electorate. Therefore, the danger of dollar-value shrinkage after emergencies is likely to remain great.

[5] This statement is not meant to deny that debt financing can to some extent shift the burden of waging war onto certain members of future generations, since those members of the current generation who are induced by the attractiveness of government bonds *voluntarily* to surrender current command over goods and services are not bearing a financial "burden" in any ordinary sense of the word.

REQUISITES FOR SECURING DOLLAR-VALUE STABILITY IN NORMAL TIMES

The likelihood of making real progress toward keeping the value of our dollar stable is materially greater in normal times. What steps are necessary to attain this end? Some economists favor simplifying our armory of policy weapons by establishing a new monetary authority to control the price level. On the other hand, there is much to be said against disturbing people by unnecessary changes in established practices and institutions. This consideration also speaks in favor of relying on cooperation between the Federal Reserve and the Treasury rather than insisting on the theoretical tidiness of a single bureau. The main thing is to choose the proper goal of monetary policy; within a considerable range, administrative details are a secondary matter.

First, Congress should be induced to pass a law designating the last officially compiled average of the prices of consumption goods as the base of an index, and terming that base 100. The new statute should make it *a mandatory duty* of the Secretary of the Treasury and the Federal Reserve Board to cooperate to keep the consumption-goods price index permanently on a horizontal trend, and to reduce variations therefrom to a minimum. At present, neither has any such duty definitely specified by law. Their actions in this field have been based primarily upon their feeling of devotion to the public weal. Apparently they have thus far considered that they have performed their duties well when they have prevented inflation (that is, when they have kept M'' from growing faster than T). Certainly they have not stabilized the index of the prices of consumption goods. Perhaps present limitations on their powers make such an accomplishment unfeasible. To secure such dollar-value stabilization, what are some of the important facts and forces which they must consider when they plan their actions, and what methods must they use in exercising their regulatory functions?

At present, our circulating medium is made up of hardly more than one-fifth currency and almost four-fifths demand deposits. As we are well aware, most sizable banks are members of the Federal Reserve System and are required by law to keep on hand in cash or on deposit at the Federal Reserve Bank in their district required percentages of reserves against all of their demand deposits outstanding—liabilities which largely originate in loans to customers. A member bank may, when necessary, bring its reserves up to the required level by borrowing temporarily at its Federal Reserve Bank. The Federal Reserve authorities have legal authority to adjust from time to time both the interest rate on such borrowings and the required reserve percentages of member banks. By lowering either or both of these figures, the Reserve authorities can facilitate lending by member banks, and thus promote an expansion of demand-deposit volume, which will tend to stop any decline in the price level and in business activity. Experience shows, however, that in times of extreme pessimism, would-be borrowers who are safe risks may be too few in number to make these measures effective. As some economist once put it, "Pushing on the lines won't make the horse go."

Vigorous use of adjustments in the Federal Reserve discount rate and in reserve requirements can presumably be more effective in combating inflation than in combating deflation and extreme pessimism. Since 1946, the Federal Reserve has been able to keep the quantity of circulating medium from outrunning the volume of trade, though it did not exercise its powers vigorously enough to offset the increase in velocity of circulation and thus did not prevent a considerable rise in the price level. Whether the Federal Reserve could have done so, I do not know.

If Federal Reserve powers did prove inadequate to keep the consumer price index from rising, it appears that Congress should authorize the Secretary of the Treasury to impose upon every commercial bank a monthly tax upon any *increase* in its volume of demand deposits. The rate of this tax should be set monthly by the Secretary of the Treasury, being raised if the current index of the prices of consumption goods stood above 100 and reduced to zero whenever that index fell below 100. It seems probable that the levying of such a tax would keep the index in question from ever running much above par.

However, should experience prove that the measures just discussed were inadequate to keep the consumption-goods price index at par, recourse should be had to open-market operations. The effectiveness of such operations depends upon the fact that bonds do not circulate as money, and hence that an increase in the volume of government bonds outstanding has practically no tendency to raise the price level. So when other measures fail to stop a stubborn rise in the above-mentioned price index, the Treasury Department should sell to private buyers at the best prices obtainable a special type of federal bond, upon whose security it would be illegal for banks to lend money, and which banks would be forbidden to own. None of the money or bank credit received in payment for these bonds should be spent by the government. All should be impounded and held for use in bond buying if the consumption-goods index later fell below par. If found necessary or desirable, these special federal bonds could be made callable.

Now, let us consider the steps necessary to prevent the consumer price index from falling below par in periods of pessimism. If and when this happened, the Federal Reserve would have to lower bank reserve requirements and reduce rediscount rates. If these measures failed to bring the consumption-goods index up to par, the Treasury, the Federal Reserve banks, or both, would have to buy government bonds in the open market, paying for them with paper money or with checks on the Federal Reserve banks. This process would be continued until the index rose to par. No forecasting would be necessary. Experimentation would soon show the extent of operations necessary to attain the desired goal. An incidental benefit of bond purchases to resist deflation would be a slight reduction of interest payments on the national debt.

It would obviously be impossible for any system to secure absolute stability in the consumption-goods index, for it takes time to collect the data and compute the price index, and later to engage in the operations indicated thereby; hence, lately, some economists have been greatly intrigued by a supposed problem of lags—lags in the diagnosis of expansionary and contractionary pressures and lags in the effectiveness of policy reversals. They have therefore contended that there is an attendant need to *forecast* in order to "lean against the wind" successfully. Otherwise, they foresee danger of error and of intensifying, rather than moderating, economic instability. They therefore consider it highly desirable to discover sensitive indicators which are capable of detecting upward or downward pressures that will show up later in the consumer price index. Prompt action to correct these pressures would, as they see it, be important.

However, as I see it, the variations in the consumption-goods price index likely to occur in the period before remedial action can take effect are not likely to be large enough to arouse much interest. Investors worry about long-time price trends—not about deviations which they know will soon be corrected. So forecasting of the type discussed would be interesting, and if successful, would be helpful, but by no means essential.

Under the policy I have outlined, we would have a standardized sound dollar. Neither creditors nor debtors would have to stand in dread of being ruined by forces for which they had no responsibility. Public-utility rate regulation would be simplified. Long-term contracts, such as life-insurance policies and annuities, could be made with confidence. Provided the average hourly earnings of labor were not pushed up faster than average hourly productivity, mass unemployment would not occur. Should not every one of us who understands the importance of stable money take pride in playing a part in attaining this goal?

· XII ·

STABLE MONETARY GROWTH

RICHARD T. SELDEN

IN the annals of monetary theory, 1936 is usually associated with John Maynard Keynes and his *General Theory of Employment, Interest, and Money*. Perhaps this is just, since a great deal of our time and energy in the past quarter-century has been devoted to issues of theory and policy raised in Keynes's classic. However, 1936 was also distinguished by publication of another, though much briefer, work—Henry Simons' "Rules versus Authorities in Monetary Policy." [1] In my judgment, monetary controversies of the future—at least in the United States—will turn much less on problems raised by Keynes than on the problem stated in Simons' title, the problem of the extent to which *discretionary* monetary-fiscal policies, rather than predetermined rules, should be used in the quest for economic stability.

The rules-discretion debate is only the latest form taken by a monetary discussion that has been going on for at least a century and a half. Broadly speaking, those who uphold the rules approach are lineal descendants of those who argued for restoration of gold, against the advocates of monetary nationalism, after World War I; those who argued for adoption of Peel's Act in 1844, against the Banking

[1] *Journal of Political Economy*, February 1936; reprinted in Henry C. Simons, *Economic Policy for a Free Society* (Chicago: University of Chicago Press, 1948).

School; and those who argued for restraint in the issuance of Bank of England notes, in opposition to the antibullionists, during the Napoleonic Wars. Each of these earlier controversies added an important increment to monetary knowledge: the necessity for establishing public control over the volume of a fiat money; the similarity between currency and deposits; and the superiority of fiat money, in a nationalistic world, to commodity money. The monetary question now before the world is: How can monetary policy make its greatest contribution to economic stability, by emphasizing or minimizing central-bank discretion?

The challenge put forward by Simons was that discretionary manipulation of money by central banks is inappropriate—politically as well as economically, although only the latter criterion shall concern us here. He and his close colleague at the University of Chicago, Lloyd Mints, favored adoption of a rule that the central bank be required to buy or sell government securities whenever a broad index of prices moved outside a specified narrow range.[2] However, both Simons and Mints mentioned several other monetary rules that in their opinion would yield better results than could be expected under a discretionary policy. The important thing in their minds was that *some* rule be adopted; they were not disposed to spend much time arguing over which one would be best.

Among the rules ranked high by Simons and Mints was growth in the stock of money at a constant rate equal to the past long-term growth rate of real national income. This proposal, which in one form or another has been taken up by Clark Warburton, Milton Friedman, and others, seems likely to emerge as the Rules Party's candidate in the continuing contest with monetary discretion. The comments that follow

[2] Lloyd W. Mints, *Monetary Policy for a Competitive Society* (New York: McGraw-Hill, 1950), pp. 224–225; and "Symposium on Fiscal and Monetary Policy," *Review of Economic Statistics*, May 1946. See also Simons, *Economic Policy for a Free Society*, pp. 174–175.

represent an attempt to explain the stable monetary growth proposal and to evaluate it both absolutely (how well would it work?) and relatively (is there a better policy?).

FRIEDMAN'S PROPOSAL

Milton Friedman's proposal that United States monetary policy consist solely of steady accretions to the quantity of money at a rate of about 4 per cent per year—regardless of season or cycle stage—is a natural outgrowth of his early training and his recent research. As a student of Mints and Simons, he has long been a critic of discretionary monetary policy. In 1948 he presented a monetary-fiscal proposal designed to eliminate nearly all central-bank discretion: the stock of money would be increased or decreased only in response to automatically generated deficits and surpluses in the federal budget, designed to be in balance whenever some agreed-upon high level of employment was attained.[3]

Friedman still thinks highly of his budget proposal. However, the research which he and Anna J. Schwartz have been conducting at the National Bureau of Economic Research on the behavior of money has convinced him that stable monetary growth would also be feasible, and that it would be simpler and easier to implement.[4] The first published indication of this modification in Friedman's approach to monetary policy came in a footnote to a paper he delivered at the National Bureau's conference on consumer credit regulation, in 1956:

> Subsequent research on monetary experience leads me to go even farther than I did in ["A Monetary and Fiscal Framework"]. On the one hand, this research has strengthened my confidence

[3] "A Monetary and Fiscal Framework for Economic Stability," *American Economic Review*, June 1948; reprinted in Milton Friedman, *Essays in Positive Economics* (Chicago: University of Chicago Press, 1953).

[4] This research is described in recent annual reports of the National Bureau.

in the efficacy of the policies there proposed; on the other, it has led me to believe that even a much less sophisticated monetary policy—namely, simply providing for a steady increase in the stock of money year by year—would be consistent with a high degree of stability and might therefore be preferable on grounds of ease of public understanding and administrative operation.[5]

In 1958, Friedman enlarged on these comments in his contribution to the Joint Economic Committee's compendium, *The Relationship of Prices to Economic Stability and Growth.*[6] There he revealed for the first time some of his major findings on the relation between monetary changes and business fluctuations, together with policy implications as he saw them. His critical finding was the existence of long and variable lags between shifts in the rate of change of the money stock and their effects on the economy. Because of these lags he concluded that discretionary policy cannot succeed, except by chance, even if initiated promptly and based on correct analyses; more often than not such policies will become effective only after they are no longer appropriate. Furthermore, the argument applies with equal force to the price-level stabilization proposal of Simons and Mints and to commodity-reserve proposals.

Friedman supplemented these views in two appearances before the Joint Economic Committee in 1959 and in his Fordham University Lectures, published early in 1960.[7] In these works he reaffirmed his belief in the desirability of 100 per cent reserves for commercial-bank deposits. Friedman

[5] Board of Governors of the Federal Reserve System, *Consumer Instalment Credit* (Washington, 1957), vol. 2, pt. 2, p. 76.

[6] "The Supply of Money and Changes in Prices and Output," in U.S. Congress, Joint Economic Committee, *The Relationship of Prices to Economic Stability and Growth*, Compendium of Papers Submitted by Panelists, March 31, 1958; subsequent references to this volume will be to "Compendium."

[7] U.S. Congress, Joint Economic Committee, *Employment, Growth, and Price Levels*, Hearings, May 25 and October 30, 1959; *A Program for Monetary Stability* (New York: Fordham University Press, 1960).

also called for freely fluctuating exchange rates, elimination of Federal Reserve discounts and advances, repeal of present limitations on payment of interest on deposits, repeal of existing gold and silver legislation and reserve requirements of Federal Reserve banks, and the payment of interest on deposits at Federal Reserve banks. Needless to say, he would ban selective credit controls, such as the power to set margin requirements on securities purchases. It is also clear that Friedman opposes any attempt to deliberately manipulate the federal budget for the purpose of offsetting business fluctuations.[8] Thus, for Friedman, stable monetary growth is the central feature of a comprehensive program of reform.

WARBURTON'S PROPOSAL

Clark Warburton arrived at stable monetary growth as the best monetary policy more than a decade before Friedman. Like Friedman, Warburton reached this conclusion only after painstaking empirical studies.[9] Unlike Friedman, however, he did not begin with an ideological predisposition to any particular approach to monetary policy.[10]

As a staff member of the Division of Research and Statistics of the Federal Deposit Insurance Corporation since 1935, Warburton has developed his position essentially as a by-product of his official duties. The FDIC wanted to find out why business recessions turn out to be severe from time

[8] For instance, see his comments in Compendium, p. 255.

[9] Warburton has presented the principal results of these studies in the following articles: "Normal Production, Income, and Employment, 1945 to 1965," *Southern Economic Journal,* January 1945; "Monetary Theory, Full Production, and the Great Depression," *Econometrica,* April 1945; "The Volume of Money and the Price Level between the World Wars," *Journal of Political Economy,* June 1945; "Quantity and Frequency of Use of Money in the United States, 1919–45," *Journal of Political Economy,* October 1946; "Bank Reserves and Business Fluctuations," *Journal of the American Statistical Association,* December 1948; and "The Secular Trend in Monetary Velocity," *Quarterly Journal of Economics,* February 1949.

[10] Warburton's unpublished paper, "Testing a Hypothesis," is a valuable source of information on the development of his thinking in relation to monetary policy. The following two paragraphs rely heavily on this paper.

to time; it was known that bank failures and losses to depositors occurred primarily on these occasions. Warburton undertook a broad program of research designed to throw light on this question. It was not until 1942 that he began the phase of this research that led him to stable monetary growth. This involved the study of cyclical changes in the stock of money and its velocity and the role of central-bank policy in these changes. In two important respects Warburton's findings were contrary to initial expectation. First:

> Scrutiny of . . . quarterly measures of quantity and circuit velocity of money, adjusted for trend, showed that the quantity of money led and its circuit velocity lagged at the turning points of business cycles. In fact, the departure in the quantity of money from a reasonable rate of growth occurred during the preceding boom phase of the cycle, and thus not only preceded a reduction in the rate of use of money but also the top of the boom. It was these observations which led to the emphasis . . . on an erratic money supply as the chief originating factor in business recessions and not merely an intensifying force in the case of severe depressions.[11]

Second, it became apparent to Warburton that departures of the money stock from "a reasonable rate of growth" were not in any significant degree the result of the decisions of businessmen or banks; rather, they resulted largely from actions of the monetary authorities.[12]

The policy implications of these findings were clear. The monetary authorities should be instructed by the legislature to aim at stable growth. Initially, Warburton set the appropriate growth rate at about 5 per cent per year—3.67 per cent to allow for rising income, because of population growth and increases in productivity, and 1.33 per cent to offset the secular decline in the velocity of money. Later he conceded

[11] "Testing a Hypothesis," p. 12.

[12] *Ibid.*, pp. 12–13. See also his "The Misplaced Emphasis in Contemporary Business-Fluctuation Theory," *Journal of Business of the University of Chicago*, October 1946; reprinted in American Economic Association, *Readings in Monetary Theory* (Philadelphia, 1951), pp. 309–311.

that the 4 per cent figure suggested by Friedman might be more nearly correct, but he is not greatly concerned over the precise number: "Pending improvement of the basic data, we may use either 4 or 5 per cent per year as a reasonable approximation to the requisite rate." [13]

COMPARISON OF THE FRIEDMAN AND WARBURTON PROPOSALS

It is not clear whether one should be more impressed with the differences or the similarities of the Friedman and Warburton proposals. In contrast to Simons and Mints, both came to stable monetary growth only after prolonged empirical study, and both emphasize pragmatic, as against doctrinal, considerations. As Friedman has said, "This seems to be about the best we know how to do with our present knowledge." [14] Another point of similarity is that neither advocates rigid adherence to stable monetary growth, regardless of results. According to Warburton, "The legislative instructions to the monetary authorities should provide for frequent review of the results of action under the foregoing rule, and for such modification of the previously calculated rate of increase in the quantity of money as may be needed for maintenance of stability in the value of money." [15] And in Friedman's words, "We are not going to avoid looking at what happens. In the course of five or ten years I would hope that we would learn more and might be able to do better. I do not mean to suggest that this is a be-all and end-all for all time." [16]

On the other hand, Friedman and Warburton disagree on

[13] "How Much Variation in the Quantity of Money is Needed?" *Southern Economic Journal*, April 1952, p. 500.

[14] *Employment, Growth, and Price Levels*, Hearings, October 30, 1959, p. 3051.

[15] "Rules and Implements for Monetary Policy," *Journal of Finance*, March 1953, p. 8.

[16] *Employment, Growth, and Price Levels*, Hearings, October 30, 1959, p. 3051.

a number of points, not all of which are trivial. A brief and partial listing follows:

1. The definition of money. Obviously, the appropriate rate of monetary expansion need not be the same for all definitions of money. Friedman's proposal is based on a concept of money that includes currency outside banks and total deposits adjusted at commercial banks, excluding those held by the federal government. Warburton agrees that time deposits should be included in money, but he takes time deposits at mutual savings banks and the postal savings system as well as those at commercial banks.

2. Seasonal variations in money. Both men approach this problem cautiously. Warburton's proposal would allow for seasonal variations: "The range of additional variation for seasonal purposes is probably not more than 3 per cent." [17] In the Compendium article, Friedman accepted the need for seasonal variations.[18] In his Fordham lectures, on the other hand, he took the opposite position: "My own tentative conclusion is that it would be preferable to dispense with seasonal adjustments." [19]

3. Structural reform of the banking system. I have already indicated that Friedman's proposal is part of a comprehensive program for monetary stability. He would eliminate fractional-reserve banking and all Federal Reserve monetary functions except open-market purchases of securities to provide for the indicated growth in money. Warburton disagrees sharply on this point.[20] He feels that with minor changes in the present institutional structure the Federal Reserve would

[17] "How Much Variation in the Quantity of Money Is Needed?" p. 508.

[18] Compendium, p. 255.

[19] *Program for Monetary Stability*, p. 92.

[20] Warburton has discussed these issues at length in "Monetary Difficulties and the Structure of the Monetary System," *Journal of Finance*, December 1952.

have no difficulty in implementing stable monetary growth. He recommends extension of member-bank reserve requirements to all banks, abolition of differential requirements among classes of banks and deposits, inclusion of vault cash in legal reserves (now accomplished), and a few other technical changes.

4. Exchange rates. Here again, Friedman favors substantial changes from the status quo, while Warburton favors only minor changes. Friedman, as we have seen, would abandon the present fixed gold parities and would permit exchange rates to be determined on unregulated and unguided foreign exchange markets. Warburton agrees that exchange rates "would be relatively stable and not subject to erratic fluctuations" under this scheme; however, he is fearful of the effects on international trade.[21] He therefore calls for perpetuation of pegged rates, under a revised International Monetary Fund, with changes in rates from time to time as this may become necessary.

5. Degree of rigidity envisaged by proposals. Although I have argued above that neither man insists on rigidly stable monetary growth, even aside from the seasonal problem, one nevertheless gains the impression that Warburton is less rigid than Friedman in this respect. For instance, Warburton has stated that occasions may arise in which short-run velocity variations should be offset by deviations from the proposed growth rate; he also speaks of spurts in production in the same vein.[22] Friedman, to my knowledge, would ignore all such variations unless evidence could be found to indicate that the variations represented modifications of secular trends that would require "permanent" modifications of the rate of monetary growth.

6. Underlying view of the economy. Even though the

[21] "Rules and Implements for Monetary Policy," pp. 18–19.

[22] See "How Much Variation in the Quantity of Money Is Needed?" pp. 502, 507.

stable monetary growth proposals must be judged fundamentally on their own merits, it is of interest to know what kind of a world their authors see when they gaze upon the monetary universe. There are two important and related differences between Friedman and Warburton here. Warburton comes close to accepting a monetary theory of business cycles, for mild and severe cycles alike.[23] Friedman, on the other hand, refers explicitly to other (nonmonetary) factors that may dominate monetary changes if the latter are small. Thus, "Even if the stock of money were to change in a highly regular and consistent fashion, economic activity and prices would nonetheless fluctuate." [24] It must be stressed, however, that Friedman, like Warburton, does have an exclusively monetary view of *severe* business contractions.

The second point of difference relates to the existence of lags in the effects of monetary changes. While Warburton shows some awareness that such lags exist, he has not emphasized them, and their existence is not crucial to his proposal.[25] For Warburton, stable monetary growth is desirable simply because unstable monetary growth in the past has caused virtually all recessions and inflations. In contrast, lags are of paramount importance for Friedman. For him, stable monetary growth is desirable because any other pattern of monetary growth is likely to intensify, rather than moderate, economic instability.

OTHER PROPONENTS OF STABLE MONETARY GROWTH

At least two other economists—James W. Angell and Edward S. Shaw—recently have advocated stable monetary

[23] *Ibid.*, p. 502. For a fuller discussion, see Warburton's "Theory of Turning Points in Business Fluctuations," *Quarterly Journal of Economics*, November 1950.

[24] Compendium, p. 251.

[25] In "Rules and Implements for Monetary Policy," p. 5, Warburton states: "Business men's expectations and plans . . . tend to follow changes in monetary policy by a noticeable lag."

growth, or something akin to it.[26] Angell recommends a constant rate of growth in bank reserves, rather than in money. However, he would deviate from this rule to meet seasonal needs and needs arising out of large Treasury financings, to restore order to the government securities markets, and to counter the threat of a money-market panic. Furthermore, he would expand selective credit controls and assign them a much greater role in stabilization policy than at present. Discretionary fiscal policy would also enjoy an expanded role under Angell's plan. In view of all this, it is obvious that Angell does not look with favor on the Warburton-Friedman proposals.

Shaw, on the other hand, has taken a position much closer to Friedman and Warburton: "It is an illusion that the money supply can be manipulated, according to the daily flux of economic statistics and their translation by men of refined intuition, into continuous equilibrium. The limit of feasibility is to ascertain the trend rate of growth in demand for money at a given price level and to set the money supply automatically on the same course." [27] However, Shaw's position appears to be based on the belief that the Federal Reserve does not have adequate powers to achieve quick policy reversals of the right magnitude. He also seems to rely more than Friedman on the argument that discretion is likely to be misused because of faulty analysis. And the fact that

[26] Angell, "Appropriate Monetary Policies and Operations in the United States Today," *Review of Economics and Statistics*, August, 1960; Shaw, "Money Supply and Stable Economic Growth," in American Assembly, *United States Monetary Policy* (New York, 1958). Shaw's paper has also been published under the title "Monetary Stability in a Growing Economy," in Moses Abramovitz, ed., *The Allocation of Economic Resources* (Stanford: Stanford University Press, 1959).

Mention should also be made of statements Senator Paul Douglas has recently made calling for monetary expansion at about the same rate as the expansion in output. See report of the Joint Economic Committee, February 29, 1960, p. 15.

[27] Shaw, "Money Supply and Stable Economic Growth," p. 62.

Shaw prefaces his discussion by saying that he is arguing "partly out of conviction and partly to arouse discussion" leaves considerable uncertainty as to where he really stands.[28]

CAN STABLE MONETARY GROWTH BE ACHIEVED?

The first question one ought to ask the proponents of stable monetary growth is, "Can it be achieved?" Under Friedman's proposal to abolish fractional-reserve banking, the answer is clearly "Yes." The central bank would purchase government securities on the open market at the desired rate and the volume of bank deposits would rise correspondingly; the reserve requirements of Federal Reserve banks would have to be removed to permit this, of course. An increased demand for currency, in relation to deposits, would have no effect on the quantity of money, since required bank reserves would fall by the full amount of currency withdrawals. Gradually the federal debt would pass into central-bank ownership, and eventually there would be a problem of how to expand the money stock when private holdings of such debt became exhausted. This would present no serious problem, however: the central bank could buy state and local government obligations, private debt, or other assets; or taxes could be reduced and the deficit financed through sale of securities to the central bank.

Under Warburton's proposal to perpetuate fractional-reserve banking, several difficulties might arise. First, the effectiveness of a given volume of reserves might be altered by variations in bank demand for reserves over time. This is possible, of course, but it does not seem to be a likely or significant source of difficulty. As Warburton has convincingly demonstrated, except during the abnormal period of the mid-1930's the volume of excess reserves has been

[28] *Ibid.*, p. 52.

remarkably small and steady.[29] Furthermore, even this good record might be improved upon if Friedman's proposal to pay interest on member-bank reserve accounts, or Tobin's proposal to pay interest on excess reserves, were adopted.[30] Under these schemes, declines in the rate of interest paid on reserves during a period of falling demand for loans and falling market interest rates would diminish the attractiveness of excess reserves in relation to loans and investments; thus banks would have an added incentive to keep their reserves fully employed. Elimination of the Federal Reserve's power to vary reserve requirements would also help by stabilizing bankers' expectations about future reserve requirements; and of course explicit adoption of stable monetary growth would work in the same direction. I see no important problem for the central bank here.

Second, the effectiveness of a given volume of reserves might be altered by shifts of deposits within the banking system. This problem is not serious even now, particularly since the recent dropping of the distinction between central reserve city and reserve city banks and the narrowing of the differential between requirements of country banks and other banks. However, with adoption of the recommendations by Friedman and Warburton that requirements be standardized for all bank deposits, the problem would vanish completely.[31]

Third, the volume of reserves might change more or less

[29] "Bank Reserves and Business Fluctuations."

[30] Friedman, *Program for Monetary Stability*, pp. 71–75; James Tobin, "Toward Improving the Efficiency of the Monetary Mechanism," *Review of Economics and Statistics*, August, 1960, p. 277. Friedman cites Lloyd Mints and George Tolley as earlier proponents of this scheme. It should be noted that Friedman justifies payment of interest on reserve accounts on entirely different grounds than that mentioned in the text.

[31] Warburton, "Rules and Implements for Monetary Policy," p. 17, n. 24; Friedman, *Program for Monetary Stability*, pp. 49–50. For details of the recent changes in reserve requirements see *Federal Reserve Bulletin*, November 1960, p. 1226.

than desired because of shifts in the demand for currency, changes in Federal Reserve float, or changes in the volume of bank borrowing from the central bank. I see no way of eliminating the first of these problems under fractional-reserve banking, but compensating open-market operations could be initiated promptly. The second problem—variations in Federal Reserve float—is probably more important. In part, these week to week variations are sufficiently regular to permit deliberate offsetting by the central bank; and even the sizable irregular movements that remain after seasonal adjustment could be diminished by adoption of more realistic availability schedules. In any case, the float problem would be no greater under fractional reserves than under 100 per cent reserves.

The final problem—changes in the volume of bank borrowing from the central bank—could be handled most simply by eliminating central-bank discounts and advances, as proposed by Friedman. Friedman is probably correct in thinking that correspondent relationships would be developed beyond their present state to take care of liquidity problems of individual banks. Nevertheless, the proposal might encounter strong opposition from bankers. A reform more palatable to bankers might be adoption of the Canadian procedure of tying the discount rate to the open-market rate on Treasury bills. This would eliminate changes in the volume of discounts and advances that result from the currently sluggish adjustments of the discount rate. And by keeping the discount rate substantially above the bill rate, say two percentage points, central-bank discounts and advances could be kept unattractive to all banks except those few that have real need for supplementary liquidity. I cannot believe that under this scheme any serious challenge would remain to central-bank control over the volume of bank reserves.

The upshot of this discussion is that stable monetary

growth certainly could be achieved with 100 per cent reserves, but that it could also be achieved with a slightly modified fractional-reserve system of the present type. The slight gain in precision of central-bank control under 100 per cent reserves would be entirely out of proportion to the turmoil that would accompany its adoption.

POSSIBLE PROBLEMS UNDER STABLE MONETARY GROWTH ACCOMPANIED BY STABLE VELOCITY

Let us imagine a situation in which the monetary authority adopts a policy of stable monetary growth at a rate of 4 per cent per year, based on an expected annual rate of growth of real income, at full employment, of 3 per cent and an expected annual rate of decline of velocity of 1 per cent, with no short-run deviations from trends. Even if velocity behaved as expected, two sorts of difficulties might arise.

1. Particularly over relatively short time periods, inflation might develop even though aggregate demand was not excessive; this is the interpretation placed on the 1955–1957 inflation by Charles Schultze, among others.[32] In brief, Schultze's thesis is this: even though *aggregate* demand is not excessive, abrupt shifts in demand may occur, with the result that demand is excessive in some markets and deficient in others. Prices will tend to rise in the former markets. However, because of administered pricing and costs that are inflexible downward, prices will not fall in the sectors of weak demand; output and employment will fall instead. Eventually, idle factories may be put to new uses or idle

[32] Charles L. Schultze, *Recent Inflation in the United States*, Study Paper No. 1, Study of Employment, Growth, and Price Levels, U.S. Congress, Joint Economic Committee, September 1959. Schultze's views on the 1955–1957 inflation go substantially beyond the relatively simple idea described in the text. It should also be stated that Schultze does not present his theory of the 1955–1957 inflation in the way that I have.

men may find jobs elsewhere; but where resources are specialized, transportation costs high, and other barriers to entry significant, such adjustments may take a long time. In the meantime the economy will suffer underemployment and inflation simultaneously, according to this thesis.

For several reasons, the possibility of demand-shift inflation should not weigh heavily against the proposal for stable monetary growth. First, the 1955–1957 inflationary episode remains open to conflicting interpretations, despite the substantial body of evidence recently brought forth in the Employment, Growth, and Price Levels investigation and elsewhere. Contrary to Schultze's view, I believe there are strong indications that aggregate demand was excessive during much of 1955 and 1956.[33] Second, and more generally, the degree to which price cuts are resisted in the face of weak demand has been greatly exaggerated by those who have been sounding the administered-price alarm in recent years. Published price data reveal the existence of substantial cross-currents in the price system at all times; even during 1955–1957, when the wholesale price index rose 8.2 per cent, prices fell in one fourth of the commodity subgroups.[34] But published data understate, to an unknown extent, the importance of price cuts since they take little account of departures from list prices and relaxation of terms, which are known to be a widespread feature of the American economy.

Finally, the remedy proposed by Schultze—increased reliance on selective credit controls—is not an attractive alterna-

[33] This is not the place for a full discussion of the 1955–1957 inflation. I have presented some of my own thoughts on this episode in "Cost-Push Versus Demand-Pull Inflation, 1955–57," *Journal of Political Economy*, February 1959.

One reason for the strong aggregate demand during 1955 and 1956 was the Federal Reserve's tardy reversal of the monetary ease it had been maintaining during the 1953–54 recession—an example, though relatively innocuous, of central-bank misuse of discretion.

[34] *Ibid.*, p. 4.

tive to stable monetary growth, or even to discretionary general monetary policy. Like general monetary policy, selective controls would not become effective immediately. Furthermore, selective controls might succeed in restraining price rises in certain sectors of strong demand, but in general this would not restore economic health to the sectors of weak demand. Demand would be redirected to other sectors, healthy as well as sick, and the area of application of selective controls would have to be widened. Aside from being costly to administer, such a pervasive system of selective controls would seriously threaten the fundamental nature of our enterprise economy, while offering little hope of success in preventing demand-shift inflation and underemployment. In my judgment, a far more rational approach is to adopt whatever monetary policy seems to make sense on other grounds and to use other aspects of economic policy (for example, antitrust policy) to assure the continued adaptability of the economy.

2. A second difficulty might arise under stable monetary growth, even if accompanied by stable velocity and even if there were no problem arising out of sudden shifts in demand: the assumed rate of growth of real income at full employment might turn out to be too high or too low, in which case secular inflation or deflation would result.[35]

It should go without saying that both Friedman and Warburton are aware that the future rate of growth of real income at full employment may differ from that of the past, although it is probably fair to say that they do not expect substantial and prolonged deviations from the past trend. We have already seen, however, that both men have stated explicitly the need for continued study of monetary behavior

[35] Lawrence Ritter, in his review of Friedman's Fordham lectures, has emphasized this possibility. See *American Economic Review*, September 1960.

if their proposal is adopted. Whenever clear evidence should become available of an acceleration or retardation in the rate of economic growth, the central bank would be directed to modify the rule accordingly. The amount of inflation or deflation would therefore be kept within tolerable limits over the long run.

This is not an entirely satisfactory solution, of course, since what is clear evidence to one observer is often not at all clear to another. Unless some arbitrary time period were established, say five years, during which the rule could not be modified, the door would be open to frequent tinkering with the rule, and the end result might be a *de facto* return to monetary discretion. It would seem wiser to me not to open this door more than the tiniest crack. An alternative to the Friedman-Warburton proposals in this regard would be to compute a new trend line for real income each year, based on data in the preceding 20 years or so. Cyclical income declines would have little effect on the computed trend line, but a persistent acceleration or retardation in the rate of growth of real income would cause gradual corrective adjustments in the rate of monetary growth, and these would become significant after a few years. In the meantime, the economy would experience some degree of price-level change, but this would be a worthwhile price to pay for greater automaticity in monetary policy.

THE POSSIBILITY OF LONG-RUN VELOCITY VARIATIONS

Having considered problems that might arise because of deviations of output from its expected trend, even with stable velocity, we turn now to the opposite problem. Suppose that the central bank's expectation of a 3 per cent annual rate of growth of real income at full employment turns out to be correct. As in the stable-velocity case, two sorts of difficulties might arise nevertheless: there might be short-run variations of velocity around its trend, and the trend of velocity might turn out to be something other than that expected. We shall begin with the latter difficulty, since it can be disposed of quickly.

As I mentioned earlier, Warburton's figure of 5 per cent per year for the appropriate rate of monetary growth assumed a secular decline in velocity of 1.33 per cent per year. This was entirely reasonable on the basis of the observed trend in velocity for more than a century up to the mid-1940's. Since then, of course, velocity has been moving fairly steadily in the opposite direction, and it is not clear whether the future trend of velocity will be up, down, or stationary.[36]

Essentially, this is the same problem we have just encountered in relation to long-run changes in real income, and the solution is the same: either deliberate adjustment at infrequent intervals or (preferably) continuous adjustment by using the trend during the preceding 20 years.

THE POSSIBILITY OF SHORT-RUN VELOCITY VARIATIONS

Let us turn now to the short-run velocity problem, which has attracted a good deal more attention. We shall analyze it in two stages, considering first why velocity has varied over short periods in the past, then how it could be expected to behave under stable monetary growth.

1. Short-run velocity variations in the past. Since the earliest systematic thinking about monetary problems it has been recognized that the velocity of circulation of money is not necessarily constant in either the short run or the long run. Recent research on the behavior of velocity has revealed a consistent pattern of rises during business-cycle expansions

[36] I have analyzed this problem at some length in "The Postwar Rise in the Velocity of Money: A Sectoral Analysis," *Journal of Finance*, December 1961, pp. 483–545, to be reprinted as an Occasional Paper by the National Bureau of Economic Research.

and declines during contractions, with turning points roughly coinciding with those of business cycles.[37]

There is nothing approaching unanimity regarding the causes of cyclical velocity variations; indeed, such unanimity probably will be achieved only as part of a generally accepted theory of business cycles. In reviewing the literature that bears on this subject, one encounters at least four distinct explanations of these velocity movements. First, there is the view implicit in much business-cycle theorizing that velocity varies cyclically because of autonomous shifts in the demand for money. The reasons advanced for these demand shifts differ greatly from writer to writer. Second, according to Warburton cyclical variations in velocity are the result of prior departures of the stock of money from its proper rate of growth.[38] Warburton finds support for this view in the writings of a number of nineteenth-century economists, as well as in his own statistical studies of lead-lag relationships since 1919. Members of the Chicago School, including Friedman, also appear to accept this view insofar as severe contractions are concerned.[39]

Third, Friedman, with characteristic ingenuity, has explained cyclical velocity variations in terms of the distinction between permanent and measured income and prices.[40] For one reason or another, there occur declines in measured real income from time to time; these may be accompanied by

[37] For instance, see Milton Friedman, "The Demand for Money: Some Theoretical and Empirical Results," *Journal of Political Economy*, August 1959, reprinted as Occasional Paper 68, National Bureau of Economic Research. See pp. 3–4 and chart 2 in the Occasional Paper (pp. 329–330 and chart 2 in *Journal of Political Economy*).

[38] Warburton has stated this view on many occasions; as an example, see "How Much Variation in the Quantity of Money Is Needed?" p. 506.

[39] This is clearly implicit in Friedman's *Program for Monetary Stability*, pp. 22–23.

[40] "The Demand for Money: Some Theoretical and Empirical Results," pp. 6–9.

declines in the price level as well. But in Friedman's view the demand for money depends on expectations of permanent, rather than measured, income and prices; and since expected permanent income and prices exceed measured income and prices during business contractions, the ratio of measured money income to the money stock (that is, velocity) will fall. Finally, according to another fairly common view cyclical velocity variations result from cyclical variations in the cost of holding money, as measured by interest rates. The latter, in turn, are attributed primarily to fluctuations in the demand for loans.[41]

It will sound hopelessly eclectic of me to say so, but I find merit in each of these views. For instance, whether or not shifts in the demand for money are important initiating factors in business fluctuations is a matter of conjecture, but it is highly plausible that such shifts occur as intensifying factors, once a cyclical change is under way. During recessions, household demand for money may rise (and velocity fall) because of increased uncertainty about job tenure; business demand for money may rise because of increased uncertainty about future monetary policy. Simons and Mints have made much of the latter possibility.

Warburton is undoubtedly correct in thinking that monetary changes are responsible for some cyclical changes in velocity; at the same time, however, it seems reasonable to suppose that other forces also may have impinged on velocity with sufficient vigor to explain some of the observed changes. Likewise, Friedman's permanent income hypothesis undoubtedly accounts for a portion of observed cyclical changes in velocity, but whether or not it accounts for all such changes is open to question. Again, strong correlations are known to exist between short-term interest rates and

[41] See Selden, "Cost-Push Versus Demand-Pull Inflation, 1955–57," p. 15, for an example.

velocity during business cycles. My own recent studies of business velocity since 1939 suggest that differential borrowing costs are a major factor explaining velocity differences (1) among industries, (2) between large and small firms in the same industry, and (3) over time.[42] These studies also suggest that nearly all of the cyclical variation in velocity occurs in the business sector. Nevertheless, it is possible to argue that both interest rates and velocity decline during business contractions because of other cyclical influences on both, so that the apparent causal connection between the two is largely spurious.

It is obvious from the foregoing remarks that the theory of cyclical velocity movements is in an unsatisfactory state. However, apart from movements associated with severe business contractions, the data do reveal a highly regular cyclical pattern in velocity over a long time span, with no discernible tendency toward greater or less volatility. Comparisons of mild cycles early in the twentieth century (such as those of 1900–1904, 1908–1911, 1911–1914, 1921–1924, and 1924–1927) with those of the postwar period are interesting in this regard.[43] These data cast considerable doubt on the theory advanced by Warren Smith, among others, that the existence of a large public debt and a set of highly developed non-bank intermediaries mean an increased volatility of velocity and a reduced effectiveness of monetary policy.[44] Nor do these data suggest that the often-discussed automatic stabilizers have had much effect on velocity so far; their main contribution seems to have been to reduce the probability of administrative mistakes.

[42] "The Postwar Rise in the Velocity of Money: A Sectoral Analysis."

[43] Friedman, "The Demand for Money," chart 2. The 1954–1958 cycle, not shown there, resembles the 1946–1949 cycle in amplitude.

[44] Warren L. Smith, "Some Unsettled Issues in Monetary Policy," in Duke University, *United States Monetary Policy* (Durham, N.C., 1959), especially pp. 14–23.

2. Cyclical velocity variations under stable monetary growth. We come now to what the critics of stable monetary growth seem to regard its point of greatest vulnerability: the possibility that velocity might suddenly decline, ushering in a recession which the central bank would not be permitted to combat. For several reasons, I do not find this a telling criticism.

First, unless adoption of stable monetary growth had the effect of intensifying cyclical variations in velocity, cyclical variations in money income would be reduced; this follows from the fact that in the past the stock of money has reinforced the effects of cyclical velocity variations by growing more slowly during business contractions than during business expansions. I cannot think of any plausible reason why mere adoption of this rule would intensify the cycles in velocity.

Second, adoption of stable monetary growth would actually remove two types of cyclical velocity variations in the past: those caused by uncertainty about the character of future monetary policy, and those caused by the tendency for deflation to set in during periods of high employment because of the Federal Reserve's failure to expand the stock of money sufficiently to permit growth in real income at stable prices. One need not agree with Warburton that such policy lapses have been responsible for each and every cyclical downturn in velocity, but there are enough clear cases (the 1920 and 1929 downturns are good examples) to indicate that the potential contribution of stable monetary growth is substantial.

Third, adoption of stable monetary growth would greatly increase the likelihood that future recessions would be mild, compared to those of 1920–1921, 1929–1933, and 1937–1938. The view that severe depressions are a thing of the past is widely accepted by economists, regardless of their differences on stabilization policy. It is based on a number of grounds. Since 1929, our monetary system has been strengthened by the enactment of deposit insurance, the elimination of thousands of weak banks, and abandonment of the gold standard. Government spending, which tends to resist cyclical declines, is a much higher portion of gross national product now. Furthermore, our tax and revenue system automatically generates sizable deficits during recessions, and the increased tendency of corporations to stabilize dividend policies works in the same direction. But quite apart from these institutional changes, the evidence presented by Friedman and Warburton is extremely powerful in showing that government policy has aggravated, rather than helped, business conditions in every severe recession we have experienced.[45] With the addition of stable monetary growth to our improved institutional structure, the possibility of a major recession seems remote indeed.

Finally, there are several ways in which the amplitude of cyclical velocity movements might be reduced in the future. For instance, countercyclical budgetary flexibility probably could be increased somewhat at both the federal and the state and local levels. We cannot take time here to pursue the various possibilities. However, I should like to endorse a different sort of proposal that has been made in recent years by a number of economists which, if adopted, might make a modest contribution toward reducing cyclical velocity movements. This is the proposal advanced by Friedman, James Tobin, and others to permit payment of interest on deposits without limitation.[46] One effect of this change would be a reduction in the cost of holding money and partial elimination of the unnecessary social cost involved in the attempt to economize a costless asset, money. But for the

[45] See Friedman, *Program for Monetary Stability*, pp. 9–23.
[46] See the works cited in n. 30, above.

present discussion another effect is more important. This yield on demand deposits and currency is zero; when interest rates fall the cost of holding money falls by the same absolute amount, the quantity of real balances demanded rises, and velocity declines. If interest were paid on demand deposits there would be some tendency for the yield to decline when other interest rates declined, and the cost of holding money, and velocity, would therefore fall by smaller amounts.

I would summarize the foregoing comments as follows. Adoption of stable monetary growth probably would not usher in a cycle-free millennium, but it would make the recurrence of severe recessions highly unlikely. Furthermore, adoption of this proposal might well result in a reduced cyclical amplitude in velocity; and in any case, cyclical *income* variations would probably be somewhat less in the future than during mild recessions of the past, simply because the rate of monetary growth would no longer decline during recessions. Finally, further development of automatic stabilizers, along with structural changes in our monetary system, might well result in a moderation of short-run velocity variations in the future. Needless to say, efforts should be made in this direction regardless of the fate of the stable monetary growth proposal.

We come at last to the acid test of stable monetary growth. Critics have concentrated on the dangers that might ensue if stable monetary growth were adopted. Friedman's answer to such criticisms is simple and direct: admittedly stable monetary growth is not perfect, but there is no better approach to stabilization policy, given our present knowledge. Furthermore, the attempt to improve upon stable monetary growth may only worsen things; it may well turn out, to use Friedman's words, that "the best is often the enemy of the good." [47]

[47] Compendium, p. 256.

Friedman introduces two types of evidence in support of his position. First, he examines past decisions of our monetary authorities and concludes that serious errors have been made with alarming frequency.[48] Evidence of this, in the form of policy-initiation lags, can be seen in the historical record. In nearly every recession since 1907 the rate of change in the money stock did not begin to increase until several months after the recession had been in progress. The postwar record indicates a decided improvement in the quality of decision-making in monetary policy; but error still creeps in, and we cannot be certain that relatively good decision-making will continue. But important though these considerations are, Friedman relies exclusively on a second type of evidence—on the existence of lags in the effects of monetary changes—to demonstrate the superiority of stable monetary growth. Before closing this paper we must briefly appraise the evidence relating to monetary lags.

LAGS IN THE EFFECTS OF MONETARY CHANGES

According to Friedman there is a fundamental difficulty in any monetary policy, whether discretionary or not, which attempts to offset business fluctuations: monetary policy operates only after a lag and may therefore become effective only when it is no longer appropriate. Conceivably the problem could be solved through advance action based on forecasting, but this is not feasible for two reasons: the average lag is much too long for present forecasting techniques to be of any use, and individual lags vary greatly in length. If Friedman is right in these contentions, his argument is unassailable. Therefore, the critics of stable monetary growth must show that Friedman's statements about lags are not factual.

Friedman's statements about lags are based on analysis of monetary changes during the 18 peacetime business cycles

[48] *Program for Monetary Stability*, chap. 1.

between 1870 and 1954.[49] The rate of change in the money stock begins to increase several months before business conditions begin to improve. Friedman's summary of findings follows:

> We have found that, on the average of 18 cycles, peaks in the rate of change in the stock of money tend to precede peaks in general business by about 16 months and troughs in the rate of change in the stock of money to precede troughs in general business by about 12 months. For individual cycles, the recorded lead has varied between 6 and 29 months at peaks and between 4 and 22 months at troughs. This is highly consistent behavior as such observations go and sufficient to pin down the *average* lead within a rather narrow range. But it is highly variable behavior for the individual episode with which policy must be concerned.[50]

Several comments may be made on these findings. First, the data themselves are relatively good, and they have been processed with great care by Friedman and his colleagues at the National Bureau. Of course it is not a simple task to determine the precise location of cyclical peaks and troughs, and one might quarrel with some of the decisions made. Examples are the trough dated early in 1908, rather than late in 1907, and the peak dated early in 1936, rather than in mid-1935. On balance, however, Friedman has probably understated, rather than overstated, the length of the lags. Second, one might object that the results have been influenced by inclusion of the 1870–1906 time segment, during which only annual money estimates are available. But Friedman has found closely similar average lags and variability of lags for 1907–1954 and for 1870–1954. Likewise, there is no significant difference in these statistics when severe recessions cycles are omitted from the analysis.[51]

[49] Compendium, pp. 249–251; *Program for Monetary Stability*, pp. 87–88.
[50] *Program for Monetary Stability*, pp. 87–88.
[51] These statements are based on unpublished data furnished the author by Anna J. Schwartz.

Third, one might question Friedman's comparison of monetary changes with business-cycle turning points as the most relevant one to make. Would not comparisons with turning points in money income, real income, or the price level be more appropriate? The question has no obvious answer in principle, and lack of quarterly income data over any substantial time period meant that only the price-level comparison was a practical alternative. Friedman found almost identical results when turning points in the wholesale price index were used in place of business-cycle turning points.[52]

Fourth, critics might agree with Friedman that a highly regular pattern exists over time between monetary changes and business cycles, while disagreeing with his interpretation of this finding. After all, one could just as well argue that the rate of change in the money stock is a lagging indicator of business cycles, rather than a leading indicator, as Friedman insists. Against this criticism Friedman has two defenses. The lagging-indicator interpretation is not consistent with what we know about monetary theory from other sources, whereas the leading-indicator interpretation is. Moreover, there is statistical evidence in favor of Friedman's view: the variability in the interval between monetary changes and preceding business-cycle turning points is much greater than that between monetary changes and succeeding business-cycle turning points.[53]

On each of the above tests Friedman's analysis of monetary lags scores high. Yet it is not entirely satisfying, because nowhere does Friedman explain why changes in monetary policy take so long to become effective; nor does he go into the precise manner in which, or channels through which, money affects the economy. The only clue we get on these

[52] *Program for Monetary Stability*, p. 87.
[53] Based on unpublished findings by Anna J. Schwartz.

points is his oft-repeated statement that the interest-rate effects of monetary changes are only incidental; it is the direct effects of increased liquidity on spending that really count.[54]

Is it reasonable that changes in monetary policy (as measured by turning points in the rate of change in the money stock) become effective with delays of as much as two years? One can visualize a slack economy in which the demand for loans has fallen sharply and the banks have re-employed their resources by purchasing securities, thus maintaining the volume of money. This in itself reduces velocity for two reasons: first, the sellers of securities are apt to be slow spenders; and second, the cost of holding money will have fallen for all holders if bond yields are reduced. Now the central bank expands reserves, and the banks buy more securities, adding to the stock of money in the process. But the new money holders, again, may be slow spenders, so for the time being the effects of the additional money may be offset completely by a decline in velocity; this is a third reason for lower velocity. In the meantime, velocity may also decline for a fourth reason: on account of gloomy expectations that pervade the economy, particularly if unemployment is rising and profits are falling. Gradually the new money holders will spend their cash, either for goods and services or for securities to replace those sold to the banks, and the ownership of cash will shift back toward the normal spenders. In short, the first and third types of velocity declines will be reversed. Even so, money income will continue to fall if the effect of the added money is swamped by the second and fourth types of velocity declines. Eventually,

[54] It is interesting to note that the only other empirical study of monetary policy lags, that of Thomas Mayer, was based on the opposite premise. Mayer's findings, however, were broadly similar to Friedman's on the length of these lags. See Thomas Mayer, "The Inflexibility of Monetary Policy," *Review of Economics and Statistics*, November 1958.

however, a new set of expectations will take hold and the rate of decline in velocity will be less than the rate of increase in the money stock; only then will the added money show up as a net increase in money income.

The preceding discussion has two important implications concerning the existence of monetary lags. First, it is clear that the adjustment process described above will require several months, perhaps even a year or more. Thus in general Friedman's findings do not seem unreasonable in the light of monetary theory. However, a second implication is less favorable to Friedman's analysis: the lags he is measuring are not those just discussed, and there is a real question whether Friedman's lags are the appropriate ones to study. Friedman's lags are between turning points in the *rate of change* in the money stock and business-cycle peaks and troughs. For peaks Friedman's procedure seems entirely appropriate; failure of the money stock to grow as fast as output will result in a downward drag on the price level, with the possibility of adverse cost-price relationships. For troughs, on the other hand, Friedman's comparison seems less relevant. The record reveals instances in which the money stock continued to fall for several months after a trough was reached in its rate of change; the most notable examples are the contractions of 1920–1921, 1929–1933, and 1937–1938. Is there any reason to expect business conditions to improve simply because the money stock is declining less rapidly than before? In my judgment, a better comparison would be between the point in time when the money stock itself, not its rate of change, stops falling, and the business-cycle trough. On this basis, the average lag between the taking of expansive monetary policies and the effects of these policies is less than Friedman has found.

However, even if one accepts this criticism of Friedman's lag analysis—and it is not at all clear that one should accept it—the practical import is not substantial. Each of the three examples cited above are related to severe business contractions. As I have already indicated, the average lag has been approximately the same for mild and severe contraction cycles. It follows that Friedman's findings are largely unaffected, as far as mild contractions are concerned.

Everything considered, therefore, I conclude that Friedman's assertions about monetary lags are, in the main, well grounded in fact, even if not completely rationalized in theory. The burden of proof now rests with his critics, who must come forward with evidence of their own.

ALTERNATIVE POLICIES COMPARED

Two attempts have been made to compare hypothetical performances of stable monetary growth and alternatives, using historical data: one by Martin Bronfenbrenner, the other by Friedman.[56] Both men are justifiably modest about the import of these tests, although they certainly add to our knowledge, and I mention them here mainly for sake of completeness.

Bronfenbrenner compared four patterns of monetary growth during 1901–1958, using annual data: the actual pattern, which he calls "the judgment rule"; stable monetary growth at 3 per cent per year; stable monetary growth at 4 per cent per year; and a lag rule, whereby money is expanded in any year at a rate determined by last year's change in velocity, the labor force, and its productivity. Bronfenbrenner limited himself to year by year comparisons, taking price-level stability as his criterion of performance. The tests were run in several different ways, with two concepts of money and two price indexes, for the period as a

[56] Martin Bronfenbrenner, "Statistical Tests of Rival Monetary Rules," *Journal of Political Economy,* February 1961; Friedman, *Program for Monetary Stability,* pp. 95–97.

whole and for four subperiods. The results were favorable to stable monetary growth, particularly the 3 per cent version, although not in every test and not by decisive margins. Bronfenbrenner appropriately points out that his test procedure was biased to some extent against the stable growth rules, since the latter are less concerned with prevention of year to year instabilities than with cyclical and long-run results.

Friedman's tests involved comparisons of actual monetary changes with those that would have been produced under the 4 per cent rule. The differences were then scored as being in the "right" or "wrong" direction, according to various criteria. One criterion was that money should grow at a less than average rate during business expansions and at a greater than average rate during contractions. On this basis, during the peacetime months from March 1918 to April 1958, "actual policy was in the 'right' direction in 155 months, in the 'wrong' direction in 226 months; so actual policy was 'better' than the rule in 41 per cent of the months." [56] A second criterion employed by Friedman was that money should grow at a less than average rate during periods of "above normal" business conditions and at a greater than average rate during "below normal" periods. This time actual policy outscored Friedman's rule in 56 per cent of the peacetime months. Finally, Friedman repeated the test for the second half of business expansions and contractions, and actual policy was "best" less than half the time again—in 45 per cent of the months. Having presented these results, Friedman goes on to indicate that they are not terribly significant, a conclusion in which we must concur.

We have reached the point at which a verdict must be delivered, though as always the decision is tentative and

[56] *Program for Monetary Stability*, p. 95.

may be reversed at any time, as new findings are uncovered. We have tried to form a judgment of stable monetary growth both absolutely and relatively, and in neither case are the answers beyond doubt. At the very least, however, we must conclude that Friedman and Warburton have presented a serious challenge to the advocates of monetary manipulation, and replies must be forthcoming. Beyond this, I am personally persuaded that stable monetary growth would yield quite satisfactory results, superior to those under any other policy proposed so far.

Some critics may argue that both Friedman and Warburton place too much emphasis on monetary policy, that it is intrinsically weak, or at least weaker than fiscal policy. This argument is irrelevant, however: even if it were true that money does not matter, we should nevertheless try to make it behave in the manner most consistent with economic stability. Other critics may be offended by the sweeping reforms Friedman seeks. But as we have argued, the additional reforms needed for implementation of stable monetary growth are few in number and limited in importance. One hundred per cent reserves and freely fluctuating exchange rates may be desirable on other grounds, but they have no necessary connection with stable monetary growth. Actually, the Federal Reserve has achieved a close approximation to stable monetary growth in the postwar period, whether by design or not. What is needed now, aside from a few technical amendments to our banking laws, is an *announcement* by the Federal Reserve that stable monetary growth is their goal.

Finally, some critics will feel that we have glossed over possible difficulties under stable monetary growth, and they may be right. Here again, however, the criticism can be answered readily. Stable monetary growth could be adopted subject to one or more provisos which would release the central bank under certain contingencies. If Friedman, Shaw, Warburton, and company are correct in their claims, as I believe they are, the contingencies will never arise, and the money stock will grow steadily at the designated rate. If they are wrong, an escape will automatically be at hand. One such proviso might be that the rule be abandoned whenever as much as 9 per cent of the labor force becomes unemployed, or whenever a broad index of prices rises at a rate of 5 per cent per year, for three months in a row. Through such devices it seems to me that stable monetary growth can be made acceptable to large elements of our populace without any important compromise of principle.

Everything considered, therefore, I agree with Malcolm Bryan that "the world is in the twilight of manipulated money systems." [57] And the chances seem very good that the successor to monetary discretion will be stable monetary growth.

[57] Malcolm Bryan, "The Sovereign, the Central Bank, and the Monetary Standard," in Duke University, *United States Monetary Policy*, p. 7.

INDEX